CHOICES

Stories for Assembly and P.S.E.

Gordon Aspland

SOUTHGATE

First published 1995 by Southgate Publishers Ltd
Reprinted 1996, 1998, 1999

Southgate Publishers Ltd
15 Barnfield Avenue, Exmouth, Devon EX8 2QE

Printed and bound in Great Britain by Short Run Press Ltd, Exeter, Devon.

British Library Cataloguing in Publication Data
A CIP catalogue record for this book is available from the British Library.

ISBN 1–85741–077–7

CONTENTS

Introduction

Throughout our lives we have to make decisions. These decisions are often in the form of choices between courses of action. Adults have a wealth of lifetime experiences to help them and even then we often get it wrong! Children do not have this advantage and therefore need to be given opportunities to explore the issues and factors that affect their choice making.

Choices is the sequel to my first book *Feelings* but can stand on its own. With 'Choices' I have tried to look at situations when children have to choose between two or more courses of action. In some cases there are obvious right and wrong decisions and in others the demarcation between right and wrong is not so obvious. The situations are developed around issues that affect many children, such as temptation, bullying, peer group pressure and unfairness. The stories are designed to stimulate children to think about and discuss the courses of action available. It is hoped that through this process of listening and thinking and putting views forward, then adopting them in the light of the responses of others, children will begin to understand how their own actions affect themselves and others.

All the stories are based around a group of children in the same class. The adults also remain the same. By this means I hope that listeners can build up a picture of the characters and their personalities as the stories are told. They might identify with one or more of them.

At the time of writing this the Government have produced a Green Paper on Drug Education. It may be that all Primary schools will have to address this issue and develop a Drug Education Policy. I have included a couple of stories that look at this, *One Puff Too Many* and *The Deadly Bag*.

I believe that these stories reflect in particular some of the moral values described in the N.C.C. Document on *Spiritual and Moral Development (1993)*. These values include: telling the truth; keeping promises; respecting the rights and property of others; acting considerately towards each other; helping those less fortunate and weaker than ourselves; taking personal responsibility for one's actions; and self-discipline.

SUGGESTIONS FOR USE

In Collective Worship

This book can be picked up and the stories used just as they are by the teacher in a hurry. They take between five and fifteen minutes to read and, with a short follow-up discussion, song or hymn and prayer, or time for silent reflection, they would occupy a full assembly for collective worship of between fifteen and twenty minutes in length. More satisfactory than this *ad hoc* use is the planning of episodes from the book into a full-term pattern of collective worship, alongside religious material from Christianity and other world faiths, so that Tuesday, say, might be the day for a visit to the world of the children in these stories, with other things happening on the other days. This would provide a coherent framework in which to set these 'broadly Christian' but essentially secular stories which would meet the requirement of the Education Reform Act that, taking a term as a whole, the collective worship must be wholly or mainly of a broadly Christian nature.

After each story I have provided questions for discussion. There is also a prayer for those schools who wish to incorporate it into their act of worship. Prayer can be introduced in an open-ended way by phrases like 'We're going to have a few quiet moments to think about ... ' or 'If you wish, share this prayer I'm going to read ... '.

As well as, or instead of, using the story in collective worship, some teachers might want to use some of the follow-up activities suggested in class.

RELIGIOUS LINKS

This book is concerned more with Personal and Social Education than with R.E. P.S.E. is no substitute for a thorough-going R.E. programme based on an R.E. Agreed Syllabus and this book makes no claim to be presenting an R.E. course or R.E. material. The Religious Links after each story are intended to link themes in the story with more explicitly religious, usually Christian, material that could be incorporated into the act of worship by the teacher if appropriate. Such links in themselves do not turn the material into R.E., for religious material is weakened when used as a tagged-on supplement or as a 'prop' for work in another subject area unless it is also dealt with fully in its own right.

In Classwork

Within the National Curriculum framework the stories might be used particularly in oral work in P.S.E. and English.

1. In pairs, the children can discuss the story. The teacher then asks one child to relate how their partner feels. This is a simple but effective way of encouraging listening as well as talking.

2. The children can be asked to write down a response to the story or how they

think it should end and then discuss what they have written in a small group. A variation on this is to split the class in half. One half sits in a circle facing outwards and the other half forms a circle facing inwards, so that each is facing someone from the inner circle. The teacher can then ask questions about the story or the children's response and the children discuss in pairs. After each question, the children in the outer circle move round so that they are facing somebody new. This encourages children to talk to someone they might not normally relate to and means that the shy child may meet someone they can talk to as the outer circle moves.

3. Some stories have a natural break in the middle for questions and discussion about the choices the character can make.

By using the Discussion questions after each story and some of the oral work mentioned above, children can start to develop skills appropriate to P.S.E. such as: predicting outcomes from different types of behaviour; empathizing with other people's feelings; reflecting on their own behaviour and feelings; and respecting the views and feelings of others.

The sub-title of this book sums up its real intention — to provide stories for use in Assembly and P.S.E., born out of my own work with children in the upper part of the primary school. I hope it will help other teachers in their work in this area.

Gordon Aspland
1995

1
The Lost Money

THEME: temptation

Prakesh arrived at Mark's house on a sunny, Friday afternoon, the last day of the half term holiday. Mark was in the back garden setting up his goalpost. It was a large garden, much bigger than his own. Prakesh lived in a flat and could only play on a small bit of grass at the front. Mark's garden was surrounded by a high hedge and it had two apple trees in the middle of it. Mark was setting up his goalpost between the trees.

"Neat goalpost," admired Prakesh as he walked over to Mark.

"I got it for my birthday a few months ago," said Mark. He finished tying the last bit of the net to the thin frame. "It's not very big but it's all right for mucking around with." Mark fancied himself as a goalkeeper and his idea was to get friends to come over and practise shooting at him.

Prakesh dribbled around a couple of bushes pretending they were defenders. He let fly with a vicious right foot kick which Mark pushed away. "Good one!" shouted Prakesh as he went to collect the ball. This carried on until Mark suggested they swapped places. He also fancied himself as a striker; in fact there were times when he thought he was the best primary school player in the country!

Prakesh easily stopped the first few shots, which rather annoyed Mark. He didn't want anybody else to be as good at goalkeeping as himself. He decided to let fly with a belter but just as he was swinging his foot to kick the ball his other foot slipped. He mis-kicked the ball badly and watched, with a sickening feeling, as it sailed over the hedge towards Mr Blackmore's greenhouse! There was a dreadful crash of breaking glass as his worst fears were realised.

Mark's mother came racing into the garden, calling out, "What have you done?"

"I, I didn't mean to, my foot slipped," muttered Mark. There was a shout from behind the hedge. Mr Blackmore was at home. Prakesh remembered that he had to go to the shop for his mum and quickly left. Mark could hear Mr Blackmore walking around to the front of his house. There was going to be a difficult scene.

Not only did Mark get a ticking off from his mother and Mr Blackmore but he was in real trouble with his Dad when he got home from work, especially since Mark had been warned before to be careful with a hard, heavy football in a garden not exactly the size of Wembley Stadium. The bill to replace the broken glass was £52.50. Mark was going to have to pay every penny of it. He didn't have £52.50, he barely had £2. Though he had £3 a week pocket money, he wasn't a very good saver. He would be going a very long time without his pocket money!

It was a long weekend for Mark and he was glad to be at school on Monday. On the way home he went by the Post Office and was just about to walk in when he remembered he had no money. He usually got his pocket money on a Sunday and then spent most of it on sweets when he was going home. That day and for the next several weeks he would have to do without sweets or his usual *Shoot* magazine.

With head down he walked on and noticed a small plastic bag on the pavement. He picked it up and noticed that it had money inside. He looked around to see if anybody was watching and put the plastic bag into his rucksack. Back home in his bedroom he had a closer look at the money. There were exactly three £20 notes. Mark was elated. This would pay for the broken greenhouse and leave a bit over. He couldn't believe his luck. There was a doubt in his mind, though. This wasn't his money so should he hand it in or was it 'finders, keepers'?

Mark has a choice, what should he do?
Should he give the money back or should he keep the money so that he can pay for the broken greenhouse ?

Mark put the money in the back of his sock drawer; he would think about it later.

That evening after tea he was reading the sports pages of the newspaper whilst his parents were listening to the news. He usually never took any notice of the news but his attention was suddenly caught when the broadcaster mentioned the sum of £60. He was talking about the need for the government to increase the Old Age Pension; he said that £60 a week was not enough for an elderly person to live on.

Mark immediately went hot all over. It must have been an elderly person's pension that he had found. He began to feel very guilty, it wasn't a nice feeling. He pictured in his mind an old lady frantically looking for her money, panicking because she could not find it. Mark knew what he must do.

The next day on the way to school Mark stopped at the Post Office and handed the money over. He said he had just found it underneath a hedge, not quite the truth but he didn't want to admit that he had found it the day before. When Mark left the shop he felt a lot better, though not completely better; he still had to pay for the glass.

When he got home from school his mother greeted him more warmly than usual. "Mark, I'm very proud of you," she said. He looked puzzled. "I was in the Post Office this afternoon," explained his mother, "and I heard all about you handing in the money. Everyone in the shop said how honest you were."

"Well," said Mark quickly, "I thought it must have been an old person's money, I couldn't keep it."

"Actually, it wasn't anyone's pension, it was Mrs Blackmore's housekeeping money. She had just taken it out of her Post Office account. Mr Blackmore was so impressed with your honesty that he said you don't have to pay for the broken glass. What do you think of that?"

Mark was speechless!

Discussion Points

1. Mark didn't know what to do. What finally made him decide to give the money back?
2. Why did Mark lie about where he found the money?
3. How did Mark's honesty finally pay off?
4. Why was Mark tempted to keep the money? Was that the right thing to do?

Prayer/Reflection

Let us pray that we can make the right choices when we are faced with the temptation to do wrong.

Here is a prayer Muslims say when they are not too sure what to do:

O Allah,
I seek your guidance
through your knowledge and ability,
through your power,
and beg your infinite bounty;
for You have power and I have none,
You know and I know not,
And You are the knower of hidden things.

Religious Links (Mark 14:12–26)

Matthew 4 : 1 – 11 describes the temptations faced by Jesus, to use his power selfishly, to set a test for God, to become a powerful worldly ruler. In each case he turns away the temptation with a quotation from the Jewish Bible. Where might we look for advice about temptation?

Follow-up Activities

1. Ask the children about times when they have been tempted to do wrong. What happened? This could be explored through role play.
2. Discuss what would have happened if Mark had kept the money. How would he have explained it to his parents? Discuss how one lie can then lead to another.

2
One Tin of Baked Beans

THEME: it's the thought that counts

Pauline looked on as the other children brought in their gifts for the Harvest Service. It was the morning before Harvest and the display of food was looking good. Pauline's friends were bringing in bags of food that they were proudly showing each other, as if it was a competition to see who could bring in the most.

"Have you brought in yours yet?" asked Sereena.

"I'll bring in mine tomorrow," lied Pauline. "I've got a huge bag of apples to bring in." Pauline didn't know why she'd said that. Her single donation of one tin of baked beans was sitting in her bag.

Things were very tight at Pauline's home lately. Her Dad was made redundant after years of loyal service and her Mum only had a part-time cleaning job. One tin of baked beans was all her mother was prepared to give her. Pauline was very embarrassed by this, she would have loved to bring more; after all, the food was going to be distributed to the local elderly. Now she had to find a bag of apples! This worried Pauline all day. More than once her teacher had to remind her to pay attention.

On the way home Pauline walked passed Mr Petrowski's house. Mr Petrowski was a rather eccentric elderly man who came from Poland more than fifty years ago. He lived alone, spending all his time tending his vegetable plot. In the corner of his garden was a large apple tree dripping with ripe Cox's apples. Pauline stood looking over the fence enviously at the tree. Surely, Mr Petrowski would not miss a few apples. Many were low down; she thought, it would only take a minute to sneak in, fill her school bag and dash away. She was very tempted.

Pauline feels desperate. She wants to give more for the Harvest Service and has told her friends that she is bringing in a bag of apples. What should she do? There they are, waiting to be picked? Should she go in and take the apples? Should she ask the owner first? Or should she walk on?

Pauline looked up and down the street. Nobody was looking, so she climbed the fence and crept around the edge of the garden. When she reached the tree she quickly began to fill her bag. A large hand grabbed her shoulder from behind.

"And what do you think you are doing, Missy?" It was Mr Petrowski. He must have been in his shed when Pauline entered the garden.

Pauline couldn't say anything. She just stood there. It was painfully obvious what she was doing, she was stealing his apples.

"Well, have you no tongue?" asked Mr Petrowski.

"I'm sorry, I only wanted them for our Harvest Service," began Pauline and then she explained all about wanting to take more than just a tin of baked beans.

"Did you think about asking for some apples?" said Mr Petrowski. "You might be surprised what you get when you ask in the proper way." He took Pauline's bag and emptied it out onto the ground. "Now, let me see," he muttered. "This is no good, see, you cannot give this apple as a gift." He held up an apple with a large bruise. He then picked eight large, beautifully formed apples and put them into Pauline's bag. "Here, take this to your Harvest and next time do not come into my garden like a thief in the night."

Pauline thanked the elderly man and walked out of his garden, this time through the gate.

The next day Pauline took the apples into school, along with her tin of baked beans. She handed them to Mrs Hunt, her teacher, who admired the apples so much that she put them to the front of the display. Somehow, Pauline wasn't very happy about this; she still felt uncomfortable about how she got the apples.

Why did she feel uncomfortable? Should she tell somebody what she had done?

After the Service all the food was put into boxes ready to be delivered to the elderly in the area. Pauline, Colin and Johnny had two boxes to deliver. She could not believe her eyes when she saw the name on the first box. It was for Mr Petrowski!

The three children walked up his path and knocked on the front door. When Mr Petrowski opened the door Colin explained that the box of food was a gift from their school.

"Well, well, what do we have here?" said Mr Petrowski, taking the box from the children. "Thank you very much. And how did you know what was my favourite food?" He picked out Pauline's tin of baked beans. "I shall enjoy this tonight!"

Discussion Points
1. What made Pauline choose to steal the apples?
2. How did Mr Petrowski show that he appreciated Pauline's tin of baked beans?
3. Pauline's teacher put the apples in the front of the display. How did Pauline feel about that?

Prayer/Reflection
Let us think about what we give to other people. What does it cost us? *Really?* .... Lord, teach us to give.

Religious Links (Mark 12 : 41–44)
People were giving money to the Treasury. Jesus saw a widow give all that she had, just a few coins. He asked his disciples, who gave more, those who gave bags of money and still had much left or the widow who gave a little and had nothing left? His point was that the value of a gift is not how great it is but what it means in cost to the giver.

Follow-up Activities
1. Talk to the children about gifts that cost very little in terms of money but can cost them a lot in other ways, such as time.
2. Discuss the peer group pressure that Pauline was under. In what other ways do the children feel this pressure?

3
The Lunch Box

Verna did not want to go to lunch. As the others filed out of the classroom she stayed behind, sitting at her desk and resting her head on her arm.

"Aren't you going to lunch?" asked Mrs Jones.

"I don't feel well," whispered Verna. She was a shy, quiet girl. Mrs Jones could hardly hear her.

"Why, what's wrong, you've been all right all morning."

"I've got a headache," was all Verna could say.

Mrs Jones was puzzled. Verna wasn't one to complain about headaches and she had seemed all right during lessons in the morning. Mrs Jones sensed that there might be another reason why Verna didn't want to go into lunch.

"Come on, Verna, let's get your lunch box. I'm sure if you try to eat something you'll feel better," she suggested.

Verna's eyes began to swell up and a tear rolled down her cheek. "I forgot my lunch box."

Many children forget their lunch boxes! Instead of pretending to be ill, what could Verna have done? What should Mrs Jones do now?

"Well, that's not such a catastrophe, said Mrs Jones. Is there anybody at home who could bring your lunch box to school?" Verna shook her head.

"Would you like a school dinner, it's chips and fish fingers today?" Again Verna shook her head. Mrs Jones was getting a bit frustrated by now. She knew that Verna should have something to eat. "Come and sit down with the others," she said. "I'll go and talk to Cook to see if she could do you a sandwich."

Verna sat down with the other girls in the class. The cook searched through her fridge and found a number of things she could make for Verna. But when Mrs Jones got back to Verna's table she had a surprise. There was Verna, smiling, with a plate of food in front of her.

"Did somebody bring your lunch box to school after all?" asked Mrs Jones.

"No," said Nina, "we've all shared our lunches with her." When Mrs Jones looked closely she saw a strange collection of food, half a ham sandwich, half a cheese sandwich, a portion of pork pie, three different types of crisps, a piece of apple and two segments of orange. Mrs Jones was sure that Verna had more to eat than any of the others!

Discussion
1. What happened to Verna's lunch box?
2. Why did Verna choose to tell a lie about having a headache?
3. How did the other children show kindness to Verna?
4. Why is it important to have something to eat at lunchtime?

Prayer/Reflection
Dear Lord, help us to share with others – it might be a pen to use or something to eat. But most important, we should share our friendship with those around us.

Religious Links
In Sikhism one of Guru Nanak's teachings was called 'Wand Chhako' which means 'sharing with others'. He taught that everyone was equal and we should all serve in the community to help one another.

Follow-up Activities
1. The children can explore other ways of 'sharing', our pencils, our time, our talents – in school and out of school.
2. Look at how rich countries can share with poorer ones.
3. Think about 'special' meals, such as at Christmas, birthdays, and so on.

4
The Tackle

THEME: bravery in overcoming adversity

When Mr Hall talked about bravery in assembly he didn't have to look far for a good example. The story of Prakesh Bannerji was always a source of inspiration for the school.

Prakesh loved football. He lived and breathed it every day. His favourite team was Manchester United and he had posters of the team all over the wall of his room. He had a drinking mug, scarf, cap, coat and a full football kit in the red colours of the club. During breaktime every day at school he organised a football game – Manchester United versus the rest. He was the captain of the school team and he was due to have a trial for the district team. It was then that football nearly ruined his life.

About twenty boys turned up for the district trials along with Prakesh. It was a cold, wintry day, the ground was frozen and the trial shouldn't have taken place but the trainer didn't want to disappoint the boys by cancelling it. He organised dribbling and shooting practice and for half an hour Prakesh was doing well and enjoying himself. The boys were then put into groups of five, with three attackers against two defenders. Prakesh liked being on the wing, so he was an attacker. Prakesh was thin and wiry, not big at all, but what he lost in weight he gained in speed. Unfortunately he wasn't fast enough that day.

Prakesh had the ball and he tried to run around one of the defenders. As this was a district trial all the boys were better than average at football. Certainly this defender was better than any at Prakesh's school. The defender eyed him as he approached and then timed his tackle to perfection. It wasn't a foul tackle but it was a hard one. Prakesh fell heavily to the the ground, his head snapped back and banged on the hard frozen ground. He lay there motionless with his eyes closed.

The other boys shouted for the trainer who ran over and immediately began to examine Prakesh. He checked that Prakesh had not choked on his tongue, that he was breathing and that his pulse was alright. He put Prakesh into the recovery position and asked one of the other adults to call an ambulance and his parents.

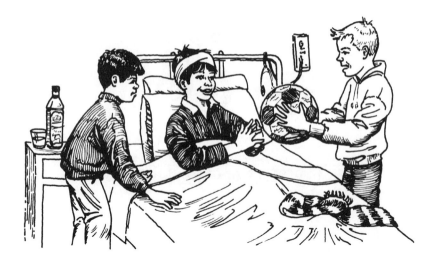

Prakesh came back to his senses during the ride in the ambulance. At first he wasn't too sure where he was, until the ambulance man reassured him. He felt the bandages around his head and then he remembered what had happened. When they reached the hospital he was taken straight to casualty. It was while the doctor was examining him that he felt real panic. He found that he couldn't move his legs.

The next week was very difficult for Prakesh. All sorts of things were done to him that he didn't understand. He had suffered a bad blow to the back of his head and neck. The doctors feared that as a consequence he had damaged the nerves that went down to his legs. They did not know when, or even if, he would regain the full use of his legs. Prakesh's mother stayed with him the whole time and his best friends, Faizan and Mark, and of course his sister Sereena visited him regularly. After a few weeks the doctors announced that he didn't need an operation and that only time and a lot of physiotherapy would determine whether Prakesh would walk properly again.

Prakesh didn't start his physiotherapy very well. He missed being able to run and play football. The physiotherapist was trying to make him move his feet and legs but the effort hurt him and he gave up very quickly. His mother began to worry about him because he wasn't making any progress.

One day, about four weeks after the accident, Mr Hall came in to visit him along with Faizan and Mark. After asking him how he was Mr Hall handed him a plastic bag. Mark and Faizan were grinning as Prakesh looked into the bag. He brought out a full sized leather football. On it were written the words, 'Please kick me', and it was signed by all the players of the Manchester United football team. Prakesh couldn't believe his eyes, as he read the names of his favourite players.

"You'll have to get better now," said Mark.

That was when Prakesh made his choice. He was determined to get onto his feet. The physiotherapist was delighted with his new efforts. It was a hard, painful process, often ending in frustrated tears. But whereas before he always gave up and would ask to go back to his ward he now insisted on working right through to the end of the session. Two weeks later when Mr Hall visited, a proud Prakesh carefully pushed himself onto his feet and stood before him. He then sat down with a bump and everybody laughed.

From then on his progress went even faster. There were hugs and tears from his mother when he took his first faltering steps. His bravery had beaten the pain and he was now on the road to a full recovery.

When he was finally discharged from hospital he took his special football into his garden. With his sister and parents watching, he gave it one good kick and everybody clapped. He then took the ball up to his bedroom and carefully placed it on his chest of drawers. He wasn't going to kick that ball again!

Discussion points
1. How did Prakesh show bravery?
2. Why did he decide to make an effort to get better?
3. Why did he only kick the ball once?

Prayer/Reflection
Let us give thanks to those who risk their lives for our safety, and pause for a moment to think about one of these people or groups of people we know, (firemen or women, RNLI, and so on). We hope that we have the strength to face the tests of life and that we'll have the courage to do what is right.

Religious Links (Acts 5 : 12–42)
Peter escaped from prison and continued to preach at the Temple about Jesus. He showed great bravery as he knew that he would be in trouble with the High Priest.

Paul, writing not entirely modestly, in 2 Corinthians 11 : 23 – 28 describes all the things he had to put up with as a Christian leader.

Follow-up Activities
1. The children could explore many different examples of bravery, such as famous people like Grace Darling and Neil Armstrong; facing physical pain and illness; the brave deeds of the rescue services; and bravery at school, when children go to school for the first time or learn to swim.
2. Is there a point when foolishness can be mistaken for bravery; for example, rushing into a burning house to save someone instead of dialling 999 and waiting for the fire brigade?
3. Children facing peer group pressure sometimes need to be brave to say 'no'.

5
Grandad

THEME: doing something you don't want to

Mark's Grandad was in hospital. He had a bad heart. For the last three weeks Mark had been going to see him on Saturday afternoons. Mark loved his Grandad but he really didn't like going to the hospital. He didn't like the antiseptic smell; he didn't like seeing all the ill people. His Grandad would lie in bed, saying very little, while Mark's mother did most of the talking. Mark had to tell him all about his week at school. He found this very difficult to do and it made him feel uncomfortable.

This had been going on for a few weeks when on Friday at school Prakesh rushed over to him and shouted eagerly, "I've got them!"

"Got what?" asked Mark.

"The tickets, dim-wit," said Prakesh. "You know, the big match tomorrow."

Mark's face lit up, "Chelsea versus Liverpool, you didn't!"

"Yea, my uncle got that job as steward at Stamford Bridge and he's sent me tickets. I've got an extra one. Do you want to go?"

Mark's heart leapt. His favourite team was Chelsea. He'd only once seen them play, that was last year. It was such a fantastic day that it seemed as if it happened yesterday. "I'll ask my Mum and give you a call tonight," he told Prakesh, "I'm sure it will be alright."

When Mark got home from school he was bursting to tell his Mum about the tickets for the football match.

"But Mark," said his Mum, "what about Grandad? You know it's the highlight of the week for him, he loves seeing you."

"He doesn't say much to me," mumbled Mark.

"But he listens to you, he likes to hear all about your week at school."

"But Mum, it's Chelsea versus Liverpool, I promise I'll go next week," pleaded Mark.

"It really means a lot to him that you make the effort to visit." She looked at the disappointment in his face. "Well, it's your choice," she said.

What would you do in Mark's position. Choose to visit your Grandad or go to the football match?

Mark could only think of one thing, the football match. To him the choice was simple. He would go to the match and see his Grandad the following week. His Grandad used to be a Chelsea supporter; Mark would tell him all about the match. He'd enjoy that.

The next day Mark was very excited. He went with Prakesh and two of Prakesh's older cousins. The train journey seemed to take ages but eventually they reached the Chelsea ground. The match was brilliant, especially as Chelsea won 2–1. That night Mark couldn't get to sleep; his mind was racing from the excitement of the day.

Early on Sunday morning Mark was woken by the telephone. He didn't take much notice until he heard his parents in the kitchen. He sensed that something was wrong and got up. His mother was sitting at the kitchen table, very upset and crying. His father was trying to comfort her. When his father saw him he said, "Mark, we've just had some bad news, your Grandad died during the night."

The news hit Mark like a hammer blow. He just couldn't believe it. "I don't understand, I thought he was getting better; that's why he was in hospital."

"He had another massive heart attack during the night," said his father. "There was nothing they could do for him."

Mark felt gutted. He ran to his room and shut the door. He lay on his bed and wept. He thought about all the good times he had had with his Grandad, playing ball in the park, going to the zoo, it all came back to him. Now he would never see him again. He wished, more than anything else, that he'd visited him the day before.

There was a knock on the door and his Dad came in. Mark sat up and said, "I wish I'd gone to the hospital yesterday. Do you think it was me not going that made him have his heart attack?"

"Good heavens, no," replied his Dad. "He would have had that attack even if the Queen had visited him. In fact he was really chuffed to hear you'd gone to the football match, so don't feel bad about it. Here's an envelope he wanted you to have. When he heard where you were going, he took this out of his bedside locker and asked me to give it to you."

Mark took the envelope and opened it. Inside, there was a blue and white card. It was a Chelsea season ticket. "I don't understand," said Mark in amazement, "I thought he hadn't been to a match for years."

"He hadn't," said his father, "but he always renewed his ticket, just in case. He was really proud to hear you had taken an interest in his old club."

Mark looked at the ticket, he put it down on his bed and said, "I'd rather have Grandad back."

Discussion
1. Why didn't Mark like going to the hospital?
2. Did his Grandad enjoy his visits?
3. Mark made the choice to go to the football match. How did he feel about that when he heard about his Grandad?
4. How did Mark know that his Grandad didn't mind that he hadn't been to visit him?

Prayer/Reflection
Lord, teach us to care for one another and help us to understand the needs of others.

Religious Links (Matthew 21 : 28 – 31))
In a story Jesus told, 'doing' matters more than 'saying'. Go on to tell the story of the two sons from Matthew 21 : 28 – 31.

Follow-up Activities
1. Sometimes we do things for other people, even if we don't like doing them, because we really care for those people. Make a list of the things that parents do for children, like washing and ironing, that perhaps they don't like doing.
2. Ask the children to write a letter to someone they know who lives on their own. Writing a letter can often be a real chore but it does give enormous pleasure to the person who receives it.

6
Mr Nanji

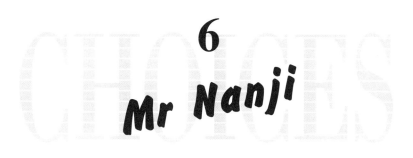

THEME: looking out for the elderly

Verna left for school at the same time every morning. As she walked down the road she would always meet Mr Nanji coming out of his house to give his old dog, Buster, a walk. Mr Nanji lived on his own; his wife had died many years ago. He was a cheerful man. Every day he greeted Verna with a comment about the weather.

"Good morning, Verna, it's a lovely day today," he would say. Or sometimes it might be, "Good morning, Verna, what dreadful weather we are having." He would always allow her to stroke Buster. Verna did not realise how much she enjoyed this meeting until one day when the man and his dog were not there.

"I'm off now," called Verna to her Mum as she went out the door. It was a dull, dismal autumn day. Leaves were blowing about on the pavement. She turned the corner of her road and walked by Mr Nanji's house. She stopped and looked. Something was strange, something not quite right. Mr Nanji was not there. His curtains were closed and his milk was still outside on his doorstep. Verna felt very uneasy. It was so unlike Mr Nanji. She didn't know what to do.

Perhaps he had just slept in. Perhaps he had already gone and she was late. She checked her watch. No, it was her usual time. Anyway, he wouldn't go out without putting his milk away. Verna looked at her watch again, she still had plenty of time to get to school, she could afford a few minutes just to check that Mr Nanji was alright. She went through his gate and then stopped. What if he was fine? He would think she was fussing over him. She hesitated, not knowing what to do and looked again at his house, with the curtains closed, then she made up her mind. She would knock on his door. If he answered and all was well she would simply ask if he wanted anything from the corner shop.

Verna ran up the path and knocked on the front door. There was no answer. She looked through the window but couldn't see anything. She went back to the front door and shouted through the letter box.

"Mr Nanji, are you there? Are you alright?" Then she heard a faint shout. Was

it for help? She ran around to the side of the house and looked through another window. What she saw made her heart race. Mr Nanji was lying at the bottom of the stairs. He was very still and there was blood coming from a wound in his head. Buster was sitting beside him not wanting to leave him.

Verna dropped her bag and raced around the block to her home. "Mum, Mum, come quickly. Mr Nanji is hurt," she shouted. Her mother came out of the lounge and, without saying another word, Verna ran out of the house and her mother followed. They both peered through the side window. Mr Nanji was still there.

"I'll pop next door and call an ambulance," said Verna's Mum. "You keep talking to him in case he can hear you. It will make him feel better." Her mother went to the house next door and rang the door bell. Mr Nanji's neighbour opened her door and Verna's mother quickly went inside.

"Don't worry, Mr Nanji, help is on its way," shouted Verna through the window. It seemed like hours but it was only a few minutes when she heard the sound of the ambulance. Her Mum, the neighbour and she were all relieved to see it. The ambulance men had to break a window in order to get into the house and then they quickly treated Mr Nanji.

After several minutes they brought him out on a stretcher, with Buster dutifully following behind. Then Mr Nanji suddenly shouted, "No, I can't go with you," and he tried to get off the stretcher.

"You've got to come with us to the hospital," replied the ambulance man. "You've got a nasty cut on the head and you may have other injuries as well." He tried to get Mr Nanji back onto the stretcher.

"What about Buster?" cried the old man. "I can't leave him."

Verna came forward and said, "I'll look after him." She took hold of the dog's collar and stroked his head. "He knows me, he'll be alright." As if to say thank you, Buster licked her hand.

"Yes, I think he'll be alright," said Mr Nanji.

Discussion

1. What three things told Verna that something was not right with Mr Nanji.
2. What is the telephone number of the emergency services?
3. Why didn't Mr Nanji want to go to the hospital?

Prayer/Reflection

Let us thank God for the wisdom and gentleness of the elderly people in our community. We pray that we can return this by being their friend, by being helpful, by being cheerful and kind and by simply being there when we are needed.

Religious Links (Galatians 6 : 9–10)

Helping your neighbour is a theme that occurs frequently in the Bible. Here is a saying from Galatians: *Let us never tire of doing good, for if we do not slacken our efforts we shall in due time reap our harvest. Therefore, as opportunity offers, let us work for the good of all.*

A Jewish proverb says "Listen to your father; without him you would not exist. When your mother is old, show her your appreciation." (Proverbs 23.22). What do you think this saying implies about how we should treat old people in general?

Follow-up Activities

1. This story is ideal for a group of five or six to act out in an assembly.
2. What else can we do to help the elderly?
3. Have the children considered an adopt-a-Gran scheme?

7
Where's Ben

THEME: appearances can be deceiving

"Pauline, can you go into town and get some shopping for me?" called Mrs Ramsey. Pauline pretended she hadn't heard and carried on watching TV. Her mother came into the living room and turned the TV off. "Come on lazy bones, we need bread and milk for tomorrow morning and you can also pop into the Post Office and get me three second class stamps."

"Can I buy a chocolate bar as well?" asked Pauline hopefully.

Her mother thought for a second and then said, "Only if you take Ben with you. You can buy him one also."

"Mum, do I have to? I can get there and back much quicker without him," moaned Pauline.

"Yes, he can do with the fresh air, now come on, off with you before the shops close."

Pauline's brother, Ben, was four years old and was a real pain. He was fine with her Mum but when Pauline had him on her own he always played up. Ben was delighted to be going to the shops, especially if he was going to get a chocolate bar.

The Ramseys lived in a small terraced house close to the centre of town. It was only a five minute walk to the main shops but it took them ten minutes because Ben walked so slowly. Ben was an inquisitive kind of boy, always asking questions: "What do the red, green and orange lights mean? What's in that window?" And so on. By the time they got to the shops Pauline was really fed up with him.

She was even more annoyed by the time they came out of the grocery shop. Ben whinged about her buying him something all the time they were in there. He kept asking for crisps, drinks and sweets. At the check-out she bought them both a packet of Rolos, which finally kept him quiet.

When they got to the Post Office Pauline decided that she didn't want to take Ben inside with her. Next to the Post Office was a toy shop with an electric train running in the window. She turned to Ben and said, "Look, you wait by this window and watch the trains. Don't wander off, I won't be long." Ben wasn't listening. He was much too interested in the trains.

Pauline's heart sank when she saw the queue in the Post Office. Though it was only a few minutes, it seemed like hours before she was served. She put the stamps and change into her purse and went out to collect Ben. He wasn't there!

Her heart started to pound. Where was he? She looked up and down the High Street but there was no sign of him. She ran into the toy shop but he wasn't there. The shop-keeper hadn't seen him either. She ran out into the street, a feeling of panic coming over her, and looked around to see if anyone could help. There were two elderly ladies walking towards her, some young skinheads leaning against a telephone box and a mother coming out of a butcher's shop with two quarrelsome toddlers. Who should she ask?

Pauline needs to get some help, what do you think she should do? What would you do?

Pauline ran up to the two elderly ladies and asked, "Have you seen a little boy in a dark blue jacket?"

"No, you should have looked after him better," one replied and they walked on. Pauline ran over to the mother with two children and asked her but she walked on muttering about having enough trouble looking after her own two children.

"He went that way," said a voice behind her. She turned and faced one of the skinheads. He was tall, with a close-shaven head and a tattoo around his neck. He had several earrings on one ear, which made him look like some evil pirate. He wore an old leather jacket and torn jeans. "Come on Joe, let's show the little lady where her brother's hiding."

The two skinheads began to wander down the High Street. Pauline didn't know what to do. She was always told not to talk to strangers, and these two certainly looked strange. She was getting desperate, she thought about dashing into one of the shops to ask for their help but found herself following the two men.

They stopped outside a newsagent and pointed inside, "There he is. If I were

you I'd give him a good hiding for going off like that." Then the two strolled on down the street.

Pauline managed to call "thank you", and then marched into the newsagent. Ben was sitting on the floor gazing at a colouring book. He looked up at Pauline, smiled and said, "Can I have this?" Pauline didn't know whether to hug him or throttle him!

All the way home Pauline thought about the two skinheads who had helped her. She thought about how threatening they looked and yet how kind they'd been. Appearances certainly could be deceiving.

Discussion Points

1. How could Pauline have avoided losing Ben in the first place?
2. Why didn't Pauline go to the skinheads first for help?
3. Was Pauline sensible to go off with the strangers?
4. Pauline initially judged them by their looks, how else should we judge others?

Prayer/Reflection

Let us not judge people by their colour, race or religion. We should care for and love them all.

Here is part of a Sikh prayer written by Guru Gobind Singh:
All people are the same although they appear different,
The light and the dark, the ugly and the beautiful.
All human beings have the same eyes, the same ears,
The same body built of earth , air, fire and water.
All human beings are the reflection of one and the same God,
Recognise the whole human race as one.

Religious Links

A Shakespeare play has the line 'All that glisters (an old fashioned word for glitters) is not gold'. What do you think it means? Read the old Jewish story of the giant statue with clay feet in the Book of Daniel (Chapter 2). Why wasn't the statue what it seemed at first? If you can get a Bible with a section called the Apocrypha, read Chapter 1 verses 1 – 22 of the Book of Bel and the Dragon. It's the oldest detective story in the world – and see why the statue in this story wasn't what it seemed.

Follow-up Activity

The story of the Good Samaritan is a good one for children to act out. Can they devise a modern version?

8
The Carol Competition

THEME: using your talents; taking part

Mr Hall stood in front of the school. It was the end of assembly. "Just one more announcement," he said, holding a piece of paper. "I've just received this letter from the local radio station inviting entries for this years 'Write a Carol Competition'. If anybody here would like to enter please come and see me."

His announcement went down like a lead balloon. After assembly, it was promptly forgotten until a few days later when Mrs Jones mentioned it again to her class.

"Mr Hall is very disappointed that nobody has volunteered to have a go with the 'Write a Carol Competition'. Surely somebody here will try?"

There was a hush in the class.

"Look, a group of you could get together and enter," she went on.

Still no reply.

"What's wrong with you lot, is it too much like hard work?" she grumbled.

One or two children shifted uncomfortably in their seats. "Mark, you're good with words, how about it?" asked Mrs Jones.

"We never win anything, what's the point?" replied Mark.

"The point is that entering a competition is all about taking part, not winning. You'll certainly not win anything with that attitude. It's your choice. Take part and give yourself a chance. Don't take part and you'll never know what you could have achieved."

Mark looked away with embarrassment.

"Let's organise this properly. Who are the musicians in the class who can work on the tune?" asked Mrs Jones. Prakesh put his hand up. He was very good at playing the piano. Then Nina and Sereena, two clarinettists, also volunteered.

"Well, that's a good start. I'm sure you three will come up with a great tune. What about the words?" said Mrs Jones, looking straight at Mark. Mark felt cornered. He shrugged his shoulders and put up his hand. Then Pauline and Verna volunteered too.

"Excellent," said Mrs Jones triumphantly. "I know Mr Hall will be pleased. The deadline is the end of the month, so you have two and a half weeks."

Why did the children initially choose to not take part? Was this attitude wrong?

The two groups of children worked separately for a week, usually during lunch times. They joined together and soon a carol began to take shape. After many ideas were written down and then thrown into the bin they finally decided to write a carol about the donkey. This was because Verna wanted to play the coconut shells in order to simulate the donkey walking along.

They wrote four verses, telling the story of the donkey bringing Mary to Bethlehem, its feelings when it watched the baby Jesus being born in a stable and the visits of the Shepherds and Wise men. The tune was a happy, lively one, especially with Verna on the coconuts.

After recording their entry on tape Mrs Jones looked at the group and said, "I am very proud of this carol, well done. I know Mr Hall will also be pleased. No matter what happens we'll sing this at our Carol Service in the church for all the parents to hear." The children looked at each other and smiled. They probably wouldn't admit it but they had really enjoyed the challenge of the competition.

Mr Hall tuned the radio just in time to hear the introduction to the 'Write a Carol Competition'. They were going to play the top five carols in reverse order. There was a hush in the school hall. Mr Hall had received a letter saying that their entry was going to be on the radio, so they were all listening intently. Even though it was only the group of six who had written and played the song, the whole school felt the excitement.

Number five was announced and played but it wasn't theirs. Then number four, then three. Theirs hadn't been played yet. The tension in the hall was tremendous. This was the moment they had been waiting for as the announcer said, "And now the carol that came second in this year's competition, 'The Donkey Song' by class J of Ford Street Primary School."

They had come second.

There was a deflated sigh around the hall but they all went quiet again as the introductory bars of the carol were played. They listened in hushed silence until the end and then let out a large cheer.

They all listened respectfully to the winning song and afterwards there was a general consensus that theirs was the best and that the judges must have had cotton wool in their ears.

Sereena and Mark went up to Mr Hall after the broadcast and said, "Please, can we enter again next year, we've got some ideas already?"

Discussion

1. Were the children pleased that they took part in the end?
2. What do you think they enjoyed about taking part? How do you think they felt when their carol was finished?
3. What effect did coming second have on them?
4. How was their carol going to be used?

Prayer/Relection

Give us the determination to do our best in all we do. Help us to face disappointment when we do not succeed.

Religious Links (1 Corinthians 9 : 24 – 25)

There can only be one winner in any race in sport – unless it's a dead heat! But some activities we can all 'win' – like giving pleasure to others. The Quran contains this passage:

O Prophet, rouse the believers ... If there are twenty amongst you, patient and persevering, they will vanquish two hundred ... For Allah (God) is with those who persevere. Sura 8 : 65, 66

Hindus have a saying that is found in the Laws of Manu, c200CE:
To be good only in the hope of being rewarded is not to be good at all.

Follow-up Activity

Everyone has a talent or interest in some area. In small groups children could discuss their own and look at how they use and develop their talent or interest. This could lead to some children giving an illustrated talk about their 'Hobby'.

Talk about the kind of pleasure they get in taking part.

9
The Smashed Plant

THEME: owning up

Nina looked down at the mess before her. She could not believe her eyes. The pot was smashed, earth was strewn everywhere, the cheese plant lay on its side, roots bare and reminding her of a goldfish out of water gasping for air. Mrs Jones had brought in the plant for her class to do some observational drawing.

Nina bit her lip and wondered how on earth this could have happened to her. She had stayed in at playtime to put the finishing touches to her drawing. She then accidentally dropped her pencil and it rolled under the table. Her table was up against another one, with the plant standing on the join between them. She had moved her table in order to reach for her pencil but this had made a gap between the two tables. It was through this gap that the plant had fallen. It was only an accident but she felt dreadful about it.

Suddenly she heard footsteps. She panicked and ducked down behind a book-case. She saw through the books that it was Colin coming into the classroom. He went to the corner to get the spare football and then, on his way out, she saw him pause and look down at the mess. She heard him mutter that someone was going to be in trouble and then he went out. Nina quickly followed, peering about nervously to see if anybody had noticed her leaving the classroom.

Out in the playground she began to feel very uncomfortable. She never normally got into trouble and really didn't know what to do. Two of her friends, Pauline and Sereena, were leaning against a wall chatting. She walked up to them and Pauline said, "What's wrong with you, you look as if you've just seen a ghost?"

"Are you all right Nina?" asked Sereena, who thought Nina was about to cry but she didn't. She told the girls what had happened.

"Mrs J will do her nut!" exclaimed Pauline, rather unsympathetically.

"What do you think I should do?" pleaded Nina, hoping that they would have some suggestion to help her out of her predicament.

"I wouldn't say nothin', you'll really get done," was Pauline's advice.

"I think you should own up," said Sereena, "it was only an accident. You'd get into worse trouble if you don't own up and then someone finds out it was you."

"How will they do that? Nobody saw you in there. Keep quiet is my advice," said Pauline.

Nina looked at each girl, she really didn't know what to do.

What should Nina do? Should she admit that she knocked the plant over and get into trouble or should she stay quiet?
What do you think might happen if she keeps quiet?

The whistle sounded and the girls went into class. There was a group of children standing around the smashed plant on the floor. Mrs Jones had Colin beside her. "Well, what do you have to say for yourself this time? You were seen going into the classroom during breaktime."

"It was already smashed when I came in here, honest it was," appealed Colin.

"I think you must have been practising your football in the classroom. How else could this have been knocked over?" said Mrs Jones whose voice was beginning to rise with anger. Colin was often in trouble for misbehaviour.

"It's not fair, I always get the blame for everything," said Colin, with tears beginning to form in his eyes.

"You can tell me all about it during afternoon break," replied Mrs Jones.

Nina began to go hot all over. Colin was getting the blame for something she had done. Pauline must have sensed how she was feeling because she whispered to her, "It serves him right, it was his fault that we had our netball confiscated yesterday." Nina still felt it was all wrong. She looked at Sereena who simply shrugged her shoulders as if to say it was up to her to make a move.

Nina decided that she couldn't live with the deception. No matter how unpopular Colin was, it still wasn't right that he should get blamed for something he hadn't done. She made her choice, walked up to Mrs Jones and said, "Excuse me, Mrs Jones, but I have something to tell you."

Discussion

1. How did the accident with the plant happen?
2. Nina's first decision was to get out of the classroom without anybody seeing her. What could she have done instead?
3. What do you think will be Mrs Jones' reaction when Nina tells her what really happened? Who should apologise to Colin?
4. Pauline and Sereena gave Nina two different choices. Whose suggestion did she eventually follow?
5. How do you think Nina will feel once she has told Mrs Jones?

Prayer/Reflection

We pray that we have the strength to do what is right, to realise that we may gain more respect from others if we own up to our mistakes.

This is from a traditional Hindu devotional prayer:
Lead us from the darkness to the light,
Lead us from lies to the truth,
Lead us from death to everlasting life.

Religious Links (Sura 42.25)

"A fool rushes into a house, while a person of experience hangs back politely."
The Quran teaches:
He (God) is the One that accepts repentance from his servants and forgives sins : and he knows all that you do. (Sura 42.25). Do you know any other religions which teach that God forgives those who are truly sorry and who intend to be better?

Follow-up Activities

1. Discuss with the children times when either they have been blamed for something they did not do or when they did something wrong and some-one else got into trouble instead. Which is worse, the actual incident or not owning up?
2. Sometimes it is not easy to make the correct choice, especially when your friends are advising you to do something that is not right. How can children make the right choice despite peer group pressure to do the contrary? This could be a good idea for role play.

10
Left Out

THEME: teasing; bullying

There is often one in every class, someone who enjoys inflicting pain on others. Colin was such a boy. He was always in trouble at school for bullying or talking back to the dinner ladies. One day he came into school in a particularly bad mood, something must have upset him at home. At lunchtime he looked around the playground to find someone to be nasty to. Then he saw just the person – Johnny.

Johnny Hwang was the smallest person in the class. He wore glasses and was very bright and always answered the teacher's questions correctly. He was a quiet boy, who usually stayed in at playtimes and preferred to get on which his work or tidy the library. Mark was probably his best friend. Mark felt sorry for Johnny, especially at games; he would often pick Johnny for his team when nobody else would. On this particular day Johnny was sitting by himself on a bench watching the other boys playing football. The other children quite liked him though they found him a little odd.

Colin had already joined in the football game. The other boys didn't really want him to but they didn't want any aggro from him so they said nothing. After a few minutes Colin managed to get the ball and kicked it towards Johnny. Everybody knew that Johnny hated sports. The ball rolled to Johnny's feet.

"Come on Shorty," shouted Colin, "kick it back." This is what Colin wanted, an opportunity to tease Johnny and call him names. Johnny tried to kick the ball back but it didn't quite go in the right direction. Colin stood there and laughed.

"You're pathetic, Titch, your glasses steamed up or something?" The other boys smirked, they were pleased Colin was not picking on one of them. Colin collected the ball with his feet and dribbled it towards Johnny.

"Look, Four Eyes, this is how you do it," he said, kicking the ball this time with a great deal of force. It hit Johnny in the stomach, winding him and bringing tears to his eyes. "Good stop, Shorty," laughed Colin.

Mark watched all this happening with increasing discomfort. Mark was an

easy-going sort of person, popular in the class. He never really understood why Colin behaved the way he did. Colin rarely bothered him as Mark was one of the biggest boys in the class. Bullies usually went after smaller prey.

Mark was Johnny's friend and he felt he should come to his rescue. But also, he did not want a confrontation with Colin. How could he help without himself getting involved in some kind of unpleasantness with Colin?

After playtime there was a Games lesson. Mr Hall was taking the boys for football.

"Can we have a proper game today?" asked Mark.

"Alright, you and Prakesh can pick the teams," replied Mr Hall.

Mark looked at Johnny, thinking about the hard time Colin had given him. He suddenly had an idea and whispered it to Prakesh. They began to pick their teams and to everyone's surprise Mark picked Johnny first. Johnny was the most surprised of all. Usually he was one of the last to be chosen. He walked over to Mark and stood beside him with a grin on his face.

The boys continued to choose players but they ignored Colin, much to his annoyance. The others sensed that this was deliberate; after all, who wanted a bully and a cheat to be on their team? Even Mr Hall realised that something was going on but he kept quiet. There were nineteen boys altogether and soon there were two teams of nine boys and one left over, a very furious Colin.

"Well Colin, it looks like you are the odd one out today," said Mr Hall. "Tell you what, you can be linesman." Colin scowled at this but there was not much he could do about it as he watched the others happily get into their positions.

Discussion
1. Why didn't Mark usually have a problem with Colin?
2. Why do you think Colin picked on Johnny?
3. How did Mark and Prakesh get even with Colin?
4. Why did the boys 'happily' get into their positions?

Prayer/Reflection
Lord, may we have the courage to help others who are being bullied and to show compassion and friendship to those who are frightened and unhappy.

Religious Links
A famous English politician once remarked 'For evil to triumph it is only necessary for good people to do nothing.' What do you think he meant? Can you think of a time in history when this has happened? William Booth, who founded the Salvation Army, believed that evil needed fighting in an organised way, the sort of way in which an army would be disciplined and organised. Find out more about the Salvation Army and how it has remained true to this belief. Teachers can write for a publications and price list to The Salvation Army Territorial HQ, Communications Department, 101 Queen Victoria Street, London EC4P 4EP.

The Chinese believed that Confucious was the wisest man in the world. When he was asked by one of his followers to sum up his ideas he put all his teachings into one word: 'reciprocity'. By this he meant that you should behave toward other people as you would wish them to behave toward you.

Further Activities
1. Children could discuss the motives of the disciples, especially Peter, about why they did nothing to help Jesus. Were they frightened, ashamed, puzzled? This could be compared to the behaviour of Christians today. Are Christians betraying Jesus by behaving badly?
2. Are those who stand by and watch bullying taking place just as guilty as those who do the bullying? This is an interesting concept for children to explore. How can they intervene without themselves getting into trouble? This could also be explored from an international point of view. Should we as a nation stand back and watch whilst one nation bullies another?

11

The Dinner Lady

THEME: respect for adults

The children in class J were not very happy. In two weeks time they were due to go away for a long weekend camping and Mrs Jones had just told them that it would have to be cancelled because there were not enough adults to accompany them.

"You and Mr Bell would be enough, surely," said Mark.

"The authority insist that for camping trips we must have at least three adults to look after the whole class. I'm afraid if none of your parents can go then we are stuck," said Mrs Jones. A note had gone home last week asking for help but no parents had come forward.

The children went off to lunch very disconsolately. "My, what long faces, what's wrong with you lot?" asked Mrs McPhee, one of the dinner ladies.

"Our camping weekend will have to be cancelled because there aren't enough adults to go with us," explained Nina.

"It's not fair," burst out Prakesh, "why do we have to have adults with us? It would be more fun on our own." All the rest of the group agreed.

"It is a shame, though, isn't it," agreed Mrs Mcphee. She went off, busying herself with some younger children.

After lunch Mrs Jones was late back into class. She rushed in, very pleased with herself, to make an announcement, "Class, I have good news for you. I have someone to go with us on camp, so the trip is on. Mrs McPhee has offered to come. "There was an excited murmur throughout the class; the gloom had lifted.

A few days later it was a windy, rainy day and the children were in a particularly silly mood at lunch time. They were talking about the camping weekend. They were also being particularly rude about Mrs McPhee and her rather thick glasses.

"We should sneak into her tent at night and take her glasses," suggested Mark.

"She's blind as a bat without them, she'll fall in the river!" said Colin, and the children burst out laughing again.

Mark and Prakesh started flicking a large grape across the table, pretending it

was a football. Mrs McPhee had her back to them, talking to another dinner lady, Mrs Dale. They were complaining how noisy and rude the children were. Colin grabbed the grape and threw it at Mrs McPhee, it hit her on the back.

Mrs McPhee whirled around and glared at the children, "If you are throwing food around I'll have to get Mr Hall." She took a step towards the children but she didn't see the grape which had split open on the floor. She trod on it with her heel and her foot slid out from under her, causing her to fall heavily onto the floor, shouting with pain. Everyone suddenly went quiet. Mrs Dale rushed over to her and told one of the children to fetch Mr Hall.

When he arrived Mrs Dale told him what had happened. He glowered at the group of children and said, "I'll deal with you later." The children watched with concern as he and Mrs Dale helped her out of the hall.

They were all very subdued for the rest of the lunch break. Later that day, just before they were due to go home, Mr Hall came into the classroom.

"How is Mrs McPhee?" asked Mrs Jones.

"Not very well I'm afraid," said Mr Hall. "Due to the stupidity of some children in the class she will be in hospital for a few days. She has broken her ankle and bruised her hip." The children were very quiet, they knew they had been naughty. "It looks like she'll have a cast on her leg for several weeks, so she won't be able to go on camp with you. I have a letter for your parents explaining why I am now cancelling your camping weekend. I think this is a very apt punishment after your extremely rude and disrespectful behaviour."

Discussion

1. What should have been the children's attitude to Mrs McPhee once she'd offered to go to camp?
2. The children were being very silly at the dinner table. Did they choose to be like that or did the incident just happen? At what point could they have chosen a different course of action?
3. What could the children do now to make amends to Mrs McPhee?

Prayer/Reflection

Let us pray that we shall learn to be sensitive to the feelings of others.
We pray that we make the right choice in our actions so that we do not offend or upset another person.
We pray that we will be kind in thought, word and deed.
Amen

Religious Links (James 3 : 5 – 6)

The children in the story were saying cruel things about Mrs McPhee. Did they realise that what they were saying could be very upsetting. This quote from the Bible seems very apt: *The tongue – it is a small member but it can make huge claims. What an immense stock of timber can be set ablaze by the tiniest spark! And the tongue is in effect a fire.*

Follow-up Activities

1. Dinner ladies are in school to help the children. Discuss with the children the role dinner ladies play in school life and what would happen if they were not there.
2. Look at other people who help us in school – the school secretary, caretaker and teachers. Discuss what we need to do to achieve harmony in the school community.

12
The Deadly Bag

Mark looked across the table at Colin. He could see his eyes drooping; he was actually about to drop off to sleep. "Hey, watch it," he whispered, leaning over the table and nudging Colin. "You'll catch it from Miss." They were in the middle of a Maths lesson and Mrs Jones was walking over to their table.

"Come on Colin," she said sternly, "you haven't got all day. I think those sums should be finished by playtime." She walked away to join other children who had put their hands up for help.

"Are you all right, Col?" asked Mark.

"Yeah, I'm just a bit tired," he replied, rubbing his eyes. "I've been out late with my brother and his mates. You ought to come, it's a good laugh."

"My parents wouldn't let me," said Mark. Mark didn't usually hang around with Colin. He preferred being with Prakesh and Johnny; they enjoyed doing the same things like playing football or riding their bikes down at the rec. All Colin did was – well, he wasn't too sure what Colin did in the evenings. As for Colin's brother, Jake, he was bad news. He had already been suspended from the senior school for bullying.

Thinking over the last few weeks he realised that Colin had been acting rather strangely. He had been absent for a couple of Mondays; he'd said he had a cold but he seemed alright. His moods seemed to change from being really lively and wanting to race around the playground, to times like now when he was tired and lethargic.

He looked closely at Colin's face. There were red sores around his mouth and nose. Mark's Mum had once said that if people had cold sores around their mouth they were a bit 'low'.

That weekend, Mark joined his friends at the rec. on Sunday afternoon to kick a football around. Johnny kicked the ball over Mark's head and it rolled up to an old rickety fence. Behind the fence were derelict gardens belonging to a row of terraced houses the council were planning to knock down. Mark ran up to the fence and picked up the ball, then he heard noises from behind the fence. He stopped and peered through a large hole. What he saw frightened him.

There were four boys, Colin, Jake and two older boys. They were staggering about the garden, giggling as if they were drunk. One boy ran through the broken door of the derelict house and then jumped out through the ground floor window, falling about laughing. Jake picked up a plastic crisp bag and put it to his nose and mouth. He breathed in deeply and then passed it to Colin who did the same.

Mark stepped back from the fence in alarm. The boys were obviously sniffing something that was making them behave in a peculiar way. No wonder Colin had been odd over the last few weeks. Mark ran over to Johnny and Prakesh and told them what he had seen. Then all three went back to the fence and peered in to watch what was going on. The four boys were still staggering about, in and out of the house, and occasionally taking deep breaths from the plastic bag.

"What should we do?" asked Johnny.

"Well, we should tell somebody, shouldn't we?" suggested Mark.

"No way," countered Prakesh, "I'm not getting involved."

"You're right," agreed Johnny, "they will do us if we snitch on them."

Mark understood why they didn't want to get involved. Jake and his friends had a nasty reputation. But he felt that what Colin was doing was wrong and he should help.

Mark was in a turmoil. He didn't know what to do. His friends said, don't get involved, but he felt he should try to help Colin. What should he do? It was a difficult decision.

Mark nodded in agreement with the other two and they hurriedly left the rec. All that evening he thought about what he had seen and during the night he woke up dreaming of the four boys dancing about like puppets without their strings.

School on Monday came as a relief for Mark. He had decided to have a talk with Colin. He nervously waited but Colin did not turn up. Now he knew why Colin had missed some Mondays from school. But he was not there on Tuesday either. Mark went up to Mrs Jones and asked, "Miss, why isn't Colin at school today?"

Mrs Jones hesitated, then she replied, "I suppose you'll all hear about it soon. Colin's in hospital. Apparently he was involved with a fire in one of those derelict buildings on Baker Street."

"Will he die?" whispered Mark.

"Oh no, but he has badly burned hands and face. He was a very silly boy."

Mark felt dreadful. A great guilty feeling came over him.

Discussion
1. Is it fair on Mark for him to feel this guilt?
2. What were the signs that showed that Colin was making himself unwell?
3. Who could you tell if you saw something like this in your neighbourhood?
4. Why do you think this story is called 'The Deadly Bag'?

Prayer/Reflection
Here is part of a prayer which has been attributed to St Francis of Assisi:

Lord, make us instruments of your peace.
Where there is hatred, let us sow love,
Where there is injury, pardon,
Where there is doubt, faith,
Where there is despair, hope,
Where there is sadness, joy.

Religious Links (Matthew 13 : 15 – 16)
It is easy to turn a blind eye but is it right to do so when as a result someone else suffers? This is an interesting point to discuss with children. How much are other people's actions our responsibility?

Read the ancient Jewish story of Cain and Abel in Genesis 4 verses 1 – 12. Cain denied that he was responsible for his brother – but do you think the story is told in such a way that it agreed with him? Why? Why not?

Follow-up Activities
1. The police have Youth Affairs Officers who visit schools and give a talk on Drug Education, either to the children or to their parents.
2. With solvent abuse the children are more likely to be hurt by their uncontrolled actions rather than the actual sniffing of the solvent. Children need to be aware of the hidden dangers, such as thinking they can fly, walking in front of traffic, starting fires, choking on their vomit, and so on.
3. Turning a blind eye can be an international problem. Do we let third world countries suffer with famine and civil war or do we try to help?

13
Up The 'Down' Road

THEME: rules are there for our safety

It was the fifth cycling proficiency lesson and Nina and Johnny were late. They were waiting outside Mark's house getting very agitated about his non-appearance. Johnny had knocked on his door and Mark said he'd be right out; that was, until he found out his bike had a flat tyre. Mark eventually arrived, rather sheepishly.

"Sorry about that, I couldn't find my pump," he explained.

"We'd better hurry," urged Nina. "Mr Hall said we must be on time for the lesson. He really did his nut with Colin last week."

The three children set off down the road in single file with Mark leading. It was six o'clock in the evening and most of the rush hour traffic was over. Two blocks further along Nina shouted for them all to stop. They were opposite a narrow, one-way road which came in from the left. They could see the school at the far end but they would have to go the long way around another block to reach it because the one-way road was against them.

"Let's go up here," suggested Nina, "there's no traffic and we might get there on time."

"Good idea," agreed Mark.

"Wait a minute," said Johnny, "you can't go up there. It's a one-way road and you would be going the wrong way."

"Look, we're going to be late if we go the long way around," said Nina. Nina Albertini had a reputation for being rather headstrong. Without saying any more she started to cycle up the narrow one-way road. Mark looked at Johnny, shrugged his shoulders and followed. Johnny hung back for a few seconds and then also followed.

The children had a choice, to take the short cut up the one-way road the wrong way and get to school on time or go the long way and be late. What would you do?

The road was narrow, with no pavement and tall buildings either side. They were half way to the end when a large blue and white van turned into the road and started coming towards them. The van driver had just finished a long day at work. He was tired, looking forward to getting home and having his dinner. He was tapping on his steering wheel to the beat of a song on the radio. The last thing he expected was to see children on bicycles coming up the one-way road towards him.

It took him a second to realise that there was very little room for the children to get out of the way. He slammed on his brakes and skidded to a halt. The first cyclist, who was way ahead of the other two, tried to get out of the way. Her front wheel hit the wall and her bicycle jack-knifed, throwing her into the middle of the road. She disappeared from view under the front of the van. The driver sat there for a few seconds, too stunned to move.

At first, Nina didn't see the van. Her head was down, trying to cycle as fast as she could to get to the end of the road. She was well ahead of the boys. It was the noise of the van's engine that made her look up. She tried to get to the side of the road but her front wheel hit the wall, buckled and threw her into the road. She was aware of the sound of brakes screeching as she hit the road, landing on her side. The van loomed over her. She could feel the heat of the engine and smell the oil. The van stopped, almost on top of her.

Mark and Johnny had shouted a warning to Nina but she obviously hadn't heard them. They jumped off their bikes and ran over to her.

"Are you alright?" asked a worried Mark.

Nina sat up, rubbing her shoulder. "I think so," she said in a small, frightened

voice. In fact she had been very lucky. Except for a grazed shoulder and elbow and a nasty gouge on her helmet she was alright.

The van driver got out. When he found that Nina was not seriously hurt his relief turned to anger. "What do you stupid kids think you're doing, cycling up this way? You could have been killed. Can't you read road signs? It said 'No Entry'."

"We were late," replied Johnny, "late for a – football practice." He didn't have the nerve to say they were late for a cycling proficiency lesson!

"Don't you think it's better to be late than not get there at all? You're a lucky girl," said the driver helping Nina to her feet.

The boys helped Nina home, walking of course. They all had some explaining to do, especially to Nina's parents and of course to Mr Hall the next day.

Discussion
1. Why was it that Johnny could not say they were going to a cycling proficiency lesson?
2. What would have happened if Nina had not been wearing a helmet?
3. The children made the wrong choice. What was the lesson the van driver gave them?
4. Why do we have road signs?

Prayer/Reflection
Rules make us safe and secure. Let us give thanks to God for the rules that protect us from thoughtless people and rules that protect us from our own thoughtlessness.

Religious Links (Romans 13: 9 – 10)
Paul, a Jew who became a famous Christian leader, summed up the Jewish religious teaching in a public letter he wrote (a bit like our letters to news-papers). This is what he said: *Thou shalt not kill, thou shall not steal, thou shall not covet, and any other commandments there may be are all summed up in one rule, 'Love your neighbour as yourself.' Love cannot wrong a neighbour; therefore the whole law is summed up in love.*

Follow-up Activities
1. Children need to be aware of the rules of the road and the dangers when they are not followed. Short plays about following the Highway Code and the Green Cross Code would make a good assembly for the school.
2. Ask the children to list their own set of rules that they need to follow in their lives in order for them to live happily with their family and friends.

14
One Puff Too Many

THEME: peer group pressure; showing love

Prakesh and Sereena Bannerji were twins. If it wasn't for the fact that they were boy and girl they might have been identical. They were very close, often knowing what each other was thinking or feeling. When they were younger they were inseparable. As they became older they began to make their own friends and develop their own interests but they still had a great love and respect for each other. One day something happened that stretched their loyalty to breaking point.

"Are you coming down to the rec. this evening?" asked Nina as she and Sereena were wandering around the playground during lunchtime. They usually practised something at lunchtime, netball or rounders, but it was too hot today.

"My parents probably won't let me," replied Sereena.

"Tell them you're coming to my house," suggested Nina. Sereena thought about it, then agreed to go. She was fed up being at home in the evenings, with Prakesh watching World Cup football and her parents working late at their shop.

That evening Sereena announced that she was going over to visit Nina and was quite pleased when her mother made no objection. She was less pleased when Prakesh asked to go to see Mark, who lived a few doors down from Nina.

As soon as they started walking down the road Sereena said to her brother, "Look, I'm not going to meet Nina at her house, we're meeting at the rec."

"Dad said you're not supposed to go there in the evenings. He said there are too many 'undesirables'," Prakesh replied.

"I've been there lots of times but don't you tell him," said Sereena.

"Well I'm coming with you," announced Prakesh. He had his football with him so he could kick it around.

"You are not!" retorted Sereena, glaring at her brother.

"You can't stop me and if you tell Dad then you'll get into trouble as well."

They walked on in silence for the next ten minutes until they got to the rec. It was a fine summer's evening and there were quite a few people about. There were

some boys racing around on bicycles, younger children being pushed on the swings by parents and a small group of girls, including Nina, sitting under a tree. The two Bannerji twins walked over to them.

"Hi," said Nina to Sereena, "this is Heather and Mandy. Why did you bring him along?" Nina nodded towards Prakesh.

"I couldn't stop him," replied Sereena. Prakesh was a little upset by his sister's attitude towards him. He wandered off to kick his ball. Heather and Mandy were two older girls who tended to dominate the others. After a while Heather brought out a small tin. "Here, do you want to try one of these?" She opened the tin and took out four small cigars. "My Dad's got hundreds of these. He gets them on the ferry boat when he comes back from France with his lorry." Mandy and Nina took one each, Sereena hesitated.

What should Sereena do? Should she take a cigar and be one of the group or should she refuse and face being teased by the others?

Sereena took the small cigar and looked around as if expecting to see her parents watching. Prakesh was staring at her, not believing what he saw. She glowered at him, daring him to say a word. Mandy brought out a box of matches and lit each cigar. There was the occasional cough as they puffed away, feeling very important. Suddenly there was a loud choking as Sereena accidentally sucked some of the smoke into her lungs. She continued to choke, unable to catch her breath. Prakesh ran over and began to smack her back. The other girls looked on, rather worried.

Sereena stopped choking but then ran behind the tree and was sick. "See what your stupid cigars do!" shouted Prakesh at the others. He had wanted to shout something at them for a while but didn't have the nerve. He went over to console his sister, who was now crying. "Come on, let's go home," he said to Sereena.

Nina muttered, "Sorry," as the twins walked away. Heather and Mandy only laughed; they thought it was a big joke. Prakesh had his arm around his sister.

When they arrived home, they tried to sneak in without their parents seeing them.

"You're back early, everything alright," asked their father coming out of the lounge as they were trying to get upstairs. "What's wrong?" he asked Sereena.

What should they do now, should Sereena tell the truth? Should Prakesh tell his father what happened? What choice should they make?

"Everything's fine," said Prakesh as casually as possible. "Our friends weren't in and Sereena got a bit of grit into her eye on the way home. We're just going to wash it out." They carried on upstairs, relieved that their father accepted their explanation. They went into the bathroom and ran the water so that Sereena could wash her face. After drying it, she turned to Prakesh and said, "I'm sorry I was horrible to you earlier, I'm glad you came along." She started crying again and the twins gave each other a long hug.

Discussion
1. Do you think the twins made the right choice at the end?
2. Why do you think Prakesh lied to his father?
3. Sereena made the choice to accept the cigar. Why did she do it? What do you think would have happened if she had not taken it?

Prayer/Reflection
Dear Lord, Help us always to do what we know is right. Give us the strength to say 'no' when we are asked to do something wrong. We pray that we can help others to make the right choices.

Here is a Hindu saying from the Ramayana:
Show love to all and you will be happy;
For when you love all, you love God,
For God is in all things.

Religious Links (Luke 20 : 19 – 26)
This is the story of the scribe who tried to get Jesus into trouble with the Romans. By a clever reply Jesus was able to turn the tables on him.

Follow-up Activities
1. After listening to the story above about Jesus the children could explore the kind of things they might say in order to get out of a difficult situation.
2. Discuss how Prakesh helped his sister. Could he have done more? This question could lead into further ideas about how we get along with our brothers and sisters.

15

The Video Nasty

THEME: brothers

Mark had an older brother, Paul. Though they constantly argued and fought, they were very close. They would always stand up for each other if one of them was in trouble. But one day Paul put Mark into a very difficult position.

It was an evening when their parents had gone out to the pub. Mark went swimming with Prakesh and his parents. It was about 9 o'clock when Mark got home and when he opened the front door with his key he was aware of frantic activity in the lounge. When he walked in, Paul gave a great sigh of relief.

"Oh, it's only you," said Paul. "I thought it was Mum and Dad coming home early." He leaned down and pulled a video cassette from under the settee. He had obviously rushed to take it out of the video machine when he heard Mark come in.

Mark was immediately suspicious about Paul's behaviour. "Why were you worried about Mum and Dad coming in? What were you watching?"

"It's a great video, called 'The Curse of the Vampires'. Do you want to watch it?" asked Paul enthusiastically.

Mark picked up the cassette case and looked at the cover. It was a horrible, gory picture of somebody being eaten alive. It made him shudder. He noticed that there was '18' on the case. "How did you get this? You're only 13 and you're not supposed to be watching this kind of film," he said.

"You know my mate, George. Well, his brother works at the video shop and he let me take it out. I've got to get it back to the shop tomorrow morning on the way to school," explained Paul.

"But you're not supposed to be watching this. Mum and Dad will do their nut," went on Mark.

"Well who's going to tell them?" threatened Paul.

Mark looked at his brother. He didn't like it when Paul was doing something wrong. He knew that if his parents found out, Paul would get into real trouble. He didn't know what to do.

"Why don't you watch it with me?" suggested Paul.

"No, I don't like that sort of thing," said Mark. "I'm going to bed."

"You're a sissy," called out Paul. "Afraid of getting nightmares?"

Mark stared at him and only said, "You're just stupid." Then he went upstairs to his bedroom. Just as he reached his room he heard the front door open; his parents had come home early. Mark smiled to himself; Paul wasn't going to be able to watch his video after all.

The next morning, when Mark came down to breakfast, his mother told him that Paul was unwell. He had a high temperature, probably the flu, and wouldn't be going to school. Before leaving, Mark went to Paul's room. He gently knocked on his door.

"Come in," said a faint voice.

Mark walked in. "Mum said you have the flu."

"I ache all over. Could you do me a favour?" asked Paul.

"Depends on what it is," said Mark.

"Would you take that video back to the shop for me?" asked Paul.

"No way, I don't want to touch it," exclaimed Mark.

"Please, George's brother said I must get it back before his boss finds out he gave it to somebody under-age," pleaded Paul. "He might phone here to ask where it is. What would happen if Mum or Dad answered it. Please Mark, do this for me?"

Mark felt he had no choice. He didn't want his brother to get into trouble, he just wanted him to see sense. "Alright, I'll take it back, but don't get one of these again."

"No of course I won't," said Paul, with a friendly smile. Somehow Mark wasn't convinced.

Discussion

1. How was Paul cruel to Mark?
2. In the end Mark felt he had no choice, but did he? What choices did he have? Did Paul deserve helping? What would you have done?
3. What would you do if you found somebody you like doing something wrong?
4. What do you think Mark should do if Paul gets another video?

Prayer/Reflection

Dear Lord, Help us to be kind and considerate to our brothers, sisters and friends. Teach us to be patient when they are intolerant; to be understanding when they are troubled; and to be loving when they are in need.
Amen.

Religious links (Philippians 4 : 4 – 9)

This passage talks about how Paul told Christians they should show a gentle attitude towards everyone. In the story about the video, Mark is kind and understanding towards Paul. In time it is hoped that Paul will learn by his example.

Follow-up Activities

There are well-known stories in the Old Testament that look at the relationships between brothers, such as Jacob and Esau (Genesis 25 : 27 – 34; 27 : 1 – 45), and the story of Joseph (Genesis 37).

16
The Dirty Football Kit

The boys were disgusted. They moaned and groaned about the filthy kit. Prakesh flinched as he slowly put on the wet, muddy top. He glowered at Mark, "Thanks a lot, Mark." Every time someone made a comment about the muddy kit, Mark went red with embarrassment. It was his fault and the others were not going to let him forget it.

At the beginning of the football season Mr Bell asked if the boys could take turns in taking the kit home to be washed. They were supposed to check with their parents to see if this was alright. When Mr Bell asked the boys a few days later, six of them said that they would take it home. Mark was one of them, though he didn't actually ask his Mum; he took it for granted that she would do it.

Three matches later, after a particularly wet and muddy game, it was Mark's turn to take the kit. "Here you are, Mark," said Mr Bell, handing him a black sack full of football kit. "Are you sure your Mum can clean them by Thursday? It's only two days time?"

"Yes," said Mark. "Don't worry, I promise we'll have nice clean kit for the match."

Mark struggled to carry it all home. He was surprised at how heavy the sack was. When he arrived home Prakesh came riding by on his bicycle. "I'm going to the rec. Do you want to come?"

Mark hesitated. He looked down at the bag of dirty kit. Nobody was home yet. He was tired of carrying the heavy bag. Should he take it into the house or leave it in the garage and take it in later? Mark decided to put the bag into the garage. He could pop down to the rec. for half an hour and still be back before his Mum. He opened the garage door, put the sack down into the corner and unlocked his bike. He cycled with Prakesh to the rec.

When Mark returned home he saw his mother's car already there, so he quickly put his bike away and went indoors.

"Where have you been?" demanded his mother.

"I had to cycle over to Prakesh's to see about some homework. What's for tea?" asked Mark. He had completely forgotten about the football kit.

It was two days later, the morning of the next match, when he remembered the kit. It was after breakfast and he was packing his bag, first with his lunch and then his football boots. He remembered the sack, rushed into the garage, and there it was, in the corner where he had left it. He grabbed the sack and rushed into the house.

"Mum, can you wash this?" he asked.

His Mum opened the sack and wrinkled her nose at the horrible wet mess inside. "Are you sure you haven't been mud wrestling instead of playing football?"

"Please Mum, we all have to take turns and I said you would do it," insisted Mark.

"Well, I suppose I'll have to, won't I?" sighed his mother. "Put it by the washing machine and I'll do them this weekend."

"But we need them this afternoon," pleaded Mark.

"You've got to be joking. I'm off to work now and you had better be on your way to school or else you'll be late."

Mark was stunned. He had promised to get the kit cleaned and he knew he had let everybody down.

Discussion

1. How did Mark let his team mates down?
2. How would you describe Mark's actions – careless, thoughtless or foolish?
3. Mark was one of the boys who volunteered to wash the team kit. When you volunteer to do something for others, is it a kind of promise? How important is it to keep this promise?
4. How do you feel when someone breaks a promise to you?

Prayer/Reflection

Dear Lord, Help us to fulfil our promises to others. Help us to realise that by breaking a promise we are betraying the trust others have in us.
Amen.

Religious Links (Exodus 19 : 1 – 20; 24 : 3 – 8)

Before God gave Moses the Ten Commandments, he told Moses to ask his people if they would make a solemn promise with God that they would live by his ways.

Follow-up Activities

1. Explore how the giving of promises occurs in important ceremonies such as weddings, confirmation and bar-mitzvah.
2. Children could explore through drama how the giving and breaking of promises could affect relationships.

17
The New Pair of Shoes

THEME: conforming to the peer group

Mrs Ramsey had a problem. Never before had Pauline not wanted to go to school. Tomorrow was the first day back after the school summer holidays and there was Pauline saying that she didn't want to go back to school. Mrs Ramsey was dumbfounded, Pauline always loved school.

"But why, Pauline?" she asked. "You must give me a reason why you don't want to go to school."

Pauline looked very uncomfortable. She looked down and muttered, "I just don't want to."

"But you love school. Don't you want to see your friends again after the holidays?"

"Yes – but I'm not wearing those!" announced Pauline.

Ah, that was the problem. Mrs Ramsey breathed a sigh of relief. She thought it was a more serious problem. Mind you, these shoes had been a bone of contention for the last two weeks. Pauline needed a new pair for school but could they find a pair that she liked? No way! Because she had grown considerably since the last pair she had, she was now into a new, older style. Gone were the lightweight, black patent shoes and in were the heavier, thick soled Doc Marten styles. The shoes Pauline wanted to choose, her mother did not agree with, and the shoes her mother chose, Pauline hated.

They looked in every shop but Pauline was not satisfied. Eventually her mother bought her a pair that the shopkeeper said was very popular with Pauline's age group. Pauline was not convinced.

"I'm not going to school wearing those!" she repeated.

"Well you'll just have to go in your slippers then, because you are going to school tomorrow and that is final!" exclaimed Mrs Ramsey.

Pauline marched off to her room muttering to herself about those horrible shoes.

The next day Mrs Ramsey was rather surprised to find a cheerful Pauline saying she was looking forward to going to school. She was even wearing her new

shoes. Mrs Ramsey decided not to say anything about them; she was just pleased that Pauline had chosen to wear the shoes.

Pauline shouted goodbye as she walked out of the front door with her new rucksack slung over her shoulder. When she was out of sight, she opened her rucksack and took out an old pair of trainers. She quickly changed shoes, putting her new ones in her rucksack, and then continued to school with a happy, smug look on her face.

When Pauline arrived at school she was greeted by her best friends Sereena and Nina. They started immediately talking about what they had been doing over the holidays but Pauline was not listening. She couldn't take her eyes off their new shoes. Sereena had exactly the same pair she had in her rucksack and Nina had a similar pair but in a different colour. She looked down at her tatty old trainers and suddenly felt very conspicuous with them on.

"I see you've got new shoes," said Pauline to the other two.

"Yea, do you like them?" asked Sereena. "They're the new style in the shops. I wasn't too sure about them at first but they are comfy."

"I've got the same pair in my bag," said Pauline. She hesitated and then said, "I didn't want to walk to school in them in case I got blisters but I'm going to put them on now." With that she went into the cloakroom and changed her shoes. They were quite nice shoes after all.

Discussion

1. Why didn't Pauline want to wear the new shoes?
2. Why did she have a smug look on her face when she changed into her trainers?
3. Why did she change back into her new shoes?

Prayer/Reflection

Dear Lord, We are thankful for the roofs over our heads, for the food on our plates, for the clothes on our backs.

We pray that those who need shelter find a good home, that those who are hungry have food, that those who are without suitable clothes are given clothing. Amen

Religious Links

Paul, a Christian leader, in a public letter (Romans 12.2) urges Christians "Do not conform yourselves to the standards of this world (which means do not copy low standards of behaviour), but let God transform you inwardly by a complete change of your mind."

Follow-Up Activities

1. Discuss with the children the concept of conformity. What kind of pressure does this put on them when it comes to fashion?
2. Discuss the role parents play in choosing clothes and shoes. Should they dictate what their children wear? Should children be allowed to have a free choice in what they wear? Is there an area of compromise here?
3. Discuss the merits and demerits of school uniform.

18
The Poem

THEME: **fairness**

The trouble with Colin was that he was always in trouble. Even when it wasn't his fault he was in trouble. Take the time when Mrs Jones left the room and Mark and Prakesh started throwing Nina's jumper about. It landed on Colin's desk and he was just about to throw it back when Mrs Jones walked in. Nina complained that Colin wouldn't give her jumper back and he got the blame for all the fuss. He had to stay in at playtime for that.

Of course, he was no angel; he often was in trouble when it really was his fault. He wasn't very popular when he deliberately kicked the younger boys' football over the fence because they got in his way. He had a reputation for being a bully, especially with younger children.

The problem was that whenever he did anything good very few would believe it. For example, there was the time when he, Johnny, Nina and Verna were working with a technology kit. They had to make a truck that had moving parts other than the wheels. It was Colin who thought up the idea of using syringes and tubes to move the dumper part of the truck. It worked really well and he was very pleased. Mrs Jones congratulated the group and, as Johnny was particularly good at technology, she asked him if it was his idea and he said, yes. This really angered Colin who then filled one of the syringes with water and squirted it at Johnny. Colin had to do 100 lines for that!

Mr Hall, the Headteacher, always treated him with suspicion. One day Mrs Jones sent Colin to Mr Hall simply to ask what time assembly was. When Colin knocked on the door Mr Hall immediately asked what had he done wrong. It just was not fair!

One day Mr Hall had a real problem. The children in Class J had entered a poetry writing competition organised by the Royal Mail. The theme was on 'Peace' and he was delighted to receive a letter from them saying that a child from his school had won. The problem was that the winning poem had no name on it. There was the name of the school and the class but the writer had not signed it.

He was not too sure what to do; then he thought that the best way forward was to read the poem to the class and ask who wrote it.

This was not as easy as he thought.

When he told Class J all about it there was a buzz of excitement. They went instantly quiet as he read the poem. When he had finished he looked up expectantly, waiting for the poet to own up. Two arms were raised, Colin's and Johnny's. Mr Hall looked at the two boys; one, a boy who was always in trouble and did not have a reputation for academic work, and the other, whose written work was always on the walls around the school.

"Are you sure you both wrote this?" asked Mr Hall. They nodded their heads.

Mr Hall didn't know what to do. Both the boys claimed that they had written the poem. How could he choose the fairest way of sorting it out?

Everybody was convinced it was Johnny's, everyone that is except Colin. At first Mr Hall thought that it must be Johnny's but then he noticed how upset Colin was becoming.

Mr Hall couldn't look at their handwriting because all the poems were produced on word processors. Then he had an idea: the Royal Mail had sent all the poems back; he would give out the poems and see who was left. Luckily all the children had taken part and he was hoping that this winning poem was the only one with no name on it.

As he called out their names the children collected their poems. About half way through there was some excitement when Johnny's name was called and he collected his poem with embarrassment. All the poems were given out and the only person without one was Colin. He had an 'I told you so' grin on his face.

"Well done,Colin, this must be yours. What gave you the idea for the poem?" asked Mr Hall.

"I saw this programme about Africa on television; it was all about how people were starving because of a war. It was easy once I got the idea," explained Colin.

Mr Hall looked at him closely, with new eyes; there was obviously more to Colin than he let on. "As I said, well done. We are all very proud of you." Colin beamed with pleasure. It wasn't often he was praised for anything and he was really enjoying it!

Discussion

1. Why was Colin always in trouble?
2. Do you think the teachers' attitude to Colin will now change?
3. Why is it important to praise people for what they do?
4. Why did Colin find life at school very unfair?
5. Colin has now won the respect of the school. What should he do in order to make sure that people's attitudes to him will change permanently?

Prayer/Reflection

Dear Lord, Please help us to have the wisdom to make fair decisions, to have the humility to say sorry if we are wrong, and to learn from our mistakes.
Amen

Religious Links (1 Kings 4 : 16 – 28)

Being fair can be difficult. The story of King Solomon giving judgement over the ownership of a baby is a well-known example.

In the story of 'The Poem', Colin needs to examine his behaviour closely. He has now got an opportunity to look to the future and improve. His way forward could be in this quote from Galatians 6 : 4: *Each person should examine their own conduct for themselves; that they can measure their achievement by comparing themselves with themselves and not with anyone else.*

Follow-Up Activities

1. Discuss the phrase 'To give a dog a bad name'.
2. The issue of 'fairness' is very strong in this story. Are there times when being fair can be very difficult? What should we do if we know we have been unfair to someone? Some of the instances that happened to Colin could be good ideas for role play. The children could explore how Colin could avoid getting into these situations.

19

Saying 'No' to Strangers

CHOICES

THEME: talking to strangers

Sereena had a very bad experience one day on the way to visit a friend. It was during the Easter holidays when it happened. If it hadn't been for her brother, Prakesh, and his friends this story could have had a very unhappy ending. Here is how Sereena described it to the police afterwards.

Sereena's story:
I was walking down Baker Street on my own. I was going to visit Pauline, she lives around the corner from Baker Street. I was going to meet her at her house, then we were going to the rec. Mum didn't want me to walk around on my own but I told her I was eleven and all the other girls were allowed out on their own.

As I said, I was walking along Baker Street when this car came past. It stopped and then came backwards towards me. I didn't think much of it. He was probably trying to find a house. When it was right beside me, the passenger window wound down. The man, it was a youngish man but not too young, leaned across the passenger seat and asked me if I knew the way to Thornton Avenue. I said I thought it was near the precinct. He then got out a map, put it on the passenger seat and opened the passenger door. I stepped back when this happened; I remembered what we were told at school about talking to strangers.

He said he was late for an appointment, he had to find an office on Thornton Avenue. He asked me if I could point it out on the map. I didn't know what to do. He seemed nice enough, he seemed like he really was lost. I remembered again about talking to strangers but I also remembered when once we were going to be late for a wedding. Dad had to ask some children the way to the church. If they hadn't helped us we really would have been late. I decided to help the man.

I stepped up to the car and leaned over to look at the map. I remember smelling strong aftershave. I was studying the map and I pointed to Thornton Avenue, when he grabbed my arm. He tried to pull me into the car. I screamed for him to let me go. He shouted at me to be quiet and get in, he said he wasn't going to hurt me. He was very strong, I just couldn't get away. He'd pulled me across the passenger seat but he couldn't close the door. It was when he was trying to do this that Prakesh and his friends arrived.

Prakesh's Story:
Me, Johnny and Mark were cycling along Fore Street; we were going to the rec. You have to go along Baker Street to get to the rec. When we turned the corner into Baker Street I saw my sister standing by a car. She was talking to someone who was leaning over the passenger seat. My first thought was it must be somebody we both knew as she is a bit shy with strangers. When we were near I told Johnny and Mark to wait a minute while I went up to the car to see who it was. I was about twenty metres away when I saw Sereena lean in, then this person tried to pull her into the car. I realised immediately something was wrong, especially when she cried out for help.

I shouted for Johnny and Mark and got off my bike and ran over to the car. Sereena was pulled into the car and was lying on the passenger seat. The man was holding onto her with one hand and trying to close the passenger door with the other. I grabbed Sereena by the waist and tried to pull her free. There was suddenly a loud banging noise. Mark and Johnny were thumping the roof of the car and shouting as loud as they could, 'Let her go!' This must have startled the man because he did let go. Sereena and I staggered back and we both fell onto the pavement. The man was really angry, he shouted something and then he revved the engine and drove off really fast.

Johnny did the best thing of all. While Mark and I helped Sereena, who was crying a lot, he memorised the licence plate number of the car. He kept saying it over and over again. We thought of knocking on a door in Baker Street to ask for

help but we didn't know anybody and half the houses are empty anyway. We decided to take Sereena home. We were only ten minutes away and when we got home my Mum telephoned the police. I hope they catch the man.

Discussion
1. Why did Sereena decide to help the man?
2. Was there a way she could have helped without putting herself into danger?
3. What do you think about how the boys reacted?
4. In what other ways do people try to lure children to their cars?

Prayer/Reflection
Dear Lord, Protect us with your wisdom and guide us when we are in difficulty. We pray that no harm will come to those who are in danger. Lead us all home safely.
Amen

Religious Links (Ecclesiasticus 2 : 1 – 2)
The Jewish Bible and some other religious books teach that one should be friendly to strangers and even offer them meals and accommodation! It is important to remember that this advice was given in a society far different from ours, in which strangers were rarely dangerous – and could easily be followed or arrested if they did do something bad when they appeared in villages and small towns where everyone knew everyone else. But the spirit of the advice about helping strangers could be translated in our society into helping strangers in countries with famine, by sending them money or food, or helping strangers at sea by giving to the RNLI, and so on. Advice to help strangers certainly referred in its day to people who had come to settle in your country and to refugees.

Follow-up Activities
1. Older Juniors could prepare an assembly for younger children about the dangers of talking to strangers.
2. The biggest problem for children is deciding who is a friend and who is a potential threat. There is no easy answer other than to treat everyone as a possible threat. The children need to discuss strategies for coping in various situations – if they themselves are approached or if they see some-one approaching another child. For example, if they witness an incident, what kind of details should they try to remember.
3. Do not forget to involve your local Community Police Officer.

PSHE & CITIZENSHIP FOR KS4

JACKIE HILL

CATHY RUSHFORTH

JILL TORDOFF

Contents

Contents (continued)

Introduction

The inclusion of PSHE and citizenship in the National Curriculum establishes what most teachers already recognise, that pupils' personal and social development goes hand-in-hand with their ability to learn and to achieve, and should be nurtured and promoted by the school.

The PSHE and citizenship frameworks help schools to focus on different aspects of this development by:

- developing pupils' confidence and responsibility and making the most of their abilities;
- helping them to develop a healthy, safer lifestyle;
- encouraging them to develop good relationships and to respect the differences between people;
- preparing them to play an active role as citizens.

In addition, the frameworks clearly set out how schools can help pupils to develop in these ways. By providing opportunities for active learning and participation, schools will enable pupils to acquire the knowledge, skills and understanding necessary for their personal and social development and to become active, informed citizens.

The main opportunities for PSHE and citizenship which promote personal and social development are:

- to acquire knowledge through real-life experience;
- to apply skills, eg making decisions;
- to explore, develop and demonstrate values and attitudes, eg taking responsibility;
- to engage with the wider community;
- to reflect on and learn from experience.

Schools already provide many of these kinds of experience, not only through their PSHE courses. The new frameworks enable schools to refocus on the real aims and purpose of this aspect of the curriculum, and to identify and build on what they already do well (and also to let go of some of the out-of-date or less relevant parts).

The newly-revised PSHE and citizenship units for key stage 4 are designed to:

- provide a range of teaching units which can be selected to meet the needs of pupils as appropriate during the key stage;
- contribute to the four aspects of personal and social development through PSHE and citizenship teaching;
- emphasize the development of skills and attitudes of practical use to the students, rather than an approach relying heavily on information;

- give examples of a structured approach to active learning and participation;
- help students to reflect on their own learning and development progressively through the programme, and assess their achievements;
- enable teachers to evaluate the impact of the programme;
- be combined with other materials including the QCA citizenship schemes of work, and Evans' *Good Thinking*.

If all the units are appropriate, they could provide material for about half the lessons in a school's designated PSHE and citizenship course in each year at key stage 4. Most teachers will be able to teach the lessons, provided they are familiar with active learning and group work techniques. Material which requires specialist training in sex and relationships education, or drug education, with resources designed for the purpose, has not been included.

Planning for PSHE and citizenship

The elements of the new curriculum give schools a radically new way to think about what used to be called PSE (Personal and Social Education).

The key to this is to plan the following three points:

1 A curriculum which will meet the needs of the pupils in a particular school, rather than cover a certain number of topics.

There is not a set course or programme which schools have to cover. Even the programme of study for citizenship is designed to be 'light touch', with schools adapting it to meet the needs of their students. Schools differ, as do their student populations. Some schools have to contend with higher rates of teenage pregnancy; in others the student population is constantly adapting to new groups such as refugees and asylum-seekers. Students in some areas are familiar with the range of illegal drugs available on the street; in others alcohol-related problems may be prevalent. Many schools provide opportunities for community involvement and service, whereas some could give students more responsibility and enable them to take part in decision-making processes in school.

a It is not possible to design one course to suit all schools. The PSHE and citizenship units do not comprise a complete course. They are designed to be used flexibly, along with other relevant materials and activities.

b The students themselves should provide the starting point for any programme. As well as asking them what they would like included, schools can ask staff, including support staff, parents and professionals who know the school and the students to identify what the students really need to learn and to develop as they progress through the school.

c The four strands of PSHE and citizenship represent students' curriculum entitlement and provide a simple framework around which schools can develop their programme.

2 A wide range of opportunities for active learning and participation across the curriculum.

Personal and social development, including becoming an active citizen, cannot be confined to, or achieved in, one lesson a week. Hence schools are recommended to take a whole-school approach in which the designated course is complemented by specific teaching in a range of subjects, and by other activities, broader in scope, which enhance the curriculum. Where a school has a tutorial programme, this provides a further context for teaching some aspects of the programme.

Schools already provide many different kinds of learning opportunities: visits, residential experience, theatre-in-education, work experience, community and environment projects, assemblies, charitable activities, field studies and surveys, exhibitions and presentations. These may be part of a PSHE and citizenship course, or of subject teaching or off-timetable activities in their own right. Once a school looks at its programme from the point of view of the students' needs and priorities, it becomes obvious that some of these activities are highly relevant to their personal and social development.

The PSHE and citizenship units can be used in any curriculum context.

3 A curriculum designed to enable pupils to achieve specific learning outcomes.

One of the reasons for the previous low status of PSE was that its purpose was not always made clear, especially to the pupils. In the new curriculum, once priorities have been established, schools should be able to say what students will be able to do (skills), to know and understand (knowledge) and to have considered (values and attitudes) at each key stage, ie what the objectives of the PSHE and citizenship programme are.

Each lesson in the PSHE and citizenship units sets out the objectives it is designed to meet in these terms.

The setting of learning objectives and identification of learning outcomes allows:

- the programme to be monitored to check that it meets the objectives;
- the programme to be evaluated to check the degree to which it achieves the desired outcomes;
- assessment of aspects of the students' progress and achievements.

Many schools are involved in a local Healthy Schools Scheme that will help them to develop a whole-school approach to PSHE and citizenship. A full school consultation and needs analysis will provide the starting point for action. Schools are also encouraged to evaluate the impact of their activities on the school and the outcomes for students and other members of the school community.

More detailed guidance about planning for PSHE and citizenship is to be found in the following sources:

PASSPORT – A framework for personal and social development. Calouste Gulbenkian Foundation, 2000 Tel: 020 7636 5313

Citizenship – A scheme of work for key stage 4. Teachers' Guide. QCA/DfES, 2002
Copies are available from QCA Publications, tel: 01787 884444, and at www.standards. dfes.gov.uk/schemes.

The units and how to use them

The key stage 4 material consists of 48 lessons grouped into 13 units which are, in turn, related to the four aspects of the PSHE and citizenship frameworks. It provides material for about half the lessons in a school's designated PSHE and citizenship course of one hour per week over the key stage.

To build a programme, schools may select from the units and lessons according to their own priorities, and combine them with other materials and activities. The units and lessons are generally suitable for use with pupils across the key stage 4 age range and can be adapted for use with particular groups. Extra flexibility can be achieved as the units can be taught in any order.

The units contain detailed plans for one or more lessons, which can be taught by specialist PSHE teachers, incorporated into subject schemes of work, or delivered by form tutors. Whatever the context, it has been shown that the most effective delivery is by teachers who have been trained in and feel comfortable with active, participatory methods.

Each unit contains lesson plans for each lesson in the unit, with learning objectives, resources needed and detailed instructions, plus photocopiable material to support the lesson. A *self-assessment sheet* is included in the introduction which can be used at the end of many lessons. Also included is a termly evaluation sheet, *For the record.*

A template, *How am I doing?*, is designed to be used to support student reflection on their personal and social development at any stage in the programme.

PSHE & citizenship strands	Number of lessons
1 Personal development	
Positive presentation (assessing and developing skills)	2
Making the most of leisure time	2
Work experience	4
Summing up my achievements	3
Planning for the future (careers)	6
2 Healthy, safer lifestyle	
Sexual health in relationships (health and welfare)	3
Coping with stress (pressure)	3
Going to the doctor	2
3 Relationships and diversity	
Relationships	4
Parenthood	3
4 Active citizenship	
Democracy and the law	4
Researching a political issue	7
Pressure groups and active citizenship	5

Assessment and evaluation

Assessment of the impact on students' learning and evaluation of the effectiveness of the programme are essential processes which enable schools to ensure that the programme is relevant and interesting for students, and that desired outcomes are being met. As part of the National Curriculum, schools are expected to monitor and record student progress in PSHE and citizenship, and report on it to parents. There is no statutory requirement for end of key stage 4 assessment in citizenship. Schools should decide on the most appropriate methods of assessing progress, recording and recognising the achievement of pupils, for example through self-assessment and peer assessment, teacher feedback and the use of qualifications, awards and portfolios. For the latest information on assessment requirements, refer to the QCA website:

www.qca.org.uk. Not only are these processes essential to the students' learning, but they will also help to raise the profile and status of this curriculum area.

Assessment and evaluation are built in to the PSHE and citizenship units. The following materials are provided to support these processes:

- Reflection on learning
- Student self-assessment and recording
- Termly assessment, recording and reporting
- Personal and social development review.

1 Reflection on learning

The approach adopted in the PSHE and citizenship units is active learning and participation. Built-in time for reflection is essential if students are to learn from their experiences. Each lesson should include some time for reflection, with an opportunity for students to record their thoughts and observations on a *self-assessment form* at the end of each unit.

Reflection can be structured around the following questions:

- What have I done?
- How do I feel?
- What did I learn? (about myself, others, the topic)
- How can I apply what I have learned?

A template to make an OHT of this agenda is given on page 8.

2 Student self-assessment and recording

The emphasis on self-assessment will be useful in training students to evaluate their own learning by reflecting upon their knowledge, understanding and new skills, and recording their achievements.

They will be able to put these skills to good use when writing their personal statement for their Progress File in year 11. The ability to assess one's own knowledge and understanding and to initiate action planning based on a set of circumstances or experiences are valuable life skills.

The *self-assessment form* can be completed by the student at the end of each series of lessons or unit. Teachers should tell the students what the main objectives of the lessons are, so that students can assess what they have achieved in terms of new knowledge or new skills. Students can also record what they felt about the lessons. The completed self assessment forms are the student's record of their learning which they can use to complete the end of term assessment and evaluation: *For the record.*

3 Assessment, recording and reporting

Each lesson in the unit has stated learning objectives ie what the student will be able to do (skills), to know and understand (knowledge) and to have considered (values and attitudes). Student reflection on their own learning and feedback to the teacher will give some indication of what the students have achieved. However teachers should plan to assess some aspects of students' learning, selected from the term's objectives, and to keep a record, which may be reported to parents and included in the student's Progress File. While student self-assessment is the cornerstone of this process, students can also demonstrate what they have learned or provide evidence of it. The lessons should include some tasks or tests in which students can use what they have learned. The units contain some of these activities; however teachers can use their knowledge and experience of assessing learning and progress in other subjects and apply it to PSHE and citizenship.

It is important to recognise that not every aspect of PSHE and citizenship need be assessed in this way. It is most appropriate to concentrate on the acquisition of knowledge and skills, as set out in the lesson objectives.

Knowledge can be assessed by:
- Tests
- Quizzes
- Games
- Presentations
- Writing leaflets; making posters; designing websites

Skills can be demonstrated through:
- Demonstrating use of previously learned skills in real or simulated activities (including role-play)
- Tests for competence
- Teaching someone else
- Writing instructions
- Diaries and records of experience

and assessed by:
- Observation by peers and teacher
- Using a checklist
- Feedback from other adults, eg employers during work experience

For the record provides the student and the teacher with the opportunity to review and reflect in more depth upon what the individual may have achieved during the term. The student can complete the form, with the teacher's help, as a record of their learning in PSHE and citizenship each term. It provides the teacher with feedback on the programme, and can form the basis of the annual report to parents.

4 Personal and social development review

It is helpful for students to step back from time to time and reflect on their personal and social development, what they have achieved, what they need now and what challenges they might take on next. *How am I doing?* (page 11) provides a structure for this reflection which may be used at any time for discussion with their teacher and form tutor, and also with friends and family. It focuses on the four dimensions of personal and social development set out in the PSHE and citizenship frameworks, and helps students to set personal goals for their learning.

Reflection on learning

Some questions to ask each lesson

What have I done?

How do I feel?

What did I learn? (about myself, others, the topic)

How can I use what I have learned?

Self-assessment

After a series of lessons on a topic use this sheet to record what you have learned. Your teacher will tell you the lesson objectives. Note down what you know more about and what you can do, also any evidence you have. Did you take a test or write an account, or did someone watch you showing what you can do?

Unit title: ....

Lesson objectives:

What I know more about:

What I have learned to do:

I enjoyed
because

I didn't enjoy
because

I would like to learn more about:

For the record

Termly assessment and evaluation

▸ Look back at your self-assessment forms before you complete this. Your teacher will remind you of this term's topics, and also what knowledge and skills have been assessed.

Name: .... Term: ....

Year: .... Class: ....

This term's units/topics were:
What I know more about:
What I have learned to do:
I enjoyed because
I didn't enjoy because
I think I did best at:
I need help with:
What was assessed? Knowledge: Skills:
Student comment:
Teacher comment:

Student signature: .... Date: ....

Teacher signature: .... Date: ....

How am I doing?

Personal and social development review

Use this form to review your progress and achievements with your teachers, friends and family.

Looking back	What have I achieved?
Developing confidence and responsibility and making the most of my abilities.	
Developing a healthy, safer lifestyle.	
Developing good relationships and respecting the differences between people.	
Becoming an active citizen.	

Looking forward	What do I need to do now?
Developing confidence and responsibility and making the most of my abilities.	
Developing a healthy, safer lifestyle.	
Developing good relationships and respecting the differences between people.	
Becoming an active citizen.	

Name: .... Date : ....

Active learning and group work

Learning through experience rather than more didactic approaches fosters personal and social development. Teachers must be familiar with active learning methods and be able to work effectively with groups of different sizes and types. Some useful strategies, most of which are referred to throughout the programme, are described below. They can be used as directed and/or at any time, as appropriate.

Classroom setting

This must support rather than hinder the lesson activities. Students must be able to move quickly into pairs and small groups, and also come together as a whole group. A circle enables everyone to participate on equal terms. If genuine discussion and interaction is to be facilitated, the teacher should avoid orchestrating the lesson from the front or from behind a desk. Find ways of joining in appropriately and move around the class to support students. Try to remove physical barriers to communication and use the space flexibly.

Ground rules

Effective personal and social development requires a climate of trust and support in the group. This can be established over time and will be helped if the class agree a set of ground rules for their behaviour in the group, ie what they would like/not like to happen. It is important for the group to come up with these themselves, but the teacher, as a member of the group, can also make suggestions. Useful rules include:

- listening;
- respecting people's opinions;
- allowing only one person to speak at a time;
- not allowing put-downs;
- accepting the right to 'pass' or remain silent.

The students should take responsibility for maintaining the rules, which can be reviewed from time to time. It may be difficult to expect young people to maintain confidentiality once a lesson is over, so it is better to encourage them to think before they speak and generally not reveal very personal information.

Brainstorming

This means making a list of related ides without thinking carefully about what springs to mind. Everything that participants shout out is recorded without discussion. No ideas are rejected. A brainstorming exercise should be spontaneous and brief. Some advantages of this technique are that:

- all ideas are acceptable;
- everybody is equal and has a contribution to make;
- it encourages imagination and creativity;
- it is a quick way of generating a lot of information;
- it can help the group leader to assess the level of understanding;
- it is co-operative and open-minded;
- it can help with problem-solving;
- it helps to develop self-confidence.

Rounds

These are a useful way for a small or large group to share their ideas or feelings. Given a sentence stem such as: 'The person I would most like to meet is.', 'I feel…', 'One thing I have learned today…', each person in a circle completes it in turn. A group member may choose to pass, and there should be no comments on any responses. A round is a useful and quick evaluation technique.

Lucky dip

Students in a circle write a question or concern about a particular issue on a slip of paper, fold it in half and place it in a hat or box. Even blank slips should be included. The slips are mixed well and the hat taken round the group, when each person takes out a new slip. They may get their own slip back, but this does not matter. Each person in turn reads out what is on the slip, and questions or concerns are recorded and grouped and can provide the basis for further discussions or activities.

Ranking

This means listing a series of statements, or pictures of objects, according to the demands of the task, eg ranking a series of statements from agreement to disagreement, ranking a series of photographs from the most to the least stereotypical images. Each statement or picture should be on a separate sheet of card or paper so that they can be manoeuvred during discussion. Items can be ranked in order, or diamond-ranked using nine pieces of paper (see below). The latter is useful with, for example, value statements where it may not be possible to create a strict hierarchy.

```
                    1st
            2nd             2nd
    3rd             3rd             3rd
            4th             4th
                    5th
```

Photographs

There are many ways in which photographs can be used, eg to help create a story, to inform a role-play, to provide discussion stimulus, to exemplify issues such as media bias, to break down stereotypes, to reinforce additional information or to offer a variety from the written form.

Snowballing

This is a way of sharing information and ensuring that everybody participates. Snowballing can take different forms, for example, a topic can be introduced, considered individually, then shared between pairs, fours, eights, etc. This process can be stopped after any stage of sharing.

Values continuum

Individuals consider where they stand on particular issues and then rank themselves physically in line. This can also be done using appropriate statements on pieces of paper – see Ranking – but the act of taking a standpoint may be more thought-provoking or committed, eg:

> strongly agree /agree /not sure/
>
> disagree/strongly disagree

Having established their relative viewpoints, students can be moved into structured discussion groups.

Role-play

Role-plays allow students to explore a situation (through the feelings and attitudes they might experience) by assuming the persona of a participant in a situation. Role-play means presenting a set of attitudes rather than any physical change or characterisation. It helps teachers to give students quick access to a topic, or generate more concern for an issue. This can take place in smaller groups, possibly followed by a reporting-back session, but it can also be an excellent medium for whole-group activities where the outcome need not be anticipated in advance. Role-play can help individuals to share emotions or concerns which they feel unable to express normally since it allows students to say how they feel and at the same time distance themselves from the emotions by putting themselves in a fictional situation.

A whole class role-play can be developed in the following way:

- the teacher presents a scenario;
- the group decides the characters that are involved;
- small groups take on a character each and develop details about who they are: name, age, where they live and work, etc;
- a fishbowl of a small circle of chairs (one per character) is placed in the middle of the room;
- one person from each group takes on the role of their character and sits in the circle;
- the teacher sets the scene to start the discussion/interaction in the fishbowl;
- after a few minutes the students in the fishbowl return to their groups and review how the situation is developing and what strategy they are going to use next;
- the same student (or another member of the group) returns to the fishbowl and continues the role-play for a few more minutes;
- the teacher may add new information about the scenario;
- this process can be repeated, and finally groups debrief the whole process.

After a role-play, particularly one that produces strong emotions, it is important to enable the students to come out of role by saying: 'My name is..., I live at... and I enjoy...'.

Visitor technique

This is an alternative to a speaker giving a talk to the group which may or may not be relevant to their interests. The students take responsibility for the visitor and are in control of the session. The aims are threefold: to allow the students to set the agenda for the visit, to provide an opportunity to work together as a group, and to interact positively with an adult, usually from outside school. The visitor should be briefed that they will not be giving a presentation, but will be asked questions during a conversation led by the students. During the visit the teacher will be present but will not intervene. At the end of the session, which the students will bring to a close, the visitor will be invited to give the group feedback on how they performed and how it felt. After the visitor leaves, the group can debrief, asking themselves what went well, what they would change, how well they worked together and what they learnt from the visitor.

In preparing to meet the visitor the group may consider the following:

- Who is our visitor?
- What do we want to get out of the visit?
- How do we think the visitor may be feeling?
- How can we make them comfortable?
- How can we involve everyone and avoid a few people taking over?

- What questions shall we ask?
- Who will meet and greet the visitor?
- Who will bring the discussion to a close?

Action research

This allows students to apply what they have learned individually, in small groups, or as a whole group, and to learn to take responsibility for their own learning. It involves the following processes:

- establishing a goal – something they want to do, find out or achieve;
- finding out what the options are and what information and support is available;
- developing a plan;
- carrying it out;
- reviewing progress with the plan and, as a result, deciding what to do next;
- deciding when the goal has been achieved, evaluating the process, and identifying what they have learned and how they can apply this in future projects.

This process can be used to plan, among other things, assemblies, class trips, charitable activities, school publications, surveys and consultations, community and environmental projects.

Evaluation activities

Graffiti sheets

Put up large sheets of paper with the following headings and ask the students to write a personal comment on each one:

- I enjoyed...
- The most difficult part was...
- I have learned...
- I would have liked...
- What next?

Evaluation voting

The teacher and/or students come up with evaluative statements about the lesson, such as, 'I enjoyed the lesson', 'I was interested in the visitor', 'I would like to do more role-play', etc.

As each statement is presented the students vote in the following way:

agree strongly	hand right up and waving
agree	hand partly up
no opinion	arms folded
disagree	thumbs down, still
disagree strongly	shaking thumbs down repeatedly

Ways of grouping students

Random groups

- Birthdays, eg everyone born in September
- Ask students to attach themselves to a set of descriptions, eg those who support a particular football team, those who support a rival team.
- Attaching numbers, ie count 1, 2, 3, 4, 5, then group all the ones, all the twos, and so on.
- House/flat numbers
- Alphabetical name order
- Class list (register order)
- Table groups
- Friendship groups
- Consciously mixed ability groups
- Team leaders pick teams – leaders may select more for competitive performance than when forming friendship groups
- Consciously mixed culture groups

Advantages and disadvantages of different types of groups

Teacher-selected groups can:

- create different/new groupings;
- break up friendship groups;
- include isolates;
- create classroom ethos;
- develop/encourage social skills;
- act as an icebreaker;
- result in 'ineffective' groups;
- facilitate mixed-ability work;
- support/enhance teacher control;
- be quick.

Student-selected groups can:

- be exclusive;
- create hierarchies;
- create a 'safe' environment for individuals;
- help with bonding of groups;
- be used competitively;
- limit integration.

Child protection notes

Read through these notes before starting certain modules, where indicated in the lesson notes.

- These lessons may raise the sensitive issue of child abuse.

- As teachers we must be aware of the possibility of students suffering such abuse. If you become concerned about a child from something they say, or reveal in a drawing, from their appearance, how they behave in school, or by a direct disclosure, you must record and report your concern to the named person in the school.

- If a child shares issues relating to child protection with you, reassure and believe the child. Do not promise to keep the information secret.

- When such abuse occurs, it is usually carried out by a person known to the victim. In the event of abuse by a stranger, the named person and the police must be informed.

- Possible sources of help include the victim's friends, parents, other family, adults they trust, form tutor, year head and helplines. Teachers should try to make students aware that while some adults can be trusted, others may not take action. The message should be, therefore, that if they are worried they must persist and tell someone else if nothing is done.

- Teachers have a general curricular responsibility to educate students to develop self-esteem, assertiveness, personal safety skills and an understanding of the responsibilities of parenthood (DES document *Working Together*).

Ground rules

To make the lesson a success try to establish the following:

- Create a climate of safety, so that each student feels secure when participating in the activities.

- Encourage students not to make assumptions about each other.

- Don't force anyone to answer or become involved in something they don't want to.

- Agree that no one will ask personal questions or make very personal disclosures.

- Let students work in friendship groups.

- Don't allow students to put each other down or discuss other students' responses outside the pair or group. Encourage them to listen and behave sympathetically.

- Circulate so that you can be aware of what is happening.

Personal rights

Make sure that students are aware of the following personal rights:

- Your body is your own.

- Other people have no right to touch you or to behave towards you in ways you do not like; if they do it's not your fault.

- People do not have the right to ask you to keep secrets which hurt you. Some secrets can be unsafe and dangerous.

- You do not have the right to touch anyone in ways they do not like.

- You do not have the right to bully others.

- Sexual or physical assault is a criminal offence and people who assault others are wrong.

- A parent/carer/brother/sister does not have the right to cause physical, sexual or emotional injury; a parent/carer should not neglect his/her child.

- It is sensible to consider and reduce the risks you take.

- Being able to say no firmly is an important skill and may help to keep you safe.

- Always seek help from someone you trust if something happens which makes you uncomfortable and afraid for your safety.

- If you are not believed, persist. If nobody listens, ring a helpline.

SECTION 1: PERSONAL DEVELOPMENT   16-84

This section focuses on personal development in five units which include 17 lessons.

The material has been designed to be used flexibly so that schools can select specific units and lessons according to their priorities, and use them alongside other materials and activities.

The units and lessons are generally suitable for use with pupils across the key stage 4 age range and can be adapted for use with particular groups. Extra flexibility can be achieved as the units can be taught in any order.

Discovering my strengths

Note: see also the lesson notes *Job search – what's available?* on page 58.

Objectives

- To help students identify what a skill is and how it might be classified.
- To help them consider what skills they may already have developed.
- To identify personal achievements which might enhance their self-esteem.

Resources

Worksheets: *Achievement and skills* (p 18), *Types of skill* (p 19), *Being interviewed* (p 20), *Interview questions* (p 21)
Three or four recent job advertisements cut from newspapers
Self-assessment sheets

1   Introduce the lesson and explain the objectives. Ask the class to discuss events and achievements in their lives, together with the skills they needed and developed.

2   Divide the class into pairs and ask each pair to complete the worksheet *Achievement and skills*. Then ask the students to come up with a definition of a skill.

3   Double up the pairs to form groups of four and ask each group to complete the worksheet *Types of skill*. Explain the instructions, giving examples of a skill which fits under each heading.

4   Briefly discuss which skills the students want to develop in the next lesson and note their responses for reference.

5   Ask the students to complete self-assessment sheets. Give them copies of the job advertisements cut from newspapers, and the worksheets *Being interviewed* and *Interview questions* to read before the next lesson.

Achievement and skills

Complete this worksheet in pairs.

- Decide who will be **A** and who will be **B**.
- Both partners think of an example of something they did that they were very satisfied with, in other words an achievement.
- First **A** then **B** describes this achievement to their partner, who writes it in the correct box below. Each person then reads back their partner's words and makes any changes they want.
- Then each of you copies your partner's achievement.

A achievement	**B** achievement

Look at both achievements and try to identify which skills have been developed.
List them in the spaces below.

....

....

....

....

....

....

Define what a skill is...

Types of skill

Complete questions 1 and 2 in small groups and question 3 individually.

1   Both sets of partners read out the list of skills they identified on the previous page.

2   The group now tries to place them under one or more of the headings below.
    Discuss between you where you think they belong.

3   Tick those skills which you wish to develop in next week's lesson.

Communication skills	✔

Social skills	✔

Organisation and study skills	✔

Physical and practical skills	✔

Being interviewed

Read this worksheet before the next lesson if possible.

Do

- Try to prepare for the interview by reading the job specification and any other information the employer may send you.

- Make sure you arrive on time and in the right place; plan this beforehand.

- Be polite to the receptionist or secretary who greets you.

- Wait patiently for the interview to begin.

- If you have to go into the interview through a closed door, always knock before entering.

- Try not to get nervous: if you do, take steady deep breaths to help calm yourself down.

- Be confident in your abilities: try to project yourself in a positive manner.

- Be pleasant with the interviewer and make eye contact.

- Think about the questions you are being asked and try to make your answers precise and to the point.

- Try to analyse which qualities the interviewer is looking for and show that you possess them.

- Speak clearly.

- Show an interest in the work and the company or institution you have applied to.

- When the interviewer gives you an opportunity, try to ask one or more relevant questions about the work.

- Say thank you at the end of the interview.

Don't

- Don't go in to the interview unprepared or you will probably make a bad impression.

- Don't be in a rush and flustered when you arrive and certainly don't be late!

- Don't be familiar or bad-mannered to anybody you meet.

- Don't be restless or noisy while you are waiting for the interview to begin.

- Don't sit down in the interview room until you have been offered a chair.

- Don't be overconfident or cocky, and make sure you have correctly read the interviewer's manner before you make any jokey remarks.

- Don't slouch or fidget: try to sit in a relaxed but upright position.

- Don't avoid eye contact by looking away all the time: on the other hand, don't stare at the interviewer!

- Don't go on at length in answer to questions and don't get off the point: try to gauge the interviewer's response to what you are saying and let them speak when they want to.

- Don't mutter and mumble.

- Don't appear bored or uninterested in either the interview or the job.

- Don't just ask questions about how much the pay is, and don't presume you have got the post before it has been offered to you.

- Don't appear to be in a hurry to get the interview over or in a rush to leave the room.

Interview questions

Complete this worksheet individually before the next lesson if possible.

1   Read through the questions below and think about what you will answer.
2   Prepare some questions which you would like to ask the interviewer:
    make sure they are relevant to the particular job you have chosen.

Some questions you might be asked in an interview...

*   Tell me a little bit about yourself.

*   Describe how you get on with your classmates at school.

*   Describe how you get on with your teachers at school.

*   What are your favourite subjects? Why?

*   What do you do in your spare time?

*   What qualities do you think will be important in this job?

*   Have you had any relevant experience?

*   What, in particular, do you have to offer? Why do you think we should choose you for the job?

*   Would you be interested in studying for recognised qualifications in this work?

*   What is your career ambition?

Some questions you might want to ask in an interview...

*

*

*

*

*

*

Tips for a good interview (to be completed at the end of the lesson)

1   ....

2   ....

3   ....

4   ....

5   ....

Developing my skills

Note: Before the lesson arrange the furniture as shown. See also lesson notes on page 53.

Objectives

- To help students to develop their ability to communicate effectively.
- To help students to project themselves in a positive way.

Resources

Worksheets: *Being interviewed* (p 20),
Interview questions (p 21), *Interview observation checklist* (p 23).
Video camera and operator (optional)
Self-assessment sheets

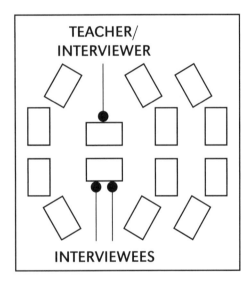

1 Start by reviewing the previous lesson and remind the students of the skills they want to develop during this one. Explain the objectives, then lead a class brainstorming on what makes for a good or a bad interview. Write responses on the board.

2 Look at the worksheet *Being interviewed*, briefly go through the dos and don'ts and ask the students to add any extra points they have thought of under the relevant heading.

3 Look at the worksheet *Interview questions* and ask for volunteers to participate in a simulated interview. During the interview the rest of the class look at the *Interview observation checklist*. Explain what is meant by each of the aspects of behaviour and how to complete the checklist. Remind the observers to stay quiet during the interview.

4 Interview (for 5-10 minutes) two students who have chosen the same job specification. If you have a video camera and operator, video the interviews. Put similar questions to both, and ask the rest of the class to make notes on the checklist.

5 Ask for feedback from the observers, and play back the interviews if they were videoed. Ask the interviewees:
• How did you feel?
• How well did you think you performed?
• Were any of the observers' comments helpful? Why?
• What did you find easiest/most difficult?
• Did you find the experience useful?
• To tell you one thing they learned.

Continue interviewing students in this way for as long as time allows.

6 Brainstorm tips for a good interview. Ask the class to vote on the five most important and write them on the bottom of the *Interview questions* worksheet. Finally, ask the students to complete self-assessment sheets.

Interview observation checklist

During each one of the simulated interviews try to observe how the interviewee performs. Put a tick in the appropriate box against each of the aspects of behaviour.

Complete one for each interviewee.

Key

− = not very good   **0** = average   + = good

Aspect of behaviour	Interviewee:	−	0	+
clarity of speech				
attitude and tone of voice				
eye contact				
posture				
ability to give clear and precise answers to questions				
relevance of interviewee's questions				

Aspect of behaviour	Interviewee:	−	0	+
clarity of speech				
attitude and tone of voice				
eye contact				
posture				
ability to give clear and precise answers to questions				
relevance of interviewee's questions				

Aspect of behaviour	Interviewee:	−	0	+
clarity of speech				
attitude and tone of voice				
eye contact				
posture				
ability to give clear and precise answers to questions				
relevance of interviewee's questions				

Leisure time

Objectives

- To help students to consider how they spend their leisure time.
- To share these considerations with others.
- To come to a definition of leisure.

Resources

Worksheets: *How I spend my day – timeline* (p 25),
How I spend my day – total hours (p 26)

1 Explain the objectives and discuss how we define leisure and why it is important.

2 Divide the class into pairs and ask each pair to complete the worksheets *How I spend my day – timeline* and *How I spend my day – total hours*. (Though these are to be completed individually, the students may find it helpful to work in pairs.) Make sure they understand the instructions.

3 Double up the pairs into groups of four and ask them to collate their information and produce a bar chart.

4 Lead feedback from group spokespeople:

- consider the range of leisure activities (sports and hobbies);

- ask individuals to think about the kind of leisure activities they do and how actively they are involved;

- discuss why time management is important;

- ask each group for their definition of leisure.

How I spend my day • timeline •

▷ **Complete this worksheet individually or in pairs.**

1 Think about how your time is spent on either a Saturday or a Sunday, mark it off against the time and write it in the space marked *activity*. The tables below represent the 24 hours (in quarters) in a day.

2 Include sleeping, meals, travel and perhaps watching TV/video, listening to radio/music, reading, hobbies/sports (name the different ones), work (house/school/paid), seeing friends, acts of worship, etc.

Day ....

Activity	*Activity*
12.00 am	12.00 pm
1.00 am	1.00 pm
2.00 am	2.00 pm
3.00 am	3.00 pm
4.00 am	4.00 pm
5.00 am	5.00 pm
6.00 am	6.00 pm
7.00 am	7.00 pm
8.00 am	8.00 pm
9.00 am	9.00 pm
10.00 am	10.00 pm
11.00 am	11.00 pm
12.00 pm	12.00 am

How I spend my day • total hours •

Complete this worksheet individually or in pairs.

1 Look at the information on the previous page and write in any additional activities on the chart below.

2 Enter the number of hours and minutes that you spend on each activity in the spaces provided, then add up all the totals.

3 Collate information in your year group or class and produce a bar chart.

Activity	hours mins	hours mins	hours mins	hours mins	Total hours mins
sleeping					
meals					
travel					
TV/video					
radio/music					
reading					
hobbies					
sport					
housework					
school work					
paid work					
seeing friends					
act of worship					
computer					
voluntary work					
Grand total					

Leisure and others

Objective

- To help the students consider the impact of their choice of leisure activities on themselves and others.
- To develop and practise negotiation skills.

Resources

Worksheets: *Leisure activities – situations* (pp 28-29)
Negotiation skills (p 30), *Leisure time role cards* (pp 31-32)
Self-assessment sheets

1 Review the previous lesson and explain the objective. Divide the class into pairs and ask them to complete the worksheets *Leisure activities – situations*.

2 Discuss each of the seven identified activities and any additions. Ask the students which activity has the most benefits and which the most problems.

3 Give the students copies of the *Negotiation skills* worksheet and go through each of the points with them.

4 Double up the pairs into groups of four and give one of the role cards to each group. Explain the rules:

   • one person reads the situation on the card to the rest of the group;

   • each person takes one of the roles;

   • the group spontaneously improvises for the next five minutes, practising negotiation skills.

   Circulate and observe the groups.

5 Select groups to perform their improvisation to the rest of the class. Follow each with a brief discussion of the disagreements and how best they can be resolved.

6 Ask the students to complete self-assessment sheets.

Leisure activities - situations

▶ Complete this worksheet in pairs.

Below are a number of different leisure activities. Discuss with your partner the benefits and problems of being involved in each situation, both for you and for others.

Look at the completed example for help.

Going on a family outing

Benefits for me   I can get to places I couldn't go on my own. Some things may not cost me any money.

Problems for me   I will not be free to do some things on my own.

Benefits for others   They will be able to share with me in doing things together.

Problems for others   There may be arguments if we can't agree on what we want to do.

Going to a youth club

Benefits for me

Problems for me

Benefits for others

Problems for others

Watching TV or video

Benefits for me

Problems for me

Benefits for others

Problems for others

Having a party

Benefits for me

Problems for me

Benefits for others

Problems for others

Leisure activities – situations continued

Meeting friends

Benefits for me

Problems for me

Benefits for others

Problems for others

Sporting activity

Benefits for me

Problems for me

Benefits for others

Problems for others

Voluntary work

Benefits for me

Problems for me

Benefits for others

Problems for others

Other...

Benefits for me

Problems for me

Benefits for others

Problems for others

Other...

Benefits for me

Problems for me

Benefits for others

Problems for others

Negotiation skills

Building relationships

Saying what each person wants and why ('I' statements)

Finding out what other people want and why (active listening)

Being aware of others' underlying feelings

Brainstorming possible solutions

Considering alternatives

Looking for consensus

Reaching agreement

Checking it is right for everyone

Leisure time • role cards •

Going on a family outing

Situation *(for three or four people)*

One or two adults want to take their two children on a day trip.

Roles

- adult who wants everyone to go
- adult who's not sure whether to let the older child stay at home
- younger child who wants everyone to go because he/she likes the company
- older child who doesn't want to go; he/she would rather go out with friends

---

Going to a youth club

Situation *(for four people)*

You attend a youth club on a regular basis and have a good time. Recently a group of youths from another club has been coming and causing trouble. The neighbours are petitioning the council to close down your club. You have to persuade the neighbours that things can be controlled and that it would be unfair to those who weren't causing trouble to close it down.

Roles

- neighbour who wants to close the club
- neighbour who is willing to listen to what the youth club has to say
- a youth club leader
- someone who attends the club

Watching TV or a video

Situation *(for three or four people)*

Your parent(s)/guardian(s) wants to introduce a locking system on the video which will control when you are able to use it.

Roles

- parent or guardian who believes that the children watch too much TV and video
- parent or guardian who isn't sure if a locking system is the answer
- young person who hardly watches TV but wants to see a video when he/she chooses
- young person who watches too much TV

Leisure time • role cards • continued

Having a party

Situation *(for four people)*

Two teenagers want to hold a party at home for their friends.

Roles

- an adult who does not want them to hold a party
- an adult who's not sure whether to let them
- a teenager who is very responsible
- a teenager who has some friends of whom the adults disapprove

---

Meeting friends

Situation *(for three people)*

Your parents or guardians are concerned about the amount of time you spend out with your friends.

Roles

- an adult who wants to limit the number of nights you go out
- an adult who wants you to limit yourself
- a young person who wants to go out as much as he/she pleases

---

Sporting activity

Situation *(for three people)*

A sports teacher/coach wants two students to spend part of their holidays at a summer training school which will only accept pairs.

Roles

- a sports teacher or coach
- the student who wants to go
- the student who doesn't want to go

Voluntary work

Situation *(for three people)*

A student enjoys doing part-time voluntary work, but is coming under pressure from a close friend to give it up.

Roles

- a student who does voluntary work
- the friend who is putting on the pressure
- the organiser of the voluntary service

Why do it?

Objectives

- To help students consider what they want from work experience.
- To help them gain from class discussion a more complete awareness of the benefits to be gained from placements.
- To help them appreciate work experience as an experience rather than training for a specific job.

Resources

Worksheets: *My hopes for work experience* (p 34),
Work experience profile (pp 35-37)
Self-assessment sheets

1   Explain the objectives, and as a warm-up play What's my line? One student volunteers, thinks of an occupation and writes it on a slip of paper. Another student mimes something about the occupation for the rest of the class. Students or groups of students take turns to ask questions (make sure everyone participates). Only yes/no answers are allowed, and if the students guess correctly within 20 questions they win. If not, the volunteer wins.

2   Ask the students to think about what they want to get from doing work experience and to record six ideas on the worksheet *My hopes for work experience*.

3   Explain that there may be benefits which they haven't thought of and ask the class to collate their ideas with a partner. The pairs then join up into groups of four and produce a list including everyone's ideas. The groups display their lists and when they return from work experience, check back against them to see what they gained. They can record this in their National Record of Achievement or Progress File.

4   Ask the students to complete the worksheets *Work experience profile* individually, calculate their scores, and refer to the 'What it means' box on the last page. Discuss the value of the objectives and how they fall into different categories, eg social skills, personal development, understanding of an organisation, knowledge of particular careers, etc.

5   Ask the students to complete self-assessment sheets.

My hopes for work experience

▸ **Complete the first part individually, the second part in pairs and the third part in groups.**

Read the list of ideas below, then:

1   record six ideas of your own;

2   discuss with a partner what you both think are the main benefits;

3   join another pair to produce a list.

- to find out about a particular occupation by working alongside people doing these jobs;

- to gain practical experience of what it is like to work: eg longer hours, having a boss, being responsible for something, etc;

- to talk to workers about why and how they chose their particular jobs;

- to use skills such as ICT skills, maths, etc, gained in school in a useful situation;

- to improve my independence, confidence, responsibility, ability to work in a team;

- to find out about working conditions, health and safety, pressures of work, etc.

What do you personally want to gain from **work experience**? Record six ideas.

1 ....

2 ....

3 ....

4 ....

5 ....

6 ....

Perhaps there are other benefits you haven't thought of. Join a partner, discuss your ideas and combine your lists.

....

....

....

....

Now join another pair. In your own words produce a sheet for class display entitled *What we hope to gain from our work experience.*

Work experience profile

This profile will tell you more about what you really want to get from your work experience. This may help you organise yourself so that you get it.

1 Complete all the boxes, add up your score for each section and enter the total.

2 Work quickly. Don't think too long about each answer.

3 Now enter your scores in the *what it means* box on the last page.

4 Report your personal priorities to your tutor. Everyone will have different priorities. The important thing is to know what **yours** are.

factor 1 For me it is ... important that on my work experience I ...	
4 = very important, 3 = quite important, 2 = not very important	**SCORE**
get used to accepting instructions at work	
learn how to get on with other people at work	
learn how to stand up for myself	
take responsibility for what other people do	
get used to working as part of a team	
learn how to help other people out	
get used to being at work	
understand how to avoid upsetting others	
understand how other people think and feel	
learn how to talk to people at work	
TOTAL	

factor 2 For me it is ... important that on my work experience I ...	
4 = very important, 3 = quite important, 2 = not very important	**SCORE**
learn how different jobs in an organisation fit together	
learn how to use my common sense at work	
experience some of the problems of life at work	
learn how different organisations relate to one another	
learn how to get a job done on time	
understand what is involved in a variety of jobs	
learn about why people work	
gain experience of working	
learn about the rules and regulations at work	
understand the differences between school and work	
TOTAL	

Work experience profile continued

factor 3	For me it is ... important that on my work experience I ...	
4 = very important, 3 = quite important, 2 = not very important		**SCORE**
learn how to use the skills and knowledge I have		
know what is needed to tackle the different jobs and tasks		
develop some new skills		
learn how to follow instructions		
understand the links between school, college and work		
learn and use new skills		
apply my skills to different jobs		
find out what I can do		
practise what I can do		
learn from those who have more skills		
TOTAL		

factor 4	For me it is ... important that on my work experience I ...	
4 = very important, 3 = quite important, 2 = not very important		**SCORE**
learn how different jobs in an organisation fit together		
learn to make the most of my time at work		
learn how to work to deadlines		
become more mature		
become more self-confident		
learn how to persuade others to my point of view		
learn how to be organised		
learn how to cope with problems		
get better at using my skills and knowledge		
become keen to learn more		
TOTAL		

Work experience profile continued

factor 5 For me it is ... important that on my work experience I ...	
4 = very important, 3 = quite important, 2 = not very important	**SCORE**
experience a possible job or career	
improve my chances of getting a job	
gain some of the skills employers are looking for	
get a better idea of what I want from work	
experience different types of work	
learn what a future job or career might be like	
try out different types of work within an organisation	
gain new skills in the kind of job I want to do	
meet people who do the kinds of jobs I want to do	
understand the differences between school and work	
TOTAL	

What it means

My total factor 1 is . . . . .   My total factor 2 is . . . . .
My total factor 3 is . . . . .   My total factor 4 is . . . . .
My total factor 5 is . . . . .   My highest score was for factor . . . . .

unimportant	not very important	quite important	very important

0   10   20   30   40

factor 1   is about learning to get on with others at work (interpersonal skills)

factor 2   is about knowing why people work (learning about the world of work)

factor 3   is about practising at work the kinds of skills you have already developed
             in school/college (links between school/college and work)

factor 4   is about standing on your own two feet and coping with work problems
             (personal development)

factor 5   is about choosing your future job and career (career preparation)

So for me the most important thing I want to get from work experience is

....

How will I cope?

Objectives

- To help students make the most of a work experience.
- To help them anticipate situations they may experience and consider what social skills they will need to employ when working alongside others.

Resources

Case study cards (pp 39-40)
Self-assessment sheets

1 Set the scene. Explain that work experience means being in a new situation and working alongside new people. Whether the placement is useful or frustrating will be determined by how well the students get on with other people. They need to show they can co-operate, work hard, and be reliable and trustworthy. They may also need to cope with people who are difficult to get on with. What will they do in these situations?

2 Divide the class into groups and distribute the case study cards in one of two ways.

Either:

Give each individual all 20 cards, but ask them to look at the first five only and write down their response. Then put one of each of the five cards face down in the middle of the group. Each pupil takes a card and gives a response. Were there any better ways of reacting?

or:

Divide the 20 cards among the groups. Each group discusses the cards and records their responses. Ask them to remember that they are practising the same listening, thinking and teamwork skills they will need on a work placement. Manage discussion between the group which has looked in depth at one situation and the rest of the class. All groups then report back on the situations they discussed.

3 Stress the need for co-operation, hard work, reliability and trustworthiness. Also mention the need to be assertive, that is to stand up for yourself if you genuinely think you are being unfairly put upon. It is a good idea for students to ask on the first day of a placement who they should go to if they have a problem.

4 Ask the students to complete self-assessment sheets.

Case study cards

1 You are being interviewed by an employer for a work experience placement. You are asked, 'Why have you chosen to work with us?' What will you answer?

2 You are on your first day of work experience. You have just met your supervisor. How will you act towards him/her?

3 On your first day you find out that one of your workmates is very lazy and asks you to do all of the work, both his/hers and yours! What could you do about this problem?

4 On the evening before your first work experience, what should you remember to do?

5 Your group keeps making racist remarks to one of the Asian workers. You like this person and don't like what is happening. What can you do?

6 You have been late for the first two days and the firm is not very happy with you. Can you do anything about this? Would you do anything about this? Explain your reasons.

7 You will be late into work because you overslept. Should you do anything? If so what should you do?

8 You are working with two people who work very hard indeed. They sometimes work through their breaks. They ask you to help them out during your own break times. What would you reply?

9 The hours of your job are 9.00 am until 5.30 pm. This is two hours longer than a school day. Over two weeks this is an extra 20 hours. How do you feel about this, and what are you going to do?

10 You are asked to make tea for the other men and women every day. Do you think that you should do this? What would you do?

Case study cards • continued •

11 The place you are working at gets very dirty during the day. One of your jobs is to help tidy up at the end of the day. This means that you get dirty every evening. Would this bother you?

12 The job you are doing becomes boring after only three days. What would you do about this situation?

13 You have done very well on work experience and the boss asks if you will work for two weeks over the summer holiday. But he/she can only pay you £20 per week. They may offer you a job afterwards. Do you take up their offer?

14 There is a great deal of work coming into the place where you work. As a favour the firm asks you to stay on for an extra hour each evening. What do you do?

15 When you arrive on your first day your boss tells you that your haircut is not acceptable. What do you do about this?

16 You are asked to work in a team of three. You dislike the other two because they mess about too much. What do you do?

17 After three days you get a cold and feel sick. You can probably get into work but feel that you need a couple of days in bed. What do you do next?

18 After two days you find that your boss is very short-tempered and shouts a great deal. How do you react to him/her?

19 You are accused of stealing some money from work. You haven't done it, but you know who has. What would you do in this situation?

20 You are bullied nearly every day at work by some of the other workers. Should you tell anyone, let the matter drop, or do something yourself?

Briefing

Note: this lesson should take place during the week before work experience starts.

Objectives

- To help students make the most of a work experience.
- To help them anticipate situations they may experience and consider what social skills they will need to employ when working alongside others.

Resources

The teacher in charge of work experience
A visiting employer (optional)
Self-assessment sheets

1 The teacher in charge of work experience should take this lesson. He/she should give a detailed briefing session. Students need to understand that they must take responsibility for details such as the directions for finding their workplace, bus/train timetables, knowing their employer's phone number, as well as the school's, in case they need it. They will also need a working alarm clock.

2 An employer could be present to give advice to the students. Details of each placement should be given to individual students.

3 Ask the students to complete self-assessment sheets.

How was it?

Objective

- To help students to reflect on their experiences, record their achievements and thank their host employers.

Resources

Video camera or audio tape (optional)
School headed notepaper
Self-assessment sheets

1 Welcome the students back. It is important to show the students that you recognise that they have managed as adults in the working world. Then have a 20-minute class discussion of what it was like and the students' feelings about their experiences. The discussion could be videoed.

2 Ask the students to write a work experience report, choosing their own format. Proper records of their work experience will ensure that students have evidence of their achievement to present when applying for further education, work or training in the future. Reports could be in a diary or log book form, possibly including photographs, plans or drawings, or in the form of a presentation with written or taped components.

3 Ask the students to write letters of thanks to their employers on school headed notepaper. Enterprising students may want to thank the employer for help received, ask permission to quote them as a referee in future job applications and maintain contact with their employer where there may be a possibility of future employment.

4 If a video camera or audio tape recorder is available, students can tape their reports. Alternatively they could make a wall display, aspects of which could be used in their Record of Achievement or Progress File.

5 If time allows, go back to the case studies from the 'How will I cope?' lesson and discuss the situations in the light of their recent experiences.

6 Ask the students to complete self-assessment sheets.

The real you

Note: see also the lesson notes *Discovering my strengths* on page 17

Objective

- To help students to reflect on and identify achievements in and out of school.

Resources

Worksheets: *The real you 1 and 2* (pp 44-45)
Examples of personal statements (pp 50-51)
Self-assessment sheets

1 Explain the objective. Remind the class of previous occasions when they have looked at their personal qualities. They may want to use some of their work on this from the previous year.

2 Explain that personal qualities are important and that everyone has different ones. Which are important and which do other people (eg employers, college lecturers) need to know about if they are going to make the best of you? Who is the real you? What makes you special? What do you have going for you?

3 Ask student to discuss these questions, using the worksheet *The real you 1* as a prompt. You could either put a student in the centre of a group and fire the questions at him/her, or ask students in pairs to take turns putting each other on the spot, using the questions for ideas. Stress the importance of being positive about yourself.

4 Introduce the idea of a personal statement. Ask the students to look at *The real you 2* (employers' and lecturers' opinions about and expectations from personal statements). Look at the examples of personal statements and decide which are best and why. These are real examples with the names changed. Groups can devise a list of things to include and omit from a personal statement.

5 Ask the students to complete self-assessment sheets.

The real you 1

What do you most like about yourself?

What do other people like about you?

If you had £1 million, what would you do with it?

What do you worry about most?

What things make you laugh?

What is the best thing you have done in your life so far?

If you were a character from history, who would it be? Why?

What qualities in yourself do you most admire?

What qualities in a person do you most admire?

In five years' time, where do you see yourself? What will you be doing?

The real you 2

What employers and colleges say about personal statements.

I like the personal statement to be refreshingly honest.

The student's personal statement is a very good document, the first thing I always read.

There are some excellent examples where the school has allowed the students the freedom to decide what achievements to include. Students must be encouraged to analyse themselves and present a very personal picture. Statements must be honest and relate to the young person concerned, not a general statement which could relate to anyone.

I wish I had had something like this when I left school.

Students should bring their Record of Achievement or Progress File to interviews and be prepared to talk proudly about the things that are in it.

I like to see evidence of the whole person. What are their aspirations and ambitions in life?

I want to know about how the student approaches the subject generally. This shows us what the student can do, what he/she has done so far, what their future goals are and what actions they intend to take in order to meet those goals.

The Record of Achievement is not only important in the interview, but also when the person is at college, university, training or in employment. It should form the basis of personal record-keeping for life.

Make the most of your chance to show these people what you are really about!

Writing about yourself

Objective

- To help students draft, write and edit a personal statement for their summative Record of Achievement or Progress File.

Resources

Worksheets: *Cartoons* (pp 47-49), *Personal statements* (pp 50-51), *Curriculum Vitae* (p 52)

1 Recap on the previous lesson, then ask individuals to note down the factual information about themselves that they would include in a personal statement, plus their personal qualities. Use the *Cartoons* as a prompt. Make sure the students consider what evidence they have to back up what they say. They could refer to their portfolios, or self-assessment sheets from the previous year.

2 Look at and discuss the examples of personal statements. It should soon become obvious that examples A, B, C and D are unacceptable, and that examples E and F are what is required.

3 Ask the students to write their first drafts. This may take longer than one lesson. Check whether students with special needs require help to do this: for example, tape recorders or computers. Also, do any students need translation facilities?

4 Ask the students to review their work using some of the following strategies. This work does not all have to take place during a class.

- Read drafts, check using the dos and don'ts checklist from the previous lesson.

- Read it to a partner and jointly edit it.

- Show it to a parent or someone who knows them well and discuss whether it gives a true flavour of themselves.

- Type it on to a word processor and use the spellchecker.

5 Students should now write their final draft. This should be photocopied, if possible, and taken home for discussion. The final statement should be typed and students can create a curriculum vitae. Suggestions for this are shown on the *Curriculum Vitae* worksheet.

Cartoons

Do any of these cartoons remind you of yourself? Think about which of your personal qualities you would like to write about in your personal statement.

You enjoy being with other people. You get on quickly with people when you first meet. You work well in a group, where you cooperate with others to carry out a task. Groups you are in work well together because you encourage everyone to do their bit and take pride in the end result.

If you say you will do something you will do it. You can be relied upon to start on time, keep to deadlines and do the best job you possibly can.

You have a good record of punctuality and attendance.

Cartoons • continued •

You are good at thinking up your own new ideas and don't copy other people. You are original and creative.

You take on new things with energy and enthusiasm.

You take care over the things you do and make sure you get them right.

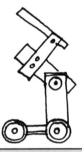

You can sort things out for yourself. You don't expect others to show or help you. You are independent and resourceful.

You have a good sense of dress and you make sure your appearance is suitable for the occasion.

continued on page 49

Cartoons • continued •

You have a lot of common sense. You are mature for your age and tend to act responsibly, thinking ahead and considering the consequences of your actions.

You are good at concentrating on a problem and seeing it through to the end. You don't give up when the going gets tough.

You listen to, understand and sympathise with other people. You think about their needs and help them where you can.

You are organised. You plan ahead, get what you need and sort out what you are going to do.

Personal statements

▷ Personal statements are intended to give other people a good idea of your qualities as a person. Read the personal statements below and comment on each of them in the box on page 51.

Person A

I am a student at .... School. I am going to do my GCSEs soon. I want to be a vet.

Person B

I am really good at working with people. I am very helpful and reliable. I like playing records and going out.

Person C

I am studying French, English, Science, Geography, Maths and Design Technology at GCSE. I like Science best. I help in the library at dinnertime. I want to go to college and then to university to study Chemical Engineering. I am a member of the School Council.

Person D

I have never been good at anything since I came here. None of the other people like me. The teachers all pick on me. I have held no positions of responsibility. All the subjects are boring but particularly French. I don't really care what job I get as long as it's well paid.

Person E

I am a person who can make friends easily and enjoy the company of both male and female friends. People say that I am warm and sensitive. I like to think that I can help anybody who needs help, and always, no matter what the situation, remember that there is someone worse off than me. I like to be with people who can take things seriously when necessary but know when and how to have fun, like myself. I enjoy being in a crowd of friends but realise that private and personal time is essential to me. I believe that family life is very important and enjoy being part of a big, happy and loving family. I really enjoy my life but take every day as it comes. I have a very determined and ambitious personality. I don't believe in planning for the future although I do have ambitions and dreams.

At the moment I am working towards my GCSEs which I will be taking in the summer. I believe I have worked to the best of my ability in my subjects. I am very interested in the creative department. I really enjoy Art, I feel it is very relaxing and fulfilling. My favourite subjects are Art, English and Business Studies. I have, so far, enjoyed my life at school. I have made many friends with students and staff. I hope to be successful in my exams and then go on to college.

I have enjoyed playing the clarinet in which I achieved up to grade four, distinction. I also played the guitar and enjoyed singing in different choirs. I really enjoyed organising several school discos for which all profits raised went to St Mary's Babycare Unit. I enjoyed the creative side of my subjects, and even though I am not taking Art A level I will continue with it in my spare time to relax and unwind. I have enjoyed being in the friendly, warm community of the school and have not only worked hard, but had a lot of fun too.

I have no settled ambitions except to be successful in anything that I do, now or in the future.

continued on page 51

Personal statements • continued •

Person F

I have been a student at this school for five years and at present I am studying for my GCSE exams. I am being entered for eight GCSEs. These are: English Language, English Literature, Science (2 GCSEs), French, Geography, Maths and Art and Design, as this and other art-related subjects are what I wish to study up to degree level when I leave. I am hoping to be accepted for a place in a Sixth Form College as I wish to study A levels in Art, Design and Technology and Photography in September. I enjoy French and Geography too, and these subjects may be useful to me later in my career. My mock examination results were good for French and Geography. I achieved 74% overall in both Geography papers. The geography coursework accounts for 25% too, and this was not included in the mock exam grade, so in the actual GCSE exams it will bring up my final grade.

I enjoy participating in extra-curricular activities, non-GCSE and other activities such as photography, amateur radio and playing my trombone in seven bands/orchestras and two groups out of school. I enjoy black-and-white photography too. I have constructed my own darkroom using the available loftspace in our house. I am involved in the Duke of Edinburgh's award scheme and have passed my Bronze and Silver Awards. I have passed my First Aid Certificate, my Bronze, Silver and Gold Awards for swimming (ASA/ASSA), and I have passed my Associated Board exams for the trombone, grades three and four with distinction and grade five with merit. I play tenor and bass trombone in the local band.

I also play squash regularly, although I only play for pleasure and exercise. I am not a member of any teams or clubs as yet. I am a member of the Incorporated Society for Amateur Radio Enthusiasts, the Radio Society of Great Britain, and I am working towards some awards associated with amateur radio.

I am applying for a place in a Sixth Form College and I should be going for several interviews in April and May. I have had to single out specific colleges that cater for my A level needs such as photography.

Which personal statements were good/bad?	Why?

Do you agree that the good ones are good because the writers have included certain statements which give a good flavour of their personalities and strengths?

Now think of a list of dos and don'ts for writing a personal statement.

Dos	Don'ts

Curriculum Vitae

What should go in your Curriculum Vitae?

Name

Date of birth

Address and telephone number

Secondary Education:	Name of school/s, address of school/s, date/s attended
Qualifications:	Examination results, subjects, level eg GCSE grades. Other qualifications eg First Aid Certificate, unit credits, music certificates, life-saving badges, Duke of Edinburgh award
Experience:	Positions of responsibility in school, community or at home. Extra-curricular interests, eg sports, clubs, leisure interests
Work experience:	Name and address of employer, nature of placement. Any paid employment, eg Saturday job, babysitting, etc
Referees:	Usually one personal and one work or educational referee with name, address, position and telephone number.

Talking about yourself

Note: see also the lesson notes *Developing my skills* on page 22

Objectives

- To help students practise speaking about their achievements to a range of people.
- To raise students' confidence.

Resources

Appointments with the students' tutor, the Careers Officer or senior staff members.
Audio or video tape-recorder (optional)

1   Arrange for the students to practise talking about themselves, expand upon their personal statements and become more fluent in describing their personal qualities and achievements. This can take place in a range of cross-curricular contexts, for example:

• as part of a review with their tutor, eg 'I see from your personal statement that you... Can you tell me more about this?'

• as the focus of a discussion with the Careers Officer;

• in groups role-playing interviews;

• as an oral component of GCSE English;

• individuals or groups practise speaking into a tape recorder, or in front of a video recorder;

• individuals take their personal statements to senior staff to discuss.

What does the future hold?

Objectives

- To give students the opportunity to research the changing nature of the job market and to anticipate likely opportunities.
- To identify reliable sources of career information.
- To consider post-16 career paths.

Resources

Information sheets: *What does the future hold? – Europe (p 55),*
What does the future hold? – family trends (p 56),
What does the future hold? – global issues (p 57)

1 Introduce the lesson by explaining that careers aren't necessarily for life. The world changes fast and some jobs which a lot of people do now may disappear. Other jobs that no one has yet heard of may be created. People need to be flexible, to think ahead, and to make sure that they have the skills society will need. Display photocopies of the information sheets *What does the future hold?* These give information about areas of change which will affect people both at work and at home.

2 Divide the students into groups and give them each an area to research. The groups report back to the class on what they have found out and how it may affect them in future. Lead a class discussion of the general skills and personal qualities that will be valued by employers in the future.

3 Ask the students to think about their own possible career prospects. Are they already sure what they want to do? Do they need to find out more about different occupations? Do they need to think about their personal interests and abilities? Do they have accurate information about possible further education and training?

4 Ask each student to write down their ideas and information on a sheet headed Action Plan. These action plans can be reviewed and revised regularly and students can choose items to discuss with suitable people. They should write an agenda for the discussions and a checklist of targets that they want to meet.

What does the future hold? • Europe •

EUROPE HERE WE COME!
Or goodbye Great Britain?

There are currently 15 members of the European Union which form a single market and have common institutions and decision-making procedures. The treaties are binding on their members, and the EU develops common policies and settles disputes throughout Europe. Eleven members have a common currency – the Euro. The EU is one of the three most powerful trading and political blocs in the world, along with the US and Japan.

How big? How united?
The European Union is seen as a success – it is economically prosperous, democratic and peaceful. Many more countries have applied to join.
Until 2004 the members are: Great Britain, Germany, Italy, Belgium, Luxembourg, Sweden, Denmark, Ireland, France, Spain, the Netherlands, Austria, Finland, Greece and Portugal.
From 2004 perhaps some or all of these countries will join: Poland, Czech Republic, Hungary, Slovenia, Estonia, Latvia, Lithuania, Romania, Croatia, Bosnia-Herzegovina, Slovakia, Turkey, Cyprus – even Albania, Russia, Serbia, Macedonia, Belarus, Ukraine and Moldova may possibly apply.

The risks
Many of these countries are much poorer and more agricultural than existing members. Big changes would need to take place first, eg cutting subsidies to farmers, or the whole budget would be taken up by paying the poor farmers of the new countries. It will be harder to reach agreement on political or economic issues with so many members.

What does the future hold? • Family trends •

Work/life balance?
Being fair to all ages?

Keeping a balance between work and personal life is becoming ever more necessary.
Did you know:

- men in Britain work the longest hours in Europe;
- the vast majority of women work, but still have not achieved equal pay and opportunities;
- relationships run into problems when work takes priority over family life;
- the number of single-person households is on the increase;
- many people are having children much later in their lives;
- the proportion of adults in work in falling;
- the proportion of elderly people is rising.

There will always be jobs in:

- childcare, as so many parents work;
- health, as elderly people face more illness and disability than younger people;
- community care, as the disabled and ill prefer to stay in their own homes;
- education, as we need to develop new skills throughout our childhood and adult lives.

Employers need to:

- consider all of us as having home responsibilities and allow us parental leave and flexible working hours;
- build in opportunities for further training and promotion whatever our age;
- not expect employees to be able to work long hours or move around the country at a moment's notice;
- support good quality childcare and holiday schemes for school-age children;
- shake up their ideas and appoint men and women to non-traditional jobs;
- promote our health and effectiveness by reducing stress and supporting healthy and balanced lifestyles.

Remember

Make sure you are in touch with what is happening and protect your rights.

What does the future hold? • Global issues •

The 2002 Johannesburg Earth Summit had these goals for global improvements by 2015

1 Halve the estimated 1.2 billion people living on less than $1 (66p) per day.

2 Bring sustainable energy supplies to up to 2.5 billion people without electricity or gas (while reducing the use of fossil fuels).

3 Open up agricultural markets and cut the £230 billion subsidies given to western farmers.

4 Remove trade barriers to goods from developing countries.

5 Halve the 800 million people without enough to eat.

6 Bring clean water to the 1.1 billion people who don't have it. Water-borne disease kills more people than any other cause.

7 Reduce infant mortality in developing countries by two-thirds.

8 Reverse the spread of HIV/AIDS, which has killed 22 million people and infected 36 million.

9 Reduce outdoor air pollution from traffic and industry and reduce global warming and climate change.

10 Protect biodiversity, including tropical forests and other habitats, and protect the oceans and their life forms.

What does this mean for us?

Sustainable development has been identified as the key to achieving these goals. Individuals and enterprises who contribute to it will have many opportunities: developing clean technology and engineering projects, biotechnology, air and water pollution controls, renewable energy, etc.

Job search – what's available?

Objectives

- To encourage students to familiarise themselves with the jobs section of the local newspaper.
- To help students discover what kinds of jobs are available locally.
- To help them to interpret job advertisements.

Resources

Copies of the local newspaper and free press newspaper.
Worksheets: *Job search: group task* (p 59); *Job search: pairs task* (p 60)

1 Explain the objectives. Divide the class into small groups of three or four and give each group a copy of the local newspaper and free press newspaper. Ask each group to complete the *Job search: group task* worksheet. Circulate and help groups as they do this.

2 Ask the groups to report back, answering the following questions:

- Which job category has the most jobs available and which the least?

- Did all the groups have similar findings? If not, why not? Were there any surprises?

- What have they learnt about the availability of jobs in the area?

- Would the selection of jobs in other parts of the UK be similar?

- How does the number of unskilled and manufacturing jobs compare with the number of skilled and service industry jobs?

- What is the likely pattern for the future?

3 Divide the groups into pairs and ask the students to complete the *Job search: pairs task* worksheet. Circulate and help the students as required.

4 Ask the students to reflect on and amend their action plan (see page 54).

Job search • group task •

Complete this worksheet in small groups.

1 Find the Jobs section in the newspaper and list all the headings or categories in the correct column below.
2 Count the total number of jobs under each category and enter them in the correct column.
3 Using the above information answer the four questions in the spaces provided.
4 Be prepared to feed back this information to the rest of the class.

Newspaper	date
Job category	**number**
Situations general	
Office and administration	

1 Which category has the most job vacancies?

2 Which category has the fewest job vacancies?

3 What can you say about the availability of jobs in this area?

4 What else have you noticed about the jobs situation? Have you been surprised in any way?

Job search • pairs task •

▷ **Complete this worksheet in pairs.**

1   Choose one job from those you have seen which you might want to apply for in the future.
2   Complete the Job information sheet below.

NB – Not all the information may be provided in the advert so you might have to leave a space blank or write N/A (not applicable).

Job information sheet	
Job category	Job title
Permanent/temporary/full/part-time (*please delete*)	Salary/pay
Age range required	Experience needed
Qualifications needed	Job training offered
Perks available (*eg extra bonuses, car, creche, etc*)	
Distance travelled: Close to home/reasonable/too far (*please delete*)	
Is it part of a Modern Apprenticeship/Careership scheme?	

▷ Look at the job advert again and discuss with your partner which of the skills below will be needed by someone to do the work: tick the appropriate answer.

	yes	*no*	*not sure*
Can use machinery	....	....	....
Can work in a team	....	....	....
Can work independently	....	....	....
Can solve problems	....	....	....
Can read well	....	....	....
Can write well	....	....	....
Can speak clearly	....	....	....
Can give instructions	....	....	....
Can carry out instructions	....	....	....
Can take responsibility	....	....	....
Can make decisions	....	....	....
Can design things	....	....	....
Can use a computer	....	....	....
Can drive a car	....	....	....
Can confidently meet new people	....	....	....

Decisions, decisions

Objective

- To encourage students to plan a personal career path.

Resources

Worksheets: *Career paths A and B* (pp 62-63), *Flow chart* (p 65),
Case studies (p 66)
Information sheet: *Glossary* (p 64)

1 Ask the students to think about their future direction. Do they have a clear idea of what it will be? Do they have some idea, eg three or four occupations they might consider? Do they have no idea? Explain that this lesson allows them to look at the possibilities for choosing a definite career path, or for putting off their decision until later by choosing a general education at 16.

2 Introduce the *Career Paths* worksheets. Divide the students into groups and give half the groups sheet A and half sheet B, but do not let them know that there are two versions. The groups read about the characters and predict their career paths. They discuss this among themselves and then report back. Reveal the difference between sheets A and B and discuss whether the gender difference affected the career paths the groups predicted. Emphasise the need to avoid stereotyping and to keep options open.

3 Explain the necessity of being clear about the options available to the students post-16. Give the students copies of the worksheets *Glossary, Flow chart* and *Case studies*, and discuss them.

4 Ask the students in pairs to use the information on the case study sheets to complete the flow chart activity. They should decide which route each character takes and draw a different coloured line for each route.

5 Ask each student to think about his or her personal aptitudes and to draw their own personal flow diagram. Alternatively they can review their action plan. Try to allay anxieties the students may have about making decisions now. Decisions can always be changed. They may discover that there are no jobs in their chosen field, that it isn't what they really want, or that they and their interests have changed. Explain that they are likely to experience career change in their lives and that they should try to make sure that the education or training they opt for now will be useful in a variety of situations.

Career paths • A •

Form _____

Date _____

Read below about a person who is in Year 11.
Decide what his future will be like by choosing a career path for him.

Jack Jones, aged 16 is:

- popular with both staff and students
- nice-looking and has a good sense of humour

He has just gained six GCSEs at grades C or above:

English Language

English Literature

Dual-Award Science, two passes

Geography

Maths

He would like to work with people.
He enjoys school but would like to start earning money as soon as possible.

Group task

Discuss what you know about Jack. Try to agree on Jack's future career path.

1   What will Jack do next? ....
....

2   At what age will he leave school? ....

3   At what age will he leave full-time education? ....

4   What do you think Jack will be doing one year after leaving full-time education? ....
....

5   What is Jack's likely career path between now and when he is 30 years old? ....
....
....
....

Career paths · B ·

Form _____

Date _____

Read below about a person who is in Year 11.
Decide what her future will be like by choosing a career path for her.

Jackie Jones, aged 16 is:

- popular with both staff and students

- nice-looking and has a good sense of humour

She has just gained six GCSEs at grades C or above:

English Language

English Literature

Dual-Award Science, two passes

Geography

Maths

She would like to work with people.
She enjoys school but would like to start earning money as soon as possible.

Group task

Discus what you know about Jackie. Try to agree on Jackie's future career path.

1   What will Jackie do next? ....

....

2   At what age will she leave school? ....

3   At what age will she leave full-time education? ....

4   What do you think Jackie will be doing one year after leaving full-time education? ....

....

5   What is Jackie's likely career path between now and when she is 30 years old? ....

....

....

....

Glossary

> Whether you fancy starting work or getting stuck into further education, there's bound to be a qualification that gives you the skills you need to get ahead in life. From Biology and English to Film Studies and Fashion, the number of qualifications and subjects on offer is huge, and there's bound to be something that grabs your attention. The good news is that the government is planning to make the options more flexible so that you will soon be able to mix and match courses – part school, part college and part work experience, so you can make your course more relevant to the career you want to follow later. But whether you'd like to study full-time or would prefer to get started with your career straight away, here are some options on offer.

Qualifications you can take at 16+

Entry Level	the first level of the national qualifications framework
Basic Skills	literacy and numeracy at five levels
Key Skills	skills you learn alongside other qualifications, eg ICT
AS Levels	equivalent to half an A level
A/A2 Levels	A2 levels combine with AS levels to give a full A level
Advanced Extension Awards (AEAs)	designed for those who will get A-grade A levels
Vocational A Levels (ACVE)	a six-unit ACVE is worth one A level
National Vocational Qualifications (NVQs)	work-based, five levels available
Foundation Modern Apprenticeships (FMAs)	work-based (paid) and worth level 2 NVQ. Need five GCSEs at A*-C including English and Maths.
Advanced Modern Apprenticeships (AMAs)	work-based (paid) and worth level 2 and 3 NVQ plus Key Skills. Aimed at people who will make management level. Need to pass employer's selection test and interview. Can be well paid.
Entry to Employment Programme	To be introduced in 2004. Can gain you a place on Foundation or Advanced Modern Apprenticeship if you have Level 1 Key Skills in communication and number.

To encourage you to stay on in education at 16 the government is to give Education Maintenance Allowances (EMAs) to students aged 16-19 whose parents are on low incomes. Up to £30 per week is available plus bonuses for good attendance.

Flow chart

▸ **Look at this flow chart in pairs.**
Read the *case studies* and use coloured pens to draw in career paths for each person.
Draw your lines on this sheet.

On another sheet try to draw your own career path.

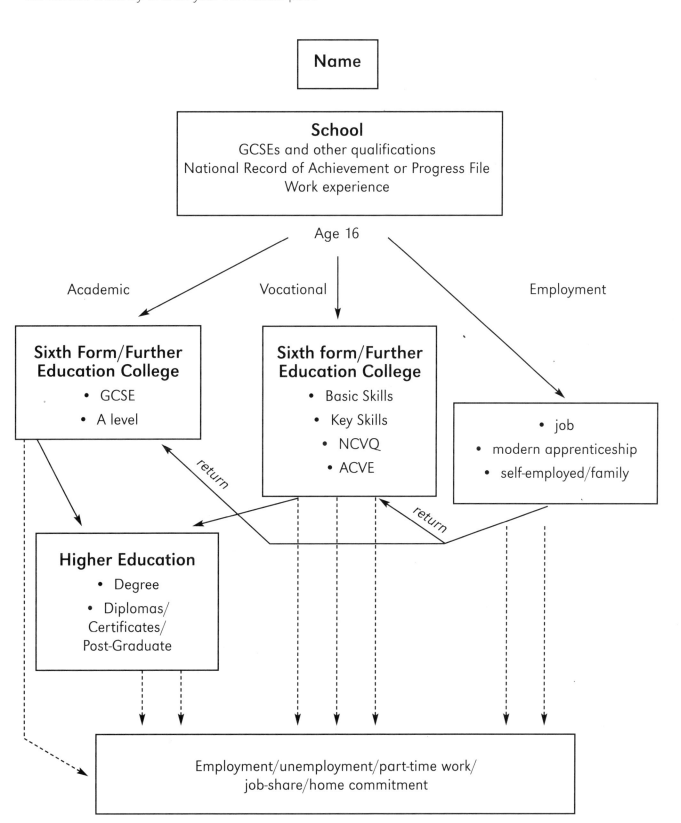

Case studies

Look at these case studies in pairs.

Work out which jobs, training courses or qualifications these people need to take if they are to achieve their ambitions.

Using a different colour for each person, draw lines on your flow chart to show what they should do.

Sharon left school with no clear idea of what she wanted to do. At the time she had had enough of school. She got a job in a local shop. After a year she found the work monotonous and no longer challenging. Although the money seemed good at first, she soon realised there were no prospects for promotion. Compared to other jobs she worked long hours and was poorly paid.

She is now determined to improve her situation by improving her qualifications.

Asif is interested in becoming an engineer. At present he is likely to get between two and four GCSE passes at grade C or above. One of these will probably be Maths. Though Physics would be useful, he is unlikely to get a grade C first time.

Claire is 16 and is interested in becoming a dentist. At present she is studying nine GCSEs and is likely to gain good grades in all of them.

Simon is interested in becoming a chef in a hotel. His attendance at school has been quite poor and he has shown little interest in academic work. He has done very well in his Food Technology option and is likely to gain a good grade in that subject. He has received good reports from his work experience placement in the catering department at the local hospital.

Getting a place

Objectives

- To give students the opportunity to write job and/or college applications and covering letters.
- To help them practise effective questioning for information, eg telephone skills.

Resources

Liaise with your Head of Careers and Careers Officer to obtain information on local deadlines for applications to post-16 education and training, for example Careerships/Modern Apprenticeships, sixth forms and sixth-form colleges, further education and local employment.
Worksheets: *Completing application forms* (p 68), *Application form* (p 69), *Application for employment* (pp 70-71), *Application for a course* (pp 72-73), *Writing a letter of application* (p 74), *Writing a covering letter* (p 75), *Telephone skills* (p 76), *Practising telephone skills* (p 77).
An internal telephone line and a tape recorder.

1 Give the students information on the deadlines for applications for post-16 education and training. Give each student copies of the worksheets and explain that it is their responsibility to make sure that they have enough practice in writing covering letters and application forms. When necessary students should fill in forms, get feedback from their tutor, amend the forms and give them to their tutor to send off. Feedback from local employers and the school's Careers Officer is also valuable. For homework ask the students to update themselves using the Radio 1 website www.bbc.co.uk/essentials.

2 Brief the students on the importance of telephone skills. Everyone should be able to ask for the information they need, and using the phone is often the quickest way of getting it. Divide the students into groups and ask them to practise these skills by arranging to visit a college, or to see someone about a course, or to find out details about what to do on the first day of their work experience. They should first look at the *Telephone skills* worksheet, then use an internal telephone to make the call to another staff member or student volunteer. Tape the conversations.

3 The students listen to themselves on tape and report back to their tutor, group and the person on the other end of the phone. They should practise further if necessary.

Completing application forms

Application forms come in many different sizes, requiring more or less information. Practise on these examples.

1   Complete the *Application form*, following the instructions.

2   Complete the *Application form for employment* and the *Application for a course*.

3   After completing these two you may like to fill in a real application for a course or a job.

4   Some application forms give you space to write about yourself and your interests. Summarise the information from your personal statement in your *National Record of Achievement* or *Progress File* and use it to fill in the box below.

Remember to make yourself sound interesting and suitable for the course or job you are applying for.

Remarks

Please give details of your interests and hobbies and any other information you feel will help your application.

Application form

1 Follow instructions.
2 Make a photocopy to practise first, or use a pencil.
3 Use black ink or type.
4 Write neatly.
5 Check the closing date and apply in time.
6 Make copies before you send it off.

Almost all application forms require the following basic information:

Job title	**permanent/temporary/full/part-time** *(please delete)*
Surname	**First name(s)**
Age and date of birth	**National Insurance Number**
Address	
Postcode	**Home telephone number**
Are you disabled? yes ☐ **no** ☐	
Do you require any special arrangements eg adaptations to premises or equipment *(please list requirements)*	
Secondary education	
Qualifications *(give details of exams taken, or to be taken, and results if known)*	
Work experience or employment	

Application for employment

Strictly confidential

Employment now sought

Surname (BLOCK LETTERS)

First name(s) in full

Full postal address (BLOCK LETTERS)

Date of birth   *Note: you will be required to produce a birth certificate*

Nationality

Full-time education

Date			
from	to	Name and type of school	Standard reached, examinations passed

Training *Give details of courses taken since full-time education ceased*

Date				
from	to	College	Subject and qualification	Type of course

continued on page 71

Application for employment · continued ·

Full particulars of employment over the last three years. Include voluntary work.

Names and addresses of employers	Dates			
	from	to	Duties	Reason for leaving

Health

Office use only

Is your eyesight good? With glasses .... Without glasses	
Is your hearing good?	
Have you suffered from:	
epilepsy	
heart problems	
any serious illness	
any accident	
If registered under The Disabled Persons Act 1944 give registered no:	

Leisure interests *(hobbies, sports, clubs, etc.)*

The information I have given above is true to the best of my knowledge and belief.

Signed .... Date ....

For official use

Suitability
(Tick as appropriate)
highly suitable   probably suitable
suitable   unsuitable
Comments on experience, special qualities, etc.
....

Application for a course

Application form for post-16 education at school or college.

Please complete this form in BLACK ink and in CAPITAL LETTERS

1 Surname .... Other names ....

2 Name of parent/guardian ....

3 Address ....

....

.... Postcode ....

4 Telephone number ....

5 Date of birth .... Male/female ....

6 Ethnic origin (*Please note this information will only be used for statistical purposes.*)

Please tick the most appropriate box:

☐	White	☐	Indian
☐	Black Caribbean	☐	Pakistani
☐	Black African	☐	Bangladeshi
☐	Black other	☐	Chinese

Other (*please specify*) ....

7 Name of present school ....

8 Name of school/college you wish to apply to ....

9 Course you wish to apply for (*Please refer to the college prospectus and discuss your choice with your Careers Teacher or Connexions Adviser – if you are not sure which course is best for you at this stage, please put 'NOT SURE'.*) ....

....

....

....

....

10 Interests and positions of responsibility, for example, sports, music, part-time jobs, membership of clubs and voluntary organisations.

....

....

....

....

....

continued on page 73

Application for a course ● continued ●

11 Career interests (*Please tell us if you have any career ideas at this stage.*)

....

....

12 Health/disability (*Please give brief details of any aspects of your health or any disability which you feel ought to be brought to our notice.*)

....

....

13 **Part A**

To be completed by the applicant:

Part B

To be completed by the school:

Subjects being studied	Course and level GCSE/unit credits/others	Estimated results

14 Reference by headteacher (*Please comment on the suitability of the candidate for the courses requested and/or submit a summative document where appropriate.*)

- **Attendance**   %

- **Punctuality**   % late

- **Comments on the course choices and any additional information:**

15 Headteacher's signature .... Date ....

16 Student's signature .... Date ....

**Please take your National Record of Achievement or Progress File
when you are invited for interview to discuss your choice.**

Writing a letter of application

Sometimes you may need to write a letter of application. You do this when:

- you need to provide more information about yourself than there is space for on your application form
- you want to stand out to a college or employer
- you think your letter may be opened by the person who will be responsible for choosing who gets the job.

When you need to write your own covering letter or letter of application, get some writing paper from your form tutor. Use the layout and punctuation shown here.

---

reference number, if given in the advert

CA/43/

**your address,
telephone number
and date**

Harbour Rd
Longsight
Manchester M13 9EQ

14 February 20_ _

name and address of person you are writing to

Mr N.S. Bell,
Bell and Co.,
Brooklands Way,
London N3 4JT.

**write something about
why you would be suitable
for this particular job**

miss a line

Dear Mr Bell,

I should like to apply for the position of trainee administrative assistant as advertised in the Evening News last Friday.

clear paragraphs

This job is of particular interest to me because I am keen to find commercial employment where I will be given the opportunity to train further and gain professional qualifications. Although I have as yet no experience in this type of work, my part-time employment as a supermarket cashier has provided a valuable opportunity to meet members of the public and deal with accounts and finance.

clear paragraphs

I enclose my CV. I shall be pleased to provide any further details required. I am free to come for interview at any time.

Yours sincerely

A.R. Anwar   **your signature**
A.R. Anwar   **your name, printed**

Writing a covering letter

You may need to write a covering letter. You do this when:

- you want to ask for more information about a job or a course you have seen in an advert (and perhaps ask for an application form);
- you want a prospectus from a college;
- you are returning a completed application form.

Remember

1 Use good quality paper.
2 If you know the name of the person you are writing to, eg Mrs Edwards, sign your letter *Yours sincerely* followed by your name. If you write 'Dear Sir or Madam', then end the letter *Yours faithfully*.
3 Write out the letter in rough first. Then check the spelling and punctuation. Keep your letter brief.

Dear Sir/Madam

With reference to the advertisement in the Evening News last Monday for the post of Trainee Manager, please send further details and an application form. I enclose a stamped addressed envelope.

Yours faithfully,

D.E. Porter

Dear Mrs Edwards

I enclose a completed application form for the post of Trainee Manager. I look forward to hearing from you.

Yours sincerely,

D.E. Porter

Dear Sir/Madam

Please send your current college prospectus and any further information you have on the ACVE (Vocational A level) course in Engineering.

Yours faithfully,

D.E. Porter

Telephone skills

▷ These pages aim to improve your ability to get the careers information you need over the telephone.

Read this example

Shahana has heard of a course that her local FE College offers. She thinks she may be interested, but doesn't know enough about it to make up her mind. Also she doesn't know whether she has the right qualifications to be able to start the course. She would like to visit the college to talk to the course tutor.

She arranges with her careers teacher to use the telephone...

Shahana	Hello. My name's Shahana Ashraf and I'm interested in...
Switchboard operator	Which department?
Shahana	Oh, er, I think it's called Business.
Switchboard operator	Putting you though now.
Voice	Hello, Business Studies.
Shahana	Hello. My name's Shahana Ashraf and I'm interested in your ACVE course in Business.
Voice	Are you a student?
Shahana	Yes, I'm 16 and still at school.
Voice	Well, you need our Student Welfare Section. I'll put you back to the switchboard.
Shahana	No, just a minute. I need some information from someone in your department. I'd like to speak to the person who's course tutor for ACVE Business.
Voice	Three modules or six modules?
Shahana	Three modules I think. I'm not sure if I've got the right GCSEs to do six.
Voice	Right, well, you need to speak to Ms Roberts. She'll sort you out. I'll see if she's available... No, I'm sorry. She's teaching until 2.30 pm. Could you ring back later?
Shahana	Yes, all right. Does she have her own extension number?
Voice	Yes. You could try her on 230. If that doesn't work, try 231, which is the general office number for our section.
Shahana	Thank you very much for your help.

How did she do? Remember you too may have to speak to several people before you get the person you want. Underline the information that she needed to make a note of as she was making the call. Now try the worksheet *Practising Telephone Skills.*

Practising telephone skills

▷ This sheet will prepare you to get some information by speaking over the telephone to people you don't know.

Decide whether you are going to **a**) ring about a post-16 course, or **b**) ring about work experience. Underline your choice, then read the correct box.

---

*Fill in these details if you have chosen the **post-16 course***

You want to speak to the course tutor for ....
You wish to arrange a visit to find out if it is the right course for you. Jot down notes of what you want to say. Be prepared to give details about yourself.

---

*Fill in these details if you have chosen the **work experience***

Your school has arranged a work experience for you at

....

You want to speak to someone there who can give you more details. Where is it exactly? To whom should you report when you get there? What are the starting and finishing times? Should you bring a packed lunch? What clothes are suitable? Jot down notes of what you want to say. Be prepared to give details about yourself.

When ready, ask your teacher if you can try out your request on a real telephone. Tape yourself.

What sort of job?

Objectives

- To help the students to focus on a particular place of work and the range of employment it offers.
- To consider the difference between specialist and transferable skills.

Resources

Worksheets: *Job categories checklist* (pp 79-80)

1 Explain the objectives and describe the range of jobs in a large institution such as a hospital, explaining the difference between specialist and transferable skills. Divide the class into pairs and ask them to complete the *Job categories checklist*. Circulate and give help as needed.

2 Ask for feedback from the pairs. Were there any jobs which were difficult to categorise? Which? How many had transferable skills? Which type?

3 Stress the importance of having transferable skills in today's job market. Introduce the idea of a new employer coming to interview the people working in a hospital. Ask each student to take the part of one member of the hospital staff and to explain to the new employer how their skills could be relevant.

4 Conclude by asking each student to revisit their action plan (see page 54) and revise and update it by adding any new occupation they want to research.

Job categories checklist

Complete this checklist in pairs.

1 For each of the jobs listed below place a tick in the category column in which you think they belong.
2 Decide also whether you think the skills involved in doing this job are easy to transfer to another job or are more specialist.

Job	Description	Category						Skills	
		Medical/nursing	Technical	Scientific	Administrative	Service general		Transferable	Specialist
Gardener	I look after the plants inside and outside the hospital.								
Pharmacist	I prepare and disperse medicines and drugs.								
Electronics engineer	I maintain sophisticated electronic equipment such as heart monitors, scanners, etc.								
Doctor	I diagnose the patients' illness and decide how to treat them.								
Radiographer	I take and examine X-rays.								
Cook	I prepare meals for the patients and hospital staff.								
Receptionist	I take care of appointments and enquiries from patients and visitors to the hospital.								
Secretary	I type letters and records, etc, for the hospital								
Librarian	I am in charge of the hospital library and take books to patients.								
Social worker	I help people with their problems, eg rent, families and children, while they are in hospital.								
Cleaner	I clean the hospital (wards, corridors, kitchens, waiting rooms, etc).								
Accountant	I am responsible for the finances of the hospital and for taking care of its budget.								
Midwife	I am a nurse who is trained in childbirth and the care of mothers and babies.								

continued on page 80 ▶

Job categories checklist • continued •

Job	Description	Category						Skills	
		Medical/ nursing	Technical	Scientific	Admin-/ istrative	Service general		Transfer-able	Specialist
Physiotherapist	I treat patients with exercise and heat.								
Machine fitter	I maintain and install machinery.								
Disc jockey	I run the hospital radio service and play requests for patients.								
Carpenter	I make and repair wooden furniture, doors, windows and gates at the hospital.								
Records clerk	I look after the records about the patients.								
Storekeeper	I am responsible for keeping and ordering supplies for the hospital.								
Security guard	I patrol the hospital and check the doors etc for security.								
Surgeon	I am a doctor who specialises in surgical treatment: carrying out operations.								
Computer operator	I enter and store all kinds of information for the hospital on to the computer and access it when it is needed.								
Porter	I move things around the hospital – patients, beds and food, etc.								
Administrator	I run the hospital and represent it at a higher level.								
Anaesthetist	I give anaesthetics to patients during operations and make sure they are breathing properly.								
Nurse	I am trained to look after people on the wards and give patients the treatment decided by the doctors.								
Medical photographer	I take photographs for doctors and students.								
Laundry worker	I take care of the dirty washing.								
Ambulance driver	I take patients to and from hospital and give emergency medical treatment.								
Nursing officer	I am in charge of the nursing staff.								

Work and pay

Objective

- To consider some of the financial implications of employment.

Resources

Information sheet: *Work and pay – definitions* (p 82);
Worksheets: *Work and pay – payslip* (p 83); *Quiz sheet* (p 84)

1 Explain the objective. Divide the class into pairs and ask them to discuss the following terms: tax code, national insurance, income tax, superannuation/pension contribution, union fees, gross/net pay, tax year. Ask each pair to come up with definitions.

2 Distribute the *Work and pay – definitions* worksheet for information and then ask the pairs to complete the *Work and pay – payslip* worksheet. Give them the answers and discuss any questions that arise.

3 Ask the students to make sure that they understand the financial implications of the career path they are choosing. To check on their financial understanding, the students can test each other with the *Quiz sheet*, or do the quiz as a class.

Work and pay • definitions •

Use the information below to check your answers to the questions on the previous page.

1 Tax code

Every worker is given a tax code when he or she is first paid. This code tells you how much you are allowed to earn before you pay tax, eg:

Personal Allowance	£4,195 = 419 L
Married Couple's Allowance	£1,900 = 190 H

- Notice the last figure of the earnings is missed off to determine the tax code
- The letter after your number defines your status, eg:

  L = single personal allowance

  H = married couple's allowance – allowed to one of the couple on top of the personal allowance

  X = emergency code, ie you haven't been assessed yet.

2 National Insurance

This is a deduction from your salary by the government used to pay for the health service, sick pay, social services, job-seeker's allowance, etc. The more you earn, the more you pay.

3 Income tax

This is a deduction from your salary by the government. It is paid as a percentage of your earnings after deductions have been made. The percentage can change from year to year. It is used by the government to run the country, eg to pay for defence, roads, civil service, etc. The more you earn, the more you pay. The very low-paid do not pay income tax.

4 Superannuation/pension contribution

This is the money taken from your wages to help pay for an occupational pension when you retire. Sometimes your employer contributes too.

5 Union fees

It is advisable to be a member of a union to help protect your rights as a worker. Some unions allow you to pay the subscription every week or month through your employer.

6 Gross/net pay

Gross pay is your total weekly/monthly wages before any deductions have been made. Net pay is how much you are left with (take-home pay) after all the deductions have been made.

7 Tax year

The tax year runs from the 6th April to the 5th of April the following year. Income tax forms may be sent at the start of the tax year.

Tax month 1 = April; Tax month 12 = March

Work and pay • payslip •

Complete this worksheet individually or in pairs.

Look at the copy of a payslip below
Answer the questions about it.

Hourly rate in pence	TAX CODE	TAX MONTH	TAX YEAR	NAME		DEPT		MAN NO
910	715H	9	02/03	Smith A		36193		75231

CUMULATIVE AMOUNTS IN CURRENT TAX YEAR					THIS MONTH		BANK	
Gross taxable pay	Tax paid	Nat insce	Supn	Supnble pay	Gross taxable pay	Subnble pay	Account	Code
15041.00	1900.00	291.04	936.04	15041.00	2688.50	2688.50	5582412	7613

Item code	£	Item code	£	Item code	£	Net pay £
1	2504.00	3	180.18	31	14.00*	1978.58
21	360.78*	22	170.52*	32	160.30*	

c Tr Form L317	* Indicates a deduction from pay	See overleaf for explanation of codes

Item code	Item code	Item code	Item code
PAYMENTS	PAYMENTS (cont.)	DEDUCTIONS	DEDUCTIONS (cont.)
1 Basic Pay	11 Boots/clothing	21 Income Tax	31 Trade Union Subscription
2 Miscellaneous/Holiday Pay	12 Car Allowanace	22 National Insurance	32 Contribution to Pension Fund
3 Overtime Pay	13 Meals/Travel Allowance	23 NI Sick Benefit	
4 Supplementary Allowances	14 Statutory Sick Pay	24 Court O	33 Social Fund
5 Bonus	15 Other allowances		

1   What is the Basic Pay of A. Smith? **£**

2   What is the take-home (net) pay of A. Smith? **£**

3   What were the four deductions taken from the salary this month?

   a   **b**

   c   **d**

4   How much was deducted this month? **£**

5   What is A. Smith's tax code? ....

6   How is the money paid to A. Smith at the end of the month?
Underline the one correct answer. *Bank/Cash/Cheque.*

7   What month is this payslip for?
Underline the correct answer. *April/September/December/March.*

8   What should A. Smith do with the payslip once it has been received?
Underline the correct answers.

   a *throw it away*   **c** *return it to the employer*

   b *keep it for reference*   **d** *check it*

Quiz sheet

▶ **Can you answer these questions?**

1 A future prospective employer wants you to send a CV. What is this?

2 Write down the addresses and phone numbers of two Careers Offices near you.

3 What is a P45?

4 What is the difference between FE and HE?

5 What is an EMA? Who is entitled to it? How do you claim it?

6 Write down the address of the local Citizens Advice Bureau.

7 Which under-19s can claim Housing Benefit?

8 Which benefits are all under-19s entitled to?

9 Can you claim Income Support?

10 What is a Contract of Employment? What is in it?

11 In a formal letter, if you start Dear Sir or Madam, how do you end it?

12 You are applying for a job. Who do you give as your referees?

13 You want a holiday job. What is the best way to go about it?

14 What is Statutory Sick Pay?

15 What does NVQ stand for?

16 Find the address of the Equal Opportunities Commission.

17 Find the address of your nearest Job Centre.

18 One of your friends is leaving home because of difficulties. Suggest an organisation which could provide help.

For further information on educational choices, interviews, CVs, money and lots more check out the Radio 1 Essentials website at www.bbc.co.uk/essentials.

SECTION 2: *HEALTHY, SAFER LIFESTYLE*   85-123

This section focuses on healthy lifestyles in three units which include eight lessons.

The material has been designed to be used flexibly so that schools can select specific units and lessons according to their priorities, and use them alongside other materials and activities.

The units and lessons are generally suitable for use with pupils across the key stage 4 age range and can be adapted for use with particular groups. Extra flexibility can be achieved as the units can be taught in any order.

Sexual health in relationships

Coping with stress

Going to the doctor

Contraception – the facts

Notes: Muslim students who are observing Ramadan will not want to study this lesson. Check the dates of Ramadan to ensure that the lesson does not fall within it.

Please read the child protection notes on page 15 before this lesson. Extra adult support for this lesson would be helpful, for example, the Head of Year or school nurse. These activities may take more than one lesson.

Objectives

- To help students to focus on future decisions, having considered their own values, ie whether to be sexually active, whether to use contraception.
- To inform students about contraception.

Resources

Worksheets: *In your opinion* (p 88), *Jumbled contraception reference* (p 89).
Information sheet: *Contraception – the facts* (p 90)
Resource box containing pictures and packets of various contraceptive devices.
Self-assessment sheets

1 Distribute the worksheets and start the lesson by pointing out that adult life involves making various decisions about one-to-one relationships which may affect our health and welfare. To help us make these decisions we each need to be clear about our own values and beliefs. The lesson is designed to help the students consider their attitudes to contraception and to inform them about different contraceptive methods.

2 Ask the students to look at the worksheet *In your opinion*. Read and explain the information about the beliefs of the different faiths. If you know that there are students of other faiths in the class, find some relevant information about these. Explain that there is no such thing as a consensus of values on these matters – what matters is that we have each carefully considered our opinions. Ask each student to complete the opinion section and then explain to a partner why they think as they do.

3 Arrange the chairs in a semicircle and sit in the middle with the resource box. Show the students contraceptive devices or pictures of them and ask them whether they can name the devices correctly. Using the information sheet for reference, give details of how each method works and any drawbacks or health hazards. Answer questions.

4 Ask the students to complete the worksheet *Jumbled contraception reference* by sorting the correct information. Give them the information on page 87 if appropriate.

5 Ask the students to complete self-assessment sheets.

Contraception – the facts continued

Name	Where they can be obtained
condom	Widely available from supermarkets, chemists, slot machines, etc. Cost – about 50p each or free from family planning clinics. To be effective must be used carefully and disposed of safely. Should be date-stamped and kite-marked. Those which contain spermicide are more reliable.
morning-after pill	Free from family planning clinics. Must be taken within 72 hours of unprotected sex.
diaphragm or cap	Free from family planning clinics. Spermicide also free or can be bought from chemists. Common brands of spermicide include Orthogynol and Orthocreme.
withdrawal	Free
vasectomy	Operation on NHS or privately. Counselling available at family planning clinics.
female sterilisation	Operation on NHS. Counselling available at family planning clinics.
IUD or coil	Free from family planning clinics. Must be fitted by a skilled doctor. Not usually suitable for young women. May not be suitable for some religious groups because it can cause irregular bleeding.
injectable methods	Free from family planning clinics. Not usually suitable for young women. May not be suitable for some religious groups because it can cause irregular bleeding.
oral contraceptive or combined pill	Free from family planning clinics or GPs. Family planning clinic usually preferable in order to get full range of check-ups, eg blood pressure and cervical smear tests.
natural methods/ rhythm method	Free advice on how the method works from family planning clinics and Catholic Marriage Advisory Service.

In your opinion

Different faiths have different views on whether or not it is acceptable to use contraception. Below are some simplified explanations. For more advice, check with your family, religious teacher, or someone who has knowledge of what these views are.

Note: All faiths see sex outside marriage as wrong, therefore it is wrong to use contraception to allow or promote promiscuous behaviour.

Christian Churches

Roman Catholic Church

Sex within marriage is a blessing but its purpose is to create children. This must always be possible. No artificial means of preventing this is acceptable. The only acceptable method is the rhythm method, 'natural family planning'.

Other Christian Churches

These hold various views but generally accept the use of contraception within marriage. Those who feel strongly that abortion is wrong may think that use of the IUD, coil or morning-after pill is unacceptable because they prevent a fertilised egg from implanting and could be seen as a very early abortion.

Islam

Sex within marriage is a blessing and having children is a prime purpose of marriage. In general therefore it is wrong for individuals to try to go against this by using contraception. However, married couples must respect and cater for each other's health and welfare. It is important that both partners are happy. There may be times when, in order to safeguard the wife's health, couples might consider using contraception – for instance, to space pregnancies.

It must be remembered that permanent change to the body – for instance sterilisation – is wrong. The IUD/coil and injectable methods may present problems because they can cause unpredictable bleeding in the middle of a woman's menstrual cycle.

Judaism (Orthodox)

Sex within marriage is a blessing and procreation is a command for men. Men should use no form of contraception. Couples may consider it necessary, in certain cases, to use female methods of contraception in order to maintain a woman's physical or mental health. In these cases they should seek advice from a rabbi. The IUD/coil and injectable methods may present problems because they can cause unpredictable bleeding in the middle of a woman's menstrual cycle.

In your opinion

Here are some different reasons people give for using contraception.
Do you think any of them are acceptable?

	acceptable	unacceptable	not sure
• to space pregnancies so that the mother's health does not suffer			
• because the couple are not ready for a baby			
• because the couple don't want any children			
• to prevent the birth of a baby which may be handicapped by a genetic condition			
• to protect themselves against sexually-transmitted infections			
• because it would be dangerous for the mother to have a baby			

Jumbled contraception reference

The comments boxes are jumbled up. Cut along the dotted lines and rearrange them in the right place.

Name	What it is	How it works	Comments
condom	rubber sheath put over erect penis	prevents sperm from entering vagina and reaching the egg	This is a permanent way of making sure a woman has no more children. Possible heavy periods. Sometimes fertility returns.
morning-after pill	hormone pills taken within 72 hours of unprotected sex	prevents the fertilised egg from implanting in the uterus and growing into a baby	It can be used in an emergency to prevent a pregnancy. Not suitable for regular use.
diaphragm or cap	rubber cap that is covered with spermicide and placed over the cervix before sex. Left in place for six hours after sex.	prevents the sperm from entering the uterus and reaching the egg	This is the only contraceptive which protects against STIs including HIV infection. It is more reliable as a contraceptive and for protection against disease when used with spermicide. Not 100% reliable. Can interrupt love-making. No side effects.
withdrawal	man pulls penis out of vagina before he ejaculates	sperm do not meet egg because man ejaculates outside vagina	It must be used with a spermicide. Needs careful fitting. No side effects.
vasectomy	simple surgery to cut vas deferens	sperm can no longer be ejaculated, only spermless semen	There is a high risk of pregnancy. (Some semen can enter vagina before ejaculation.)
female sterilisation	surgery to cut fallopian tubes	eggs can no longer reach sperm	This is unpredictable as you can't predict when fertility will return. Possible unpleasant side effects such as irregular bleeding.
IUD or coil	plastic/metal device inserted into uterus	prevents fertilised egg from implanting in the uterus and growing into a baby	Is the only method allowed by RC Church. Only works if woman has regular periods. No artificial barriers or hormones.
injectable methods	injection of a hormone every three months	changes woman's body so that fertilised egg can't implant in the uterus	This is a permanent way of making sure a man fathers no more children.
oral contraceptive or combined pill	pill containing two female hormones taken daily as instructed	prevents ovulation (release of egg)	This is only suitable for women who have had a baby. Risk of pelvic infection and heavy periods. Occasional failures.
'natural' methods/ rhythm method	close observation of woman's body and no sex when fertile	relies on natural cycle of woman's body to allow couple to avoid sex when she is fertile	Is the most effective preventer of pregnancy if taken as directed. Needs monitoring for side effects. Not for women over 45 or for women over 35 who smoke. Not safe to be taken by all women.

Contraception – the facts

These are the right answers. Use them to check whether students have the facts right.

Name	What it is	How it works	Comments
condom	rubber sheath put over erect penis	prevents sperm from entering vagina and reaching the egg	This is the only contraceptive which protects against STIs including HIV infection. It is more reliable as a contraceptive and for protection against disease when used with spermicide. Not 100% reliable. Can interrupt love-making. No side effects.
morning-after pill	hormone pills taken within 72 hours of unprotected sex	prevents the fertilised egg from implanting in the uterus and growing into a baby	It can be used in an emergency to prevent a pregnancy. Not suitable for regular use.
diaphragm or cap	rubber cap that is covered with spermicide and placed over the cervix before sex. Left in place for six hours after sex.	prevents the sperm from entering the uterus and reaching the egg	It must be used with a spermicide. Needs careful fitting. No side effects.
withdrawal	man pulls penis out of vagina before he ejaculates	sperm do not meet egg because man ejaculates outside vagina	There is a high risk of pregnancy. (Some semen can enter vagina before ejaculation.)
vasectomy	simple surgery to cut vas deferens	sperm can no longer be ejaculated, only spermless semen	This is a permanent way of making sure a man fathers no more children.
female sterilisation	surgery to cut fallopian tubes	eggs can no longer reach sperm	This is a permanent way of making sure a woman has no more children. Possible heavy periods. Sometimes fertility returns.
IUD or coil	plastic/metal device inserted into uterus	prevents fertilised egg from implanting in the uterus and growing into a baby	This is only suitable for women who have had a baby. Risk of pelvic infection and heavy periods. Occasional failures.
injectable methods	injection of a hormone every three months	changes woman's body so that fertilised egg can't implant in the uterus	This is unpredictable as you can't predict when fertility will return. Possibly unpleasant side effects such as irregular bleeding.
oral contraceptive or combined pill	pill containing two female hormones taken daily as instructed	prevents ovulation (release of egg)	Is the most effective preventer of pregnancy if taken as directed. Needs monitoring for side effects. Not for women over 45 or for women over 35 who smoke. Not safe to be taken by all women.
'natural' methods/ rhythm method	close observation of woman's body and no sex when fertile	relies on natural cycle of woman's body to allow couple to avoid sex when she is fertile	Is the only method allowed by the RC Church. Only works if woman has regular periods. No artificial barriers or hormones.

Sexually-transmitted infections

Note: Muslim students who are observing Ramadan will not want to study this lesson. Check the dates of Ramadan to ensure that the lesson does not fall within it.

Please read the child protection notes on page 15 before this lesson.

Objectives

- To inform students about sexually-transmitted infections.
- To establish how people get sexually-transmitted infections and how to reduce the risk of catching them.

Resources

Information sheets: *STI facts* (pp 92-93)
Worksheets: *Questionnaire* (pp 94-95), *STIs* (p 96)
Self-assessment sheets

1 Explain the objectives of the lesson and ask each student to check what he or she knows by completing the *Questionnaire*. In pairs, the students check the answers against the STI facts. You may need to go through the information, especially with poorer readers, to make sure they understand.

2 Lead a class discussion of how the risk of catching STIs can be reduced.

3 In pairs, ask the students to complete the *STIs* worksheet. Ask for feedback and see whether there is a consensus on what action is most appropriate for each situation.

4 Conclude with a class discussion and ask the students to complete self-assessment sheets.

STI facts

Answers to questionnaire. Photocopy these pages for students if appropriate for your class.

1   STI stands for sexually-transmitted infection.
2   Infections which affect the genital/urinary organs include the following:

Gonorrhoea

This causes painful urination and often a discharge from the penis in men.
Often there are no symptoms in women. Sometimes women experience a vaginal discharge and painful urination.
If left untreated gonorrhoea is serious. It can often cause pelvic infection and infertility in women so that they
cannot have children, and it causes blindness in babies through infection during birth.

Chlamydia

The most common and rapidly-growing infection. Not much is known about it and it is difficult to detect. It can
cause an early-morning discharge from the penis in men. Women often have no symptoms. If left untreated
chlamydia is serious: it can often cause pelvic infection and infertility in women so that they cannot have children,
and it causes eye, ear and throat infections in babies. A simple dose of antibiotics cures it. In some areas one-fifth
of sexually-active young people have it without knowing.

HIV (human immunodeficiency virus)

The virus which destroys our immune system and our ability to fight infection. It survives only in blood, semen and
vaginal fluid. You have to have this virus in order to develop AIDS. HIV infection is one of the fastest-growing sexually-
transmitted infections and has been found in all parts of the world. In many countries AIDS is the largest single cause
of death for those in the 20–40 age group. There is no cure for HIV infection or AIDS. Babies can be born with HIV.
Usually those with HIV have no symptoms. Broken skin on the genitals caused by other STIs helps spread HIV.

Warts

A common STI. Causes warts on the penis/scrotum and anus in men and on the vulva/vagina areas and anus
in women. Treatment by special lotions is necessary. Women who have warts must have frequent cervical smear
tests since there is a link between warts and cervical cancer.

Herpes

This causes blisters or 'cold sores' on the penis/scrotum and anus in men and on the vulva/vaginal areas or anus
in women. Treatment by special drugs is necessary to make them heal more quickly. There is no cure for herpes.
Women with active genital herpes usually have to have babies by Caesarian section. Women who have genital
herpes must have frequent cervical smear tests since there is a link between herpes and cervical cancer.

Thrush

Very common. Often caused by pregnancy, the pill, being on antibiotics, etc, but can sometimes be passed
on sexually. Causes an itchy white discharge and soreness around the vaginal and vulval area in women.
Treatment by cream, tablets or pessaries from pharmacists.

NSU (non-specific urethritis)

Very common. Causes discharge from the penis and pain on passing urine in men. Often no symptoms in women.
Treatment is by antibiotics.

Hepatitis B

Caused by a virus transmitted through sexual contact or blood to blood, eg shared needles. Can cause serious
liver disease or death. Some carriers may have no symptoms. There is a vaccine which can protect against it.
More infectious than HIV.

Syphilis

A serious but now uncommon STI. Causes hard, infectious, painless sores on the genital areas or mouth.
Eventually fatal if left untreated. Children born to infected mothers are handicapped. Pregnant women are
routinely tested for syphilis.

continued on page 93

STI facts • continued •

Answers to questionnaire continued

3   STIs in general are caught from intimate bodily contact, although herpes may be spread by active cold sores on the mouth. Some STIs are hard to get, eg HIV, where there has to be an exchange of bodily fluids through penetrative sex.

4   Men who have STIs sometimes have symptoms. Things that may worry a man are pain, lumps, swellings, discharge, sores or blisters. They should seek help from their doctor or from the genito-urinary unit at their local hospital.

5   HIV infection usually causes no symptoms. It can take from six months to ten years to develop AIDS, ie lose the ability to resist the disease.

6   Women who have STIs sometimes have symptoms. This is serious because if left untreated they can:

   a   develop pelvic infection and become infertile, ie unable to have babies.

   b   pass on infection during birth to their babies – this means that men must tell their partners about any infection.

7   See 5

8   **False**. This decision needs thinking about carefully. People may not be able to cope with a positive result. Insurance companies discriminate against anyone who has had a test. Sometimes people do not react with sympathy. Anyone who is considering having a test should first ring a counselling service such as Aidsline in order to talk this over.

9   **True** – Some STIs can be fatal, eg HIV and syphilis.

10 **True** – See 6 above.

11 **True** – Cervical cancer is linked to genital warts and other factors such as smoking, occupation, personal hygiene and whether condoms are used. Cervical cancer is on the increase – women who are sexually active are recommended to have a check-up every three years.

12 **True**. Gonorrhoea causes blindness. Syphilis causes handicap. HIV can cause illness and death.

13 **True**. Most STIs are treatable. Some have no cure, eg HIV and herpes, although drug treatments with anti-retrovirals can keep people well for many years.

14 **STIs are increasing**. The most dramatic increase is in HIV. There is evidence that the rate of new infection in homosexual men is increasing again. New infection among heterosexual men and women is increasing rapidly and is recognised as a major health problem in most countries in the world.

   Chlamydia and cervical cancer are also increasing, especially among young women. The increase in this and gonorrhoea is worrying because it shows that some people continue to risk unsafe sex. Female infertility will be the result, and HIV infection is an ever-present risk.

15 Treatment at a genito-urinary clinic is **confidential,** but people will be given help as to how to discuss it with their partners.

16 All three apply if a person has an STI.

Questionnaire

Follow the instructions to find out how much you know about STIs.

1 Underline what STIs stand for: Sexually Transmitted Infections

                                       Scottish Transport Institute

2 Underline those infections which affect the genital/urinary organs (penis, vagina and reproductive organs).

measles	chlamydia
flu	HIV
gonorrhoea (clap)	chickenpox
syphillis (pox)	acne
whooping cough	warts
herpes	thrush
non-specific urethritis (NSU)	malaria
Hepatitis B	TB

3 Underline the correct answer. STIs can be caught from:

a kissing someone who has one;

b toilet seats;

c swimming pools;

d sharing cups;

e having unprotected sex with someone already infected;

f shaking hands/touching someone.

4 Underline the correct answer. Men who have STIs:

a rarely have symptoms;   c sometimes have symptoms;

b usually have symptoms;   d always have symptoms.

5 Underline the correct answer. Men who have HIV infection:

a rarely have symptoms;   c sometimes have symptoms;

b usually have symptoms;   d always have symptoms.

NB: Thrush, which causes an itchy discharge in women and may cause irritation in men, is often not sexually transmitted, but could be caused by anaemia, pregnancy, taking antibiotics, etc.

continued on page 95

Questionnaire • continued •

6   Underline the correct answer. Women who have STIs:

   a rarely have symptoms;   **c** sometimes have symptoms;

   b usually have symptoms;   **d** always have symptoms.

7   Underline the correct answer. Women who have HIV infection:

   a rarely have symptoms;   **c** sometimes have symptoms;

   b usually have symptoms;   **d** always have symptoms.

8   Anyone who is worried they may be HIV-positive should go right away for a test.
   (Delete as appropriate)   TRUE / FALSE

9   Some STIs can be fatal. (Delete as appropriate.)   TRUE / FALSE

10 Some STIs cause infertility in women. (Delete as appropriate.)   TRUE / FALSE

11 Some STIs can cause cervical cancer in women. (Delete as appropriate.)   TRUE / FALSE

12 Some STIs can infect babies. (Delete as appropriate.)   TRUE / FALSE

13 Most STIs can be cured by antibiotics if treated early. (Delete as appropriate.)   TRUE / FALSE

14 Underline the correct answer. The number of STIs is:

   a increasing;   **b** decreasing;   **c** staying the same.

15 Underline the correct answer. Treatment at a genito-urinary clinic is:

   a not confidential;   **b** confidential;   **c** made known to your GP.

16 Underline the correct answer. If you have an STI you have a responsibility:

   a to yourself;   **b** to yourself and others;   **c** to seek help.

STIs

In pairs read these situations and answer the questions.

1   Someone has an active cold sore (herpes) on his/her lip. What should he/she do?

   ....

   ....

   ....

2   Someone has a discharge from his penis. What should he do?

   ....

   ....

   ....

3   Someone has thrush and in spite of using cream from the doctor it keeps coming back.
   What should she/he do?

   ....

   ....

   ....

4   Someone has gone to the genito-urinary clinic and has found that he/she has gonorrhoea.
   What should he/she do?

   ....

   ....

   ....

5   In the past, someone had unprotected sex. Now, he/she is in a stable sexual relationship.
   Is there anything to worry about and if so, what should he/she do?

   ....

   ....

   ....

Health and welfare dilemmas

Note: Muslim students who are observing Ramadan will not want to study this lesson. Check the dates of Ramadan to ensure that the lesson does not fall within it.

Please read the child protection notes on page 15 before this lesson.

Objectives

- To discuss responsibility and moral values in relationships.
- To help students apply the knowledge they have gained to decision-making in personal relationships.

Resources

Information sheet: *What are the consequences?* (p 98)
Worksheets: *Health and welfare case studies 1 and 2* (pp 99-100), *Attitudes quiz* (p 101)
Self-assessment sheets.

1 Brief the class on the objectives of the lesson. Explain that they have been given a lot of information about contraception and STIs, and in this lesson they will apply that information to decisions made by individuals and couples about their behaviour.

2 Brainstorm the possible consequences of making a relationship sexual. Refer to the information sheet *What are the consequences?* to ensure that all suggestions are adequately covered.

3 Divide the students into groups of five and ask each group to answer questions from at least three *Health and welfare case studies*. They will need to apply all they know about relationships, contraception and STIs to do this.

4 Ask for feedback from each group. Collate answers, correct misinformation and ask for further responses if necessary. Hold a class review: which groups had best protected people's health and welfare in their case study answers?

5 Ask the students to complete the *Attitudes quiz* individually.

6 Finally, ask the students to complete self-assessment sheets.

What are the consequences?

pregnancy: – wanted
– unwanted

pleasure: giving and receiving

cervical cancer

herpes/warts

orgasms

gonorrhoea

our bodies

protectiveness

anxiety

jealousy

stability

status

guilt

joy

conflict

commitment

partner

babies

your parents

partner's parents

family

others eg health professionals

friends

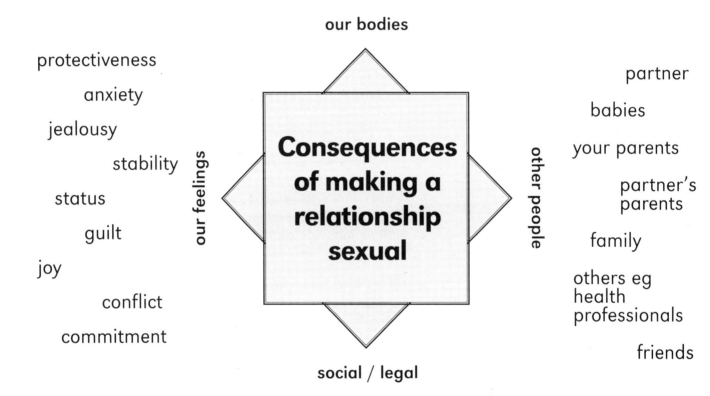

our feelings

other people

Consequences of making a relationship sexual

social / legal

age of consent – heterosexual
– homosexual

reputations

family structures

religious values

moral values

cultural values

National Health Service

Health and welfare case studies ● 1 ●

Sharon has just discovered, to her horror, that a former boyfriend is now injecting drugs. She has started a new relationship with Dave.
Why do you think she is worried?
What advice would you give Sharon and Dave?
Would your advice protect this couple's health and welfare?

Eric knows that he is HIV-positive.
He has fallen in love with Mandy.
He is very worried that if he tells her he is infectious, she will end the relationship.
What advice would you give Eric?
If the relationship continued, should they ever consider having children?

With two small children to look after, Parveen and Shafiq are feeling pretty run down. Parveen has one cold after another and can't seem to shake them off. They don't think Parveen could cope with another pregnancy right now. They are both Muslim. Do you think Parveen and Shafiq should consider using contraception?
If not, why not?
If so, what methods do you think they should consider?

Sue got drunk at a party last night and ended up having sex with someone she met there. They took no precautions.
What advice would you give Sue?
List the risks that Sue took.

Ron is 17 and boasts a lot about the number of girls he has had sex with.
He's not afraid of AIDS or getting a girl pregnant and says it's up to girls to sort that out.
What are your reactions to Ron?
What advice would you give any girl Ron meets?

Lisa is 17 and feels sure that she is lesbian, but so far has had no relationships.
She is attracted to somebody who she feels sure feels the same way.
What advice would you give Lisa?
Are lesbians more at risk from AIDS than heterosexuals?

Health and welfare case studies • 2 •

Dave and Linda have been going out with each other since they left school. Dave wants to have sex with Linda but Linda is not sure. When she asks Dave about condoms he says they can think about that later. Why do you think Linda is worried?
Comment on Dave's attitude.
What advice would you give Dave and Linda?

Maria and Tony have just got married. Both have been married before.
They now have three children, two from Maria's previous marriage and one from Tony's. Tony is sure he doesn't want any more children. Maria doesn't want to make her mind up just yet.
What advice would you give Maria and Tony on **a** contraception, **b** health?

Alex is 17 and feels sure that he is gay but so far has had no relationships.
He is attracted to somebody who he feels sure feels the same way.
What advice would you give Alex?
Are gay men more at risk from AIDS than heterosexuals?

Ahmed and Rizwana are getting married soon. They are both happy about this but Rizwana is worried. Someone has told her that, although he has settled down now, Ahmed used to hang around with quite a wild bunch of friends.
Why do you think Rizwana is worried?
Do you think she should raise her worries with **a** Ahmed, **b** anyone else?
What advice would you give this couple?

Sean and Theresa have a four-month-old baby. They do not want another child yet. They are practising Catholics. Do you think they should consider using contraception?
If not, why not?
If so, what method/s would you advise and why?

Attitudes quiz

Test your own attitudes by underlining the statements you most identify with. Then check with someone you trust to see whether they think you have the kind of attitudes which will protect your health and welfare in the future.

How safe is this attitude?   safe ——————→ unsafe

1 'People with infectious diseases should be locked up and then the rest of us would be safe.'

....

2 'I think it's important to be open with a partner about any previous sexual experiences.'

....

3 'As long as I stick to one partner I'll be all right.'

....

4 'I shall always put my own health first, no matter what my partner may say.'

....

5 'Men should wear condoms when having sex.'

....

6 'You need to use condoms for a few months till you are really sure about your relationship – then go on the pill.'

....

7 'I'd be really embarrassed to carry condoms.' .

....

8 'I prefer to be celibate.'

....

9 'We shouldn't just assume that our partners tell us everything.'

....

10 'If people are mature enough to make a relationship sexual they should be mature enough to talk about health and contraception beforehand.'

....

Do you suffer from stress?

Objectives

- To help students define the meaning and effects of stress, including positive and negative aspects.
- To identify situations which may cause individuals stress.
- To become aware of external factors which influence the level of stress.
- To explore different ways of reducing stress.

Resources

Information sheets: *Stress performance curve* (p 104), *Stress – what is it?* (p 106)
Worksheets: *Stressful situations for students* (p 105), *Individual stress* (p 107), *Potentially stressful situations* (pp 108-110), cut up and stuck on to card.

1 Brainstorm the word stress. What comes into your mind when you think of the word? Ask the students to look at the *Stress performance curve* and the list of *Stressful situations for students*. In pairs, ask the students to rank the situations starting with those they consider most stressful. They can go on to compare their answers with the definitive list *Stress – what is it?*

2 Ask each student to complete the worksheet *Individual stress*. Make it clear that this is for their information only. Follow this with a show of hands to determine levels of stress within the class. Who thinks they suffer symptoms of stress: never, sometimes, often, most of the time or all of the time?

Note: although the *Individual stress* worksheet is confidential, it may alert you to students who are suffering from severe stress. You should support these students and give them an opportunity to talk to someone else in the school or another agency. One of the best ways of relieving stress in the short term is to talk to someone.

3 Divide the students into groups and give each group a set of *Potentially stressful situation* cards. The students place each card under one of three headings: 'Within your control', 'More difficult to control' or 'Not sure'. The group should discuss each situation briefly before placing the card.

4 Look at the cards under the heading 'Within your control'. Ask each group to make a list of ways in which they think these areas could be reduced or eliminated.

5 Next look at the cards under the heading 'More difficult to control'. Is it difficult to decide what action to take when looking at these? Discuss the example on the following page and how to choose the best solution. Then ask the students to record three situations in which they agree that it is hard to decide what to do in the same way.

6 Ask the whole class to give feedback on the activity. Try to extract from them the key ways of dealing with stress.

continued on page 103

Do you suffer from stress? continued

Example	*Why might it be difficult to decide on a plan of action?*	*List the possible courses of action you could take*	*Which is the best choice?*
One of your parents is becoming increasingly violent to the family at home	1 Interferes with privacy of family. 2 Could bring shame upon the family. 3 Could break up the family. 4 Things could get worse and you are dependent on the family. 5 You are not sure who to turn to. 6 This is something totally new and you don't know anyone else who has had this experience. 7 You love your parent.	1 Talk to the parent who is being violent. 2 Consider your behaviour and make sure you avoid confrontation. 3 Talk to someone else in the family. 4 Talk to someone outside your family, eg doctor/teacher/ neighbour community leader. 5 Run away from home. 6 Call the police. 7 Remove all the family to a family refuge centre.	

Stress performance curve

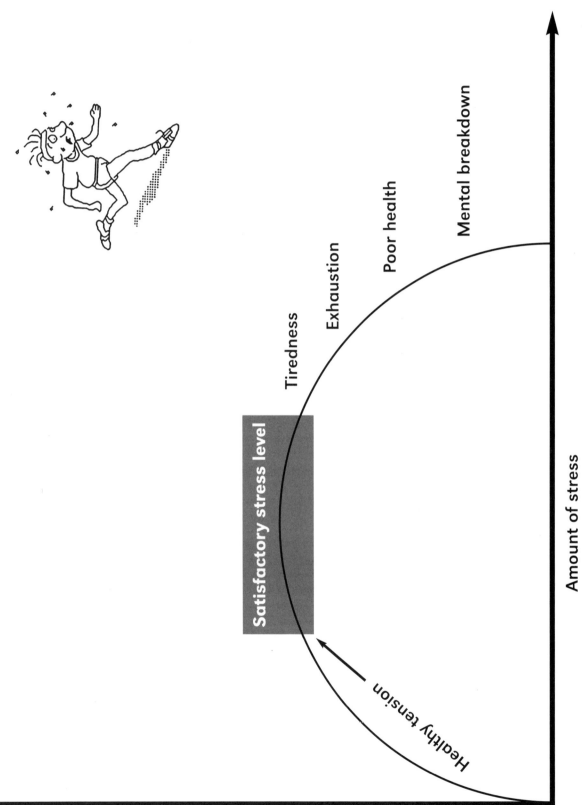

Satisfactory stress level

Tiredness

Exhaustion

Poor health

Mental breakdown

Healthy tension

Amount of stress

Level of performance

Stressful situations for students

Look at the list below of possible stressful situations. Rank them in order of importance, writing in the most stressful at the top.

We think the most stressful are...

Lack of privacy

Concern about appearance, weight or identity

Conflict with parents

Difficulty in making decisions

General feelings of frustration

Death of a parent

In trouble with the law

Interviews or starting a new job

Sexual difficulties

Not part of the crowd

Death of a close friend

Serious health problems, eg surgery

School pressures, exams, deadlines

Recent move: home, school, college

Parents having rows or in financial trouble

Engagement or marriage

Insecurity about the future

Loss of a parent through divorce

Break up with boy- or girlfriend

Unemployed, financial trouble

Driving test

Death of a close relative

Stress – what is it?

Current thinking shows that young people find the following situations stressful. The list begins with the most stressful. If people experience too many of these changes over a short time, they are more likely to become ill, either physically or mentally. The dictionary definition of stress is: stress, n. strain; pressure; force.

Death of a parent
Death of a close relative
Loss of a parent through divorce
Death of a close friend
Parents having rows or in financial trouble
Serious health problems – surgery/pregnancy
Engagement or marriage
Conflict with parents
In trouble with the law
Unemployed, financial trouble
Break up with boy or girlfriend
Interviews or starting a new job
Insecurity about the future
Sexual difficulties
Not part of the crowd
Lack of privacy
Driving test
School pressures, exams, deadlines
Difficulty in making decisions
Concern about appearance, weight or identity
Recent move: home, school, college
General feelings of frustration

A certain amount of stress is beneficial. People need stress in order to perform well, eg a tennis player before a big match (see *Stress performance curve*) or a student before an exam.

Everyone has a different stress level at which they perform well, but going beyond that level of stress will lead to problems, eg tension, exhaustion, concentration and memory problems, anger, anxiety, depression or ill-health.

Industry is severely affected by stress-related illnesses. One recent estimate has put the total cost of stress to industry at £28 billion a year in terms of lost hours, accidents and substandard work.

As we have seen, stress is normal and a certain amount can have positive effects. But when excessive stress occurs it is important to *recognise it* and *deal with it*.

You can deal with it by relaxation, by changing the situation which is causing it, or by seeking help.

Individual stress

Find out how stressed you are by filling in this questionnaire.
Don't show the results to anyone else.

Do you ever	never	sometimes	often	most of the time	all of the time
sleep badly					
feel moody					
get headaches					
find it difficult to concentrate					
get anxious					
feel irritable					
take days off school					
feel depressed					
lose your sense of humour					
feel things are your fault					
have difficulty concentrating					
get physically tense					
feel ill					
overeat or lose your appetite					
feel you don't care about anything					
get annoyed with your family or friends					
feel unable to cope					
lose your self-confidence					
get angry					
stop seeing your friends					
Total ticks					

If you have a lot of ticks in the last three columns you may be living with more stress than is good for you. Find out about some ways of reducing your stress.

Potentially stressful situations

Put the three heading cards Within your control, More difficult to control, and Not sure at the top of your table. Take it in turns to pick up a card, read it out and discuss which heading you should place it under. Then place the card under the heading you have agreed on.

Within your control

More difficult to control

Not sure

On the morning of your exam your alarm clock doesn't go off and you oversleep.	You have forgotten your homework, again.
Someone has borrowed your coursework. Your teacher wants to mark it but your friend has not returned it.	A teacher constantly rings your parent or guardian.
The family has been unable to keep up the payments on its house and is threatened with eviction.	Your eldest brother has not paid his fine for a driving offence and faces a court case or prison.

continued on page 109

Potentially stressful situations · continued ·

For moral reasons you decide you want to become a vegetarian. This causes problems within your family.

You are expected to work long hours in the family business at the expense of school work.

Someone calls you a racist name.

Someone bullies you.

Someone in your class constantly disrupts lessons and you can't get on with your work.

You have revised for a test and the teacher is absent.

A difference arises between a group of friends and you are left out.

You are told off for being late. The reason you are late is that your teacher overran the previous lesson.

Coursework deadlines are drawing near and it is impossible for you to get the work in on time.

Being the eldest, you are expected to look after younger children and have to take time off school.

Your parents are planning to separate.

At the end of the school day you have to change a pair of expensive trainers which are damaged. You have no receipt, but would like a new pair.

continued on page 110 ▶

Potentially stressful situations • continued •

You hear screams from next door most nights. You think a child is being hit.

Your parent is made redundant.

You have nowhere quiet to do your homework at night.

You are looking forward to watching a TV programme and someone else wants to watch another channel.

Parents insist you visit relatives when you want to do your work at the weekend.

Your family is being harassed by a local teenager.

You can't sleep because you are worried about a test tomorrow.

It is painful when you go to the toilet and you need to go to your doctor to discuss it.

A close relative suddenly dies.

You have to care for a sick parent.

You can't do your homework because you have to cook the meal.

Dealing with stress

Objectives

- To help students recognise moments of stress in their lives.
- To identify different ways of coping with stress in the short term.
- To practise relaxation methods.

Resources

Worksheet: *Individual stress* (p 107)
Information sheet: *Dealing with stress* (p 112)
Phone directories

1 Look at the worksheet *Individual stress*. Ask the students whether they have any of these stress reactions. If so, how do they cope with them? Brainstorm coping methods and record them on the board. Be ready for negative as well as positive responses and be ready to deal with the implications of negative choices such as the use of drugs or alcohol.

2 Ask the students to think of four or five recent situations which have caused them concern or stress, for example mock exams, records of achievement, not getting a work experience placement, being fed up with school, pressure from parents, course work deadlines, interviews, planning for a career, applying for a college place or job.

Ask the students in pairs to discuss how they can relieve pressure for themselves.

3 From group feedback compile a list of strategies. Add any strategies from the list below which have been omitted.

- Personal organisation, eg organising time, setting deadlines, asking for help. This could include asking other people to take on your responsibilities at home for a short time while you revise.

- Altering the physical environment, eg no bells between lessons, carpets in classrooms, asking others to turn off the TV when you are working.

- Relaxation.

- Seeking emotional support, eg from friends, family, teacher or other agencies.

4 Follow this with a practical session on dealing with stress as outlined in the information sheet *Dealing with stress*.

Extension: Agencies which help us
In class brainstorm agencies which offer support and list them. Look in the phone directory and information from your local Community Health Council for further ideas. Ask students to select an agency which interests them and write requesting information, for example, on who they help, opening hours, where they are, whether they run a helpline, etc. Each student should approach a different agency. Students should explain in their letters that they are compiling a guide for young people on agencies which can help them. This could be a homework task. Compiling the booklet could be a group or class task.

Dealing with stress

Most people are far from relaxed. We often tense muscles out of habit and are unaware of the resulting tension. The aim of these techniques is to introduce the skills of muscle relaxation and mental calming which lead to feeling more in control. Successful relaxation regulates rapid heart rate, uneven breathing, sweating, dry mouth, churning stomach and other sensations related to anxiety. Many people use relaxation techniques, eg top athletes, chess grand masters, etc. The aim should be to use relaxation techniques automatically and unselfconsciously when the need arises. The more you practise, the easier it becomes.

Relaxation techniques

1   **Relaxing where you are**. Sit on your chair with your feet on the ground. Lean forward so that your elbows rest firmly on your knees. Lean forward slightly. Let your hands hang loose and your head drop forward. Alternatively, lean forward on to your desk. Keep your fingers relaxed. Keep your feet flat on the ground. Let your head rest on your arms or your hands. Choose the most comfortable alternative and get into that position.

2   **Breathing to relax**. Breathe calmly. Breathe in deeply and out slowly, six to ten breaths a minute. When we are upset we breathe fast. Sixteen or more breaths a minute can lead to hyperventilation (overbreathing) which makes you feel worried and strange. Keep your body relaxed as you breathe in and out. Breathe slowly for a few minutes.

3   **Mental calming**. Say firmly to yourself 'Stop' (worrying, fussing, shouting, etc). Take a breath in and breathe out slowly. Relax your shoulders and hands. Talk to yourself again. 'I feel calm. There is no need to worry.' Take another breath and as you breathe out relax your lips and jaw. Repeat and talk to yourself again.

4   **Hand relaxation**. Clench your hands and fists tightly. Then shake your hands loose, stretching your fingers. Rest your hands in a comfortable position, in your lap or on the desk top. Can you feel the tension being released when you shake your hands?

5   **Shoulder relaxation**. Tighten your shoulders slightly, then release. Shrug your shoulders up and down. Wriggle them until they feel relaxed. Let your shoulders droop as low as they can, then relax.

6   **Deep relaxation**. Sit comfortably in a chair or lie down if preferred. Close your eyes. Calm your mind. Breathe slowly. Let your breath out gently. Breathe gently in and out. Feel your back relax into the chair or on to the floor.

    Start at your feet. Tense them, then relax. Tense them, then relax.
    Now your ankles, Tense them, then relax. Tense them, then relax.
    Now your knees. Tense them, then relax. Tense them, then relax.
    Feel the tension coming out as you breathe out.

    If your mind wanders, say to yourself, 'Relax, calm'.

    Now your stomach muscles. Tense them, then relax. Tense them, then relax.

    Now your chest muscles. Tense them, then relax. Tense them, then relax.

    Now your fingers. Tense them, then relax. Tense them, then relax.

    Now your elbows. Tense them, then relax. Tense them, then relax.

    Now your shoulders. Tense them, then relax. Tense them, then relax.

    Now open your mouth wide, relax. Open, then relax.

    Now frown. Tense your forehead, then relax. Tense, then relax.

    Take in a deep breath. Blow out. Open your eyes. Get up slowly and shake yourself.

Doctor, doctor

Objectives

- To increase students' critical awareness of prescribed and over-the-counter drugs.
- To practise explaining their health problems clearly to a doctor.
- To help students understand any advice given, and to ask for and get clarification where necessary.
- To help students gain knowledge about common forms of medication.
- To increase awarensss of the risks of not following instructions when taking drugs.

Resources

Worksheets: *Card sort cards* (pp 115-118), *Role-plays 1-3* (pp 119-121), *Options and consequences* (p 123)
Information sheet: *Main messages* (p 122)

1 Introduce the lesson by making the following points:

- You are sixteen or almost sixteen. At this age you have the right to go to your doctor and ask for confidential treatment and advice. You can give consent for your own treatment, for example, an operation. You may be given drugs on prescription.

- This means your health is now in your own hands. You are responsible, not anyone else. If you don't ask the right questions about your treatment no-one else will do it for you. You need to know about and understand what you are putting into your body. You need to make sure your needs are met.

- Drugs can affect your body in powerful ways. If misused they can be very dangerous. This unit will make you more skilled and confident in asking the right questions about all sorts of drugs and treatments.

2 Divide the students into groups of four and give each group a set of *Card sort cards*. They need to match the front and back of the cards, ie the name of the drug with its details. The groups should discuss their choices. Circulate and help them as needed. The correct answers are:

1 Antibiotics B	2 Antiseptics C	3 Decongestants G
4 Anti-anxiety drugs J	5 Anti-depressants A	6 Anti-histamines D
7 Antacids E	8 Analgesics H	9 Steroids F
10 Topical I.		

3 Ask the students to think about how they feel when they walk into a doctor's surgery. Nervous? Anxious? Many people find it hard to make the most of their time with the doctor. There is one thing that you know more about than the doctor and that is how you feel: what exactly has made you concerned enough to visit the doctor? You need to explain this clearly if you want the doctor to help. You then need to make sure you understand the doctor's advice and ask further questions if you are not clear. Use the role-plays to practise being clear and confident.

continued on page 114 ▶

Doctor, doctor • continued •

4 Divide the students into groups of four and ask each group to work on *Role-plays 1* and *2*, each person in the group taking a part. The groups then analyse the behaviour of the characters, answer the questions on the worksheet and rewrite the scripts on the worksheet *Role-play 3* so that the patients take a more assertive role. Ask them to perform the new scripts.

5 Discuss as a class the questions we should ask when we go to the doctor. What are the potential risks of not following instructions? Look at the information sheet *Main messages* and ask the students to add any further points they would find it useful to remember.

6 Ask the students to check their understanding of prescribed drugs by working in groups on the *Options and consequences* worksheet. The answers are as follows:

Safe bets: 1c, 2b, 3b, 4a, 5b, 6c, 7a, 8a

Definitely dodgy: 2c, 3a, 6b, 7c, 8c

Downright dangerous: 1a and b, 2a, 3c, 4b and c, 5a and c, 6a, 7b, 8b

Notes

These activities will take two lessons to complete. The lessons concentrate on prescribed drugs, an area often ignored in drugs information packs. This is relevant to all young people, as at this age they become legally responsible for consenting to treatment.

Sometimes students request further drug education because of local issues that arise from their neighbourhood's sub-culture on drugs. If that happens, respond to the need as it is defined at the time, drawing on the local community drugs team and voluntary agencies for help.

Card sort

ANTIBIOTICS

ANTISEPTICS

DECONGESTANTS

ANTI-ANXIETY DRUGS

ANTIDEPRESSANTS

ANTI-HISTAMINES

Card sort • continued •

ANTACIDS

ANALGESICS

STEROIDS

TOPICAL

Card sort • continued •

J DETAILS

- These are called relaxants or tranquillisers.
- At a lower dose they calm you down, act as a sedative.
- At a higher dose they send you to sleep, act as a 'hypnotic'.
- A common sort, the benzodiazepines, are habit-forming and should only be taken for a short period of time. They have side effects and can affect ability to drive or operate machinery.

  In the past many people were prescribed these, and addiction is a common problem.

H DETAILS

- Pain-relieving drugs for mild to moderate pain: aspirin and paracetamol.
- For moderate pain: ibuprofen.
- For severe pain control morphine and morphine-related medicines can be prescribed. These have side effects such as constipation and can be habit-forming.

  Aspirin should be avoided by those with stomach problems. Many people with a history of asthma are allergic to aspirin.

  It is dangerous to take more than the recommended dose of any of them.

A DETAILS

- Treat the symptoms felt by people who are very depressed, but do not deal with the cause of depression.
- One sort, the monoamine oxidase inhibitor drugs (MAOI), are dangerous if taken with certain foods so a strict diet advised by the doctor must be followed.
- Can have a variety of side effects.

F DETAILS

- Drugs similar to the hormones produced by your body in the adrenal gland.
- Can be used against allergies or asthma.
- Can be used against pain or inflammation in the joints.
- If taking corticosteroid tablets you must carry a card with you at all times and show it to doctors, nurses and dentists every time you are treated.
- You must never just stop taking them (very dangerous) unless your doctor knows.
- After-effects can last up to several years.
- Found in several skin creams; relieves symptoms but can make skin thinner.

D DETAILS

- Act to reduce the body's reaction in case of allergy, eg hay fever.
- Can be in tablets, creams or cold medicines.
- If they cause drowsiness, do not drive or operate machinery.
- Can in themselves cause allergic reactions and should not be used for long periods.
- Found in skin creams such as Anthisan and Wasp-Eze.
- Found in Actifed, Benylin, Night Nurse and lots of other cold medicines.

E DETAILS

- Are often taken to relieve the discomfort of indigestion or ulcers.
- They neutralise stomach acids and this stops the pain.
- Tell your doctor what you are taking for indigestion if he/she proposes to prescribe you a medicine for something else. Antacids affect the way your stomach absorbs things, and should not be taken for a long time without your doctor knowing.
- Some act as laxatives and some make you constipated.

Card sort • continued •

B DETAILS

- Very useful for infections caused by bacteria.
- Useless against viruses.
- Some people are allergic to one of the commonest: penicillin. They must not take it. It could kill them.
- Must be used long enough to kill each bacterium, otherwise the bacterium adapts and becomes resistant to that antibiotic. This is why you must finish taking all the medicine even if you feel better.

C DETAILS

- Used to kill or prevent the growth of an organism on the surface of the body, eg the skin. Sometimes called germicides. Found in creams and lotions.

G DETAILS

- Used to unblock nasal, sinal or bronchial passages so that you can breathe more easily.
- One sort, the sympathomimetics, relax bronchial muscles. These are found in lots of over-the-counter cold medicines, eg Actifed, Lemsip, Sudafed. People with high blood pressure, heart disease or diabetes shouldn't take them without their doctor's knowledge.
- Lozenges and linctuses help to relieve sore throats.
- Expectorants make phlegm more watery.

I DETAILS

- A medicine applied directly to the skin, eyes or ears. Never lick or swallow it.
- Could be a cream, lotion or powder.
- Must never be given to a friend; skin is sensitive and this could cause itching, rashes or allergies.
- Depending on what it is prescribed for, could contain antibiotics, anti-fungal drugs, antihistamines or antiseptics, corticosteroids, local anaesthetics, etc.
- Sometimes says 'For External Use Only'.
- Should not be kept in a cupboard for longer than the use-by date.

Role-play 1

**Doctor writing at desk...
there is a knock on the door**

Doctor	Come in.
Patient	(enters room hesitantly)
Doctor	(without looking up) Sit down.
Patient	Er, good morning doctor.
Doctor	(continues to write)
Patient	(looks increasingly nervous) Erm, I've had a problem with my back.
Doctor	(without looking up) Mr Jones is it ?
Patient	(smiling faintly) Yes doctor.
Doctor	Well, what's the trouble Mr Jones?
Patient	Well, I've had a bad backache over the past...
Doctor	Back eh? (looks up briefly)
Patient	Yes, you see...
Doctor	Right, take one of these three times a day. (starts to write out a prescription)
Patient	Oh right. When should I...
Doctor	Right, that should help. Good day. (hands over prescription and continues to write on notepad)
Patient	(uncertainly) Well, thank you doctor. (leaves room)

Discuss among yourselves

Was this a useful appointment? How did the doctor behave? What was his/her tone of voice?
How would the doctor's body language affect the patient? How would the layout of the room
affect the patient? What do you think the patient expected to happen?

Role-play 2

**Doctor writing at desk...
there is a knock on the door**

Doctor   Come in.

Patient   (enters room hesitantly)

Doctor   (looking up and smiling) Do take a seat.

Patient   Good morning doctor.

Doctor   Good morning. Mr Jones isn't it?

Patient   Yes doctor.

Doctor   Now, what seems to be the trouble?

Patient   Well doctor, I've had trouble with my back.

Doctor   Oh dear, when did this start?

Patient   Well, a few days ago.

Doctor   Where exactly does it hurt?

Patient   (indicates spot in the small of the back) I've been decorating recently. It may have been caused by that.

Doctor   Very possibly. Not to worry. We'll soon sort it out.

Patient   Well, what exactly do you think I have done?

Doctor   You've probably pulled a muscle. I'll give you a prescription. (starts to write)

Patient   What treatment are you giving me?

Doctor   Oh, just something to take the pain away.

Patient   I prefer not to have any sort of sedative.

Doctor   Don't worry Mr Jones. This will sort you out. (hands over prescription)

Patient   Well... (takes prescription but seems worried) erm...

Doctor   Right. Goodbye Mr Jones.

Patient   Oh. Goodbye doctor. (leaves room)

Discuss among yourselves

Was this a useful appointment? How did the doctor behave? What was his/her tone of voice? How would the doctor's body language affect the patient? How would the layout of the room affect the patient? What do you think the patient expected to happen?

Role-play 3

Doctor writing at desk...
there is a knock on the door

Doctor

Patient

Doctor

Patient

Doctor

Patient

Doctor

Patient

Doctor

Patient

Doctor

Patient

Doctor

Patient

Doctor

Patient

Doctor

Patient

Doctor

Patient

Main messages

I'd like an appointment please

You have the right to see a doctor at your GP's surgery at any time during surgery hours. If there is an appointment system you could be given one for a later surgery as long as the delay wouldn't risk your health. The receptionist is there to ensure access to the doctor. You don't need to give details of your symptoms to the receptionist. If you know you will need an examination you could mention it. Some doctors allow longer appointments for this.

It's OK

You are entitled to seek help and feel that you have had a decent service.
When you come out of the surgery you should feel that:

- you were listened to and understood;
- you made the most of your time with the doctor;
- you gave clear information;
- you understand the advice you were given;
- if given a prescription you know how to use the medicine safely and effectively.

But... I'm still not better

Go back and explain this, eg:

- if your medicine doesn't work or has effects you weren't expecting;
- if you don't understand what is wrong with you and you are worried;
- if you would like a second opinion about what is wrong with you;
- if you don't understand the advice you were given;
- if you are feeling worse or have developed new symptoms.

Do	Don't
• find out the name of the medicine; • ask what it is for; • ask if there are food, drinks or other medicines you should avoid while taking it; • ask when you should take it, how often and how many at a time; • ask how long you should continue taking it; • ask if there are any side effects you should know about; • ask if there are things not to do, eg driving or operating machinery; • ask what you should do if you miss a dose • report any side effects; • tell the doctor of any allergies to medicines; • tell the doctor if you are already taking some medicines.	• delay once you realise you need medical help: make an appointment; • be put off by the mystique of the doctor; tell him/her exactly how you are feeling; • leave the surgery if you are not clear about the advice or treatment you have been given – write it down if necessary; • ignore the instructions on the bottle; • forget what you have taken: get a little box and put the correct dosage for the day in it if you know you are forgetful; • let anyone else use medicines prescribed for you; • keep old medicines in the cupboard – they can lose their effect or become harmful.

Options and consequences

1 **You've been sick after taking three tablets. Do you:**

   a carry on taking them despite your sickness;
   b stop taking them and hope you get better;
   c contact your doctor and explain the problem.

2 **You can't remember how many antibiotic tablets you've taken today. Do you:**

   a play safe and take another;
   b assume you've taken enough and continue the course;
   c think 'Oh, I've missed one now. I might as well stop'.

3 **You go down with what you think is the same bug your sister has had. Do you:**

   a help yourself to her left-over medicine;
   b make an appointment for yourself at the doctor's;
   c do nothing.

4 **You are feeling down and fed up. Someone offers you a 'pick-me-up'. Do you:**

   a say 'no thanks – I don't like taking pills';
   b say 'OK then';
   c take it because you don't want to offend them.

5 **Your skin is very sore. There is some cream in the medicine cabinet. Do you:**

   a use it;
   b go to your doctor or pharmacist and explain your symptoms;
   c read the instructions carefully and check the sell-by date.

6 **You have been prescribed something but then hear something about it on TV that concerns you. Do you:**

   a assume it's scaremongering and continue to take it;
   b throw it in the bin;
   c go back and ask your doctor about it.

7 **Your eye is very sore. You see some suitable-looking drops in the medicine cabinet. Do you:**

   a think 'never use someone else's medicine' and go to ask the pharmacist's advice;
   b use them;
   c Look at the sell-by date, check the seal, if opened check how long they have been open, and go ahead, taking care not to touch your eye with the bottle.

8 **You develop a skin rash and pains in your joints while taking some prescribed medicine. Do you:**

   a phone the doctor to report this;
   b carry on regardless;
   c stop taking the medicine and hope you get better.

SECTION 3: RELATIONSHIPS AND DIVERSITY 124-148

This section focuses on relationships and parenthood in two units which include seven lessons.

The material has been designed to be used flexibly so that schools can select specific units and lessons according to their priorities, and use them alongside other materials and activities.

The units and lessons are generally suitable for use with pupils across the key stage 4 age range and can be adapted for use with particular groups. Extra flexibility can be achieved as the units can be taught in any order.

Please read the child protection notes on page 15 before these lessons.

What do people think?

Please read the child protection notes on page 15 before this lesson.

Objectives

- To help students to feel at ease when discussing relationships and to have adolescent feelings affirmed.
- To help students realise that different people have different perspectives when looking at relationships.

Resources

Worksheets: *What do people think?* questionnaire (pp 126-127), *Scruples dilemmas 1* (p 128)
Self-assessment sheets

1 Set the scene with a brief class discussion, trying to establish agreement that different people have different moral and family values and that it is important to respect other people's views.

2 Ask the students to complete the questionnaire *What do people think?* They should complete the first column with the statement they most agree with. They then predict the statement their chosen adult would most agree with in the second column. They go on to share their answers with a partner, highlighting similarities and differences.

3 Ask the students to divide into groups of four or five. Give them the worksheet *Scruples Dilemmas 1* and explain the rules, using one group as an example. The students should consider the dilemmas on this page only.

4 Ask each group to report back on one dilemma and the issues that arose. Were they good at predicting what people thought? Were there lots of different views within the group, or were they similar? Highlight the need to find out what people actually think, not just to assume what they might think.

5 Ask the students to complete self-assessment sheets. For homework they could interview the adult whose predictions they recorded in part B of the questionnaire, recording the adult's answers on a blank questionnaire. Ask the students to bring completed questionnaires to the next lesson. Stress the importance (and interest) of doing this. It is an ideal opportunity for students to talk to their parents or guardians about these issues.

What do people think?

First read the questions and write in column **A** the statement that you most agree with for each question.
Then in column **B** write the statement that you think your named adult would most agree with.
Write here the name of the adult whose answers you are predicting in the **B** part of each question.

....

	A (my view)	B (an adult's view)
1 I am most influenced in the clothes I wear by... *parents friends other relatives the media other*		
2 If I were involved in a one-to-one relationship I would... *still be close to my friends tend to be less close to my friends*		
3 The age that a daughter should be allowed to go out independently in the evening is... *5–9 years 10–12 years 13–14 years 15–16 years 16+ years never*		
4 The age that a son should be allowed to go out independently in the evening is... *5–9 years 10–12 years 13–14 years 15–16 years 16+ years never*		
5 My family should play... *some part in the choice of my partner no part in the choice of my partner a large part in the choice of my partner*		
6 It is reasonable for a girl to become involved in a one-to-one relationship when she is... *Under 16 16–18 years 19–21 years 22–25 years 26–30 years 30+*		

continued on page 127

What do people think? · continued ·

	A (my view)	B (an adult's view)
7 It is reasonable for a boy to become involved in a one-to-one relationship when he is... *under 16 16–18 years 19–21 years* *22–25 years 26–30 years 30+*		
8 It is best to build a relationship... *before marriage after marriage*		
9 It is a good idea for a woman to start a family when she is... *under 16 16–18 years 19–21 years* *22–25 years 26–30 years 31–40 years* *whenever she feels she wants to*		
10 It is a good idea for a man to start a family when he is... *under 16 16–18 years 19–21 years* *22–25 years 26–30 years 31–40 years* *whenever he feels he wants to*		
11 If I had a personal problem I would talk to... *my parents other relatives* *friends other adults*		
12 The qualities I would look for in a partner would include		

Take home a blank copy of the questionnaire, use it to interview the person you were thinking about when you wrote the **B** answers. Make sure you bring your homework to the next lesson!

Scruples dilemmas 1

▶ **Rules**

First person **A** reads Dilemma 1 and secretly records his/her answer on rough paper. The others in the group predict **A**'s answer to this dilemma and each place their initials against their prediction.

A then reveals his/her real answer and records it on the sheet. Other group members mark the accuracy of their prediction with a cross or a tick. The group discusses the answers.

Next person **B** repeats the exercise with Dilemma 2. Go round the group until all have had a go.

Dilemma 1 You are out with your partner shopping for some clothes for yourself. Do you:
  a buy what you like?
  b buy what your partner likes?
  c wait until you find something you both agree on?
  d other – please describe.

Dilemma 2 Your best friend tries to use you as an alibi to stop him/her being prosecuted for stealing. Do you:
  a go along with it?
  b challenge him/her later?
  c deny all knowledge?
  d other – please describe.

Dilemma 3 Your friend offers to drive you home. He/she has been drinking and is, you think, over the limit. Do you:
  a accept the lift?
  b refuse the lift?
  c suggest you both get a taxi?
  d other – please describe.

Dilemma 4 You had arranged to meet your partner. At the last moment your mates give you a ticket for a big game. It is too late to let her/him know. Do you:
  a go to the match, then lie and say you were ill?
  b meet her/him as arranged?
  c go to the match and leave her/him a message at the meeting place?
  d other – please describe.

Dilemma 5 Your partner wants you to dress up to meet her/his family for the first time. You feel daft in your best clothes. Do you:
  a dress to please your partner and her/his family?
  b insist on wearing clothes you feel comfortable in?
  c refuse to go?
  d other – please describe.

Talking about relationships

Please read the child protection notes on page 15 before this lesson.

Objectives

- To help students to feel at ease when discussing relationships and to have adolescent feelings affirmed.
- To help students realise that different people have different perspectives when looking at relationships.
- To consider the role of open communication and shared values in forming good relationships.
- To develop respectful attitudes to all the positive ways in which people express their sexuality.

Resources

Worksheets: *Scruples dilemmas 1-3* (pp 128, 131-132)
Large sheets of paper
Self-assessment sheets

1   Ask the students to divide into the same groups as for the previous lesson. They can then review each other's homework, answering these questions:
  • Were there any questions they found difficult to predict?
  • In general, how accurate were their predictions?
  • Were there any questions from adults which surprised them?
  • What did they learn from doing this?

2   Explain that they are going to play the *Scruples dilemmas* game again, this time using questions about one-to-one relationships. Using the same rules, the students deal with all the dilemmas. Circulate, and make sure you raise and help with any of the following issues which may arise from the groups:

Q6 The safest behaviour re HIV/AIDS and other sexually-transmitted infections (STIs) is to be open with your partner about your past and to require the same of him/her.

Q8 Personal space is important. If students voice adverse comments about homosexuality, for example, clarify the point of the lesson. Remind them that they should accept all relationships as valid if they are 'positive' relationships.

Q9 Remember that pain like this can be a symptom of some STIs. It should never be ignored.

Q16 Stress that students should never be frightened of seeking help from others in school, agencies for child protection or phone helplines. No one has the right to treat them like this. They can change the situation but first they have to speak out.

continued on page 130 ▶

Talking about relationships continued

Q18 The school's position must be clear. All personal comments are unacceptable. All people should be valued, regardless of their sexual orientation. There may be students in the class who are in this situation and will be noting our attitudes, both verbal and non-verbal. Explain that this is an opportunity for students to explore their feelings about sexuality. They should not pass judgement on others.

3 Ask the groups to discuss and list on large paper six factors which promote one-to-one relationships and six which hinder them. Display the sheets. Is it possible to arrive at a class consensus on three factors which promote good one-to-one relationships?

4 Ask the students to complete self-assessment sheets.

Scruples dilemmas 2

Dilemma 6 You are newly married. Your partner does not know how sexually experienced you are. Do you:
  a tell her/him?
  b say nothing?
  c lie?
  d other – please describe.

Dilemma 7 You are in a one-to-one relationship. A friend of yours is making your partner embarrassed. Do you:
  a let her/him sort it out?
  b ask your friend to stop?
  c join in with your friend?
  d move away?
  e other – please describe.

Dilemma 8 A friend comes up to you and greets you by touching you. Do you:
  a object?
  b accept it as normal?
  c not say anything although you don't like it?
  d other – please describe.

Dilemma 9 You have a pain when you urinate. Do you:
  a tell your partner first?
  b ignore it?
  c seek professional advice?
  d other – please describe.

Dilemma 10 You are quite happy not having a one-to-one relationship. Do you:
  a explain this to your friends?
  b tell your friends that you are looking for the right person?
  c say nothing – it's your own business how you feel?
  d say nothing but feel left out?
  e other – please describe.

Dilemma 11 You are in a one-to-one relationship and intend to make it sexual. Do you:
  a say if you have had sexual experience so that you can both decide whether it's necessary to think about ways to prevent either of you from being at risk from sexually transmitted diseases such as HIV/AIDS?
  b refuse to think about it and hope for the best?
  c suggest using condoms until you are ready to start a family?
  d worry secretly but say and do nothing?
  e other – please describe.

Dilemma 12 You find a condom in your partner's pocket. Do you:
  a praise him/her for being sensible?
  b assume he/she is seeing someone else?
  c think 'Good, I was wanting to discuss this anyway'?
  d finish with him/her because you obviously don't share his/her views?
  e other – please describe.

Scruples dilemmas 3

Dilemma 13 Your family is particularly keen for you to develop a relationship with someone. Do you:

    a trust your family and go along with their wishes?

    b politely ignore your family's advice?

    c risk a family argument/rejection by refusing to take their advice?

    d other – please describe.

Dilemma 14 You feel very comfortable having a non-sexual friendship with a boy/girl. Your friends think something else is going on. Do you:

    a ignore them and carry on regardless?

    b finish the friendship?

    c see him/her in secret?

    d other – please describe.

Dilemma 15 Your friends are being cruel and calling you names because they think you are missing out by not going out with boys/girls. Do you:

    a explain your point of view?

    b feel hurt/upset?

    c agree in public, disagree in private?

    d feel embarrassed?

    e other – please describe.

Dilemma 16 Someone in your family is behaving violently towards you. Do you:

    a keep it to yourself?

    b seek help?

    c try to sort it out between you and the person?

    d other – please describe.

Dilemma 17 You are in a one-to-one relationship and intend to become sexually active but do not want children yet. Do you:

    a discuss with your partner what sort of contraception you should use?

    b not bother with any contraception?

    c assume that your partner has taken the necessary precautions?

    d provide contraceptives for yourself?

    e other – please describe.

Dilemma 18 Someone in your class is being taunted with names such as 'gay', 'queer', 'lesbian'. Do you:

    a tell the class to stop making personal comments? It is everyone's right to have his or her sexuality respected and not to be persecuted by others.

    b join in with the class?

    c feel sorry for the person but say nothing?

    d other – please describe.

- Were there any particular questions which were difficult to predict?
- In general, how accurate were the predictions?
- Were there any answers which were surprising?
- What did you learn from doing this?

Teenage feelings

Please read the child protection notes on page 15 before this lesson.

Objectives

- To help students to feel at ease when discussing relationships and have adolescent feelings affirmed.
- To realise that different people have different family and moral values.
- To consider the role of open communication and shared values in forming good relationships.
- To develop tolerant and respectful attitudes to all the positive ways in which people express their sexuality.
- To explore stereotypes about normality.

Resources

Worksheets: *Looking back on teenage pressures* (p 134),
Sexual rights and responsibilities (p 135)
Self-assessment sheets.

1   Explain and discuss the objectives then ask the students whether they can think of any ground rules which would help to create the right atmosphere for the rest of the lesson, eg listen to others, no put-downs, the right to privacy, respect for confidences, not making personal disclosures, etc. Write their suggestions on the board. Be firm about respecting these ground rules. Enable the group to take responsibility for managing their behaviour using this agreement.

2   Ask for definitions of the following terms: celibate (someone is celibate if they have chosen not to be involved in a sexual relationship), virgin (someone who has not had full sexual intercourse), homosexual (someone who is sexually attracted to people of his or her own sex – describes both men and women), lesbian (another name for homosexual women), heterosexual (someone who is sexually attracted to people of the opposite sex), bi-sexual (someone who is sexually attracted to people of the opposite sex and people of his or her own sex), coming out (telling family and friends that you are homosexual or lesbian). Ensure that students understand the terminology and can use it correctly.

3   Give the students copies of the worksheet *Looking back on teenage pressures*. Hold a class discussion and ask the students to respond to the questions.

4   As a class or in groups, read through the worksheet *Sexual rights and responsibilities*. Ask the students to discuss and record any rights and responsibilities they think are important when considering sexual behaviour. Encourage them to record these and create a visual display, eg a large Venn diagram in poster form, or a presentation.

5   Ask the students to complete self-assessment sheets.

Looking back on teenage pressures

▷ Read these comments which people have made about their feelings as teenagers.
Use them to think about the pressures that you feel and to answer the questions.

'I now realise that everyone has sexual feelings. You don't have to be young and beautiful to enjoy a good sex life. You don't have to be handsome to be a good lover.'

'If only someone in my school had said it's OK to have homosexual or lesbian feelings: For years I thought I was the only person who was gay... Now I realise others in my school must have felt the same way.'

'I even used to join in with the jokes because I was scared people would turn round and call **me** names if I didn't.'

'As a teenager I was never that interested in sexual relationships. I was made to feel odd though, because everyone else always seemed to be talking about sex.'

'I used to think that my parents were old-fashioned and too protective, now I release they were right to be worried about the pressures young people face.'

'Nobody would ever talk honestly about it. People bragged, and you never felt they were telling the truth.'

'I had very strong sexual feelings but felt ashamed of them. "Nice girls" weren't supposed to feel that way.'

'My body was changing but emotionally I was just confused.'

Questions

Do you feel that society (or your own friends) pressurises young people to conform to certain norms about sexuality?

If so, how does society or peer pressure do this?

Do these pressures help young people feel comfortable about their own feelings?

Do the pressures help them to build good relationships?

Sexual rights and responsibilities

Read the information below. Then use the word collage below to help you do your own Venn diagram showing the ways people ought and ought not to behave towards each other sexually.

Don't forget that some pressures can become a risk to people's physical and mental health, for example:

- feelings of depression or guilt;
- discrimination in jobs or housing;
- threat and reality of physical violence;
- graffiti written on people's property;
- stereotyping/isolation of those who don't conform;
- hurtful jokes;
- people finding they are rejected by their families or places of worship.

On the other hand, most people survive the pressures of their teenage years and successfully build caring, loving relationships.

How can we sort out some rules for sexual behaviour which will help us to feel comfortable that we are expressing our sexuality without harming that of others?

Look at the word collage. Add any words or messages you think are important concerning sexual behaviour. Leave out any you don't think are helpful in saying what you want.
On a large piece of paper create a Venn diagram to show what you think are the main messages.
Display your messages for the rest of the class.

Word collage

laws	consent	*passion*	**repression**	morality
force	**security**	two-timing	religion	....
exploitation	sharing	**media**	sexism	....
trust	prostitution	intimacy	pornography	....
maturity	**violence**	**honesty**	*trust*	....
romance	**faithfulness**	life partner	**fun**	....

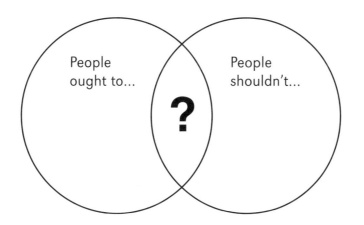

Case studies of different relationships

Please read the child protection notes on page 15 before this lesson.

Objectives

- To help students to feel at ease when discussing relationships and have adolescent feelings affirmed.
- To realise that different people have different family and moral values.
- To consider the role of open communication and shared values in forming good relationships.
- To develop tolerant and respectful attitudes to all the positive ways in which people express their sexuality.
- To explore stereotypes about normality.
- To consider moral and family values concerning relationships.

Resources

Worksheet: *Case studies of different relationships* (p 138)
Self-assessment sheets

1   Ask the class to consider their own experience of times when they felt under pressure from friends and other people. Ask for examples of situations and identify types of pressure. Record them on the board.

2   Divide the students into groups and brief them as follows:

- Each group selects a situation from the list identified.

- In their groups the students role-play the situation in two different ways: first giving way under pressure from peers, parents or others, then, with the same situation but different people playing the various parts, showing the person resisting pressure in a positive manner.

Circulate and watch each group in turn. Ask the groups to report back on strategies used to resist pressure.

3   Explain that you will now be focusing on wider circumstances in which pressures can arise in a one-to-one relationship. Brainstorm what these pressures might be and record them on the board. Examples you might expect include:

- starting a new relationship when one or both partners has children from a previous one;

- whirlwind romance;

- parental opposition;

- conflict of cultures and/or religions;

- arranged relationships versus a free choice of partner;

continued on page 137

Case studies of different relationships • continued •

- shortage of money;

- settling down at a young age;

- the pressures of parenting a young baby;

- conflict of personalities;

- changing ambitions or expectations.

4   Introduce the idea of a storyboard. In pairs, ask the student to select their own example of a couple in a one-to-one relationship who are experiencing problems and develop a storyboard of up to 12 frames. The example could be from the list on the board or from the *Case studies* sheet. The storyboard should show how the people involved try to make the relationship work despite the pressure. As an alternative to drawing, students could cut and paste drawings or photos from magazines they bring in.

5   Hold a whole-class discussion. What strategies do people use to overcome problems and make their relationships more successful?

6   Display the storyboards and ask the students to complete self-assessment sheets.

Note

Students should not be put under any pressure to disclose private feelings. However, they may appreciate knowing about sources of advice they could use if they wanted to, both inside and outside school. You could provide your own contacts and display them in tutor rooms, as well as making them available to all students. The numbers can be found at the front of your local phone book. Alternatively, students could use a search engine such as Yahoo to access websites such as Women's Aid.

Case studies of different relationships

▷ Choose one of the case studies below, or one of your own, and develop it into a storyboard.
The storyboard should show how the people involved try to make their relationship work despite the pressure.
Happy endings are allowed!

Couple A have only known each other for one month. It has been a whirlwind romance and both feel deeply involved. They want their relationship to continue. However, ...'s father is against the relationship and thinks they are both too young. They are talking about what to say to him tonight when he comes in from work.

Couple B have just got married. They didn't know each other well before the marriage but are both committed to making it work. It is two months after their marriage and both have realised that being married has made a big difference to their lives. She has been offered a place on a good college course. They are discussing the offer.

Couple C have been seeing each other for a few months but have kept their relationship secret because they fear the disapproval of their families and friends. They have been seen together by a friend and are discussing what they should do.

Couple D have been together for several months and both want a permanent relationship. He still enjoys spending several evenings a week going to the pub with his mates. She would like them to spend more of their leisure time together and is finding that she resents the amount of money that he is spending on drink. Their joint bank statement has just arrived.

Couple E have been going out for a number of weeks and really like each other. Their friends know they are going steady and are constantly asking if they have had sex yet. Although both are aware of this pressure, neither has liked to raise the subject first. Her best friend has just told her that one of his mates has said that it is common knowledge that they have had sex. She is looking upset when she next meets him.

Mike is a single parent who is looking after his children aged two and five. He enjoys caring for them and watching them grow up but is finding that he feels isolated from other adults and has no opportunities to develop new one-to-one relationships. He is talking to a friend about how he can develop his social life without letting his children down.

Parents' needs

Please read the child protection notes on page 15 before this lesson.

Objectives

- To make students aware that parents have a joint role in promoting their child's health and welfare.
- To gain experience of researching issues of antenatal care.

Resources

Worksheet: *Checklist for talking to parents* (p 140)
Self-assessment sheets

1 Start with a whole-class discussion about parenthood and its responsibilities. Then ask the students to prepare lists of questions to ask parents of small children, about their care and the parents' responsibilities. Give them copies of the worksheet *Checklist for talking to parents* to help them.

2 Ask the students to carry out interviews based on these questions as homework. Encourage the students to interview their mothers if possible – most will be only too pleased to talk about their experiences.

3 Ask the students to prepare a display of their findings, either as a whole class, or in groups.

4 Review the displays and commend those who have done a thorough research job and successfully carried out their interviews. Ask the students to file the information carefully. Discuss what they have learned from this exercise.

5 Ask the students to complete self-assessment sheets.

Checklist for talking to parents

> Your task is to think of some questions you would like to ask anyone who is, or has been, the parent of a young baby. Write your questions down and prepare to carry out one or more interviews.

Perhaps you have some questions you could ask your own mother or father about their experience of having you? Do you know someone who is pregnant or who has recently had a baby who would be prepared to talk to you?

Some things you may like to ask about:

- length of pregnancy;
- problems during pregnancy;
- what the pregnancy was like;
- antenatal care;
- labour and birth;
- feelings about birth;
- the first few days;
- being a parent;
- what a new baby is like.

Write your questions and the person's answers here.

....

....

....

....

....

....

....

....

....

....

....

....

....

....

....

....

What do children need?

Please read the child protection notes on page 15 before this lesson.

Objectives

- To help students focus on their own expectations and experience of parenthood.
- To identify what being a parent involves and what a child needs from a parent.
- To identify those personal qualities in a relationship which will help them in their future role as parents.

Resources

Worksheet: *Child's needs checklist* (p 142)
A large sheet of paper
Self-assessment sheets

1 Ask the class to consider the following statements. In this room there are:
   - some people who will choose not to be parents for a variety of reasons;
   - some people who will choose to be parents for a variety of reasons.

2 In pairs ask the students to complete the worksheet *Child's needs checklist*. They then initial the activities they can see themselves doing for a child. They should note the differences and similarities between them.

3 Ask for feedback from the pairs and record on a large sheet of paper how many students initialled which statement. Raise and discuss the following.
   - Is there a general pattern?
   - Do you think girls/boys would give different answers?

   In a single-sex school ask what the opposite sex would say if they saw what had been put down. Optional homework: check this out with a girl/boy.

4 In boys' groups try to agree on:
   - three hard things about being a father;
   - three good things about being a father.

   In girls' groups try to agree on:
   - three hard things about being a mother;
   - three good things about being a mother.

5 Ask for feedback from the groups, then ask individuals around the class to complete the sentence: I think parents should be...

6 Ask students to complete self-assessment sheets.

Child's needs checklist

Think about what a child needs at various ages and tick the boxes.
Then initial those things you could see yourself doing for a child.

A child needs a parent...	Age 1	Age 5	Age 11	Age 16	Age 21+	Initial
• to provide money						
• to provide the right food						
• to change his/her nappies						
• to wash him/her every day						
• to play with and stimulate him/her						
• to talk to						
• to cuddle						
• to show how to do things						
• to listen						
• to read a story at bedtime						
• to put to bed						
• to tell what to do and what not to do						
• to consider safety						
• to provide adequate clothing						
• to provide adequate housing						
• to take him/her to school						
• to take an interest in his/her education						
• to encourage independence						
• to give warmth						
• to enjoy his/her company						
• to provide rewards/give punishment						
• to lay down rules						
• to show interest in what he/she is doing						
• to help through problems						
• to give advice based on experience						
• to encourage reading and other skills						
• to provide care and comfort when ill						
Any other things?						

What is a family?

Please read the child protection notes on page 15 before this lesson.

Objectives

- To help students focus on their own expectations and experience of parenthood.
- To identify what being a parent involves and what a child needs from a parent.
- To identify those personal qualities in a relationship which will help them in their future role as parents.
- To consider the family structures that exist in the real world.

Resources

Worksheets: *What is a family?* (p 144),
Family situation illustrations (pp 145-148) enlarged to A3 size.
Self-assessment sheets

1   Start by explaining that children are brought up in a variety of different types of family situation and that you will be looking at illustrations depicting this.

2   Divide the class into groups of four. Give each student a copy of the worksheet *What is a family?* and ask them to consider the following questions about one of the families shown.

- Describe what they think the relationship is between these people.
- Comment on who seems to do what to care for others in the family.
- Give the illustration a caption which sums it up.

3   Ask each student in turn to report back to the group, describing their picture. Then the groups select the illustration they find most interesting and report back on it to the class.

4   Give each group a different *Family situation* illustration. Ask the groups to discuss what is happening and answer the questions. More creative students could use the blank page to create their own illustration.

5   Ask for feedback on the following:
- the feelings people have in different illustrations;
- ways of coping with difficult situations and the personal qualities needed to deal with them;
- where people can turn for help in difficult family situations;
- the possible consequences of not seeking help.
Note that at some time everybody needs help in bringing up children and that those who have little help in the home should not be afraid to seek support from family/friends/external agencies, etc.

6   Ask the students to complete self-assessment sheets.

What is a family?

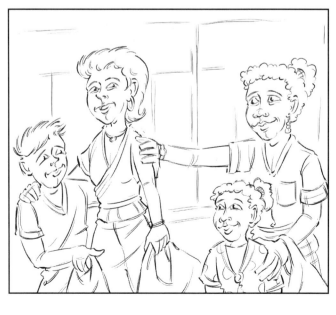

Family situations • 1 •

At 2 o'clock in the morning

What do you think is happening in this picture?

What are the feelings of the people involved?

Can you suggest ways of coping with this problem and where people could seek help?

What personal qualities are needed to help and deal with such difficulties?

What could be the consequences of not doing anything?

Family situations • 2 •

A hectic day

What do you think is happening in this picture?

What are the feelings of the people involved?

Can you suggest ways of coping with this problem and where people could seek help?

What personal qualities are needed to help and deal with such difficulties?

What could be the consequences of not doing anything?

A hectic day

Family situations • 3 •

'I want some sweets...'

What do you think is happening in this picture?

What are the feelings of the people involved?

Can you suggest ways of coping with this problem and where people could seek help?

What personal qualities are needed to help and deal with such difficulties?

What could be the consequences of not doing anything?

Family situations • 4 •

What do you think is happening in this picture?

What are the feelings of the people involved?

Can you suggest ways of coping with this problem and where people could seek help?

What personal qualities are needed to help and deal with such difficulties?

What could be the consequences of not doing anything?

SECTION 4: ACTIVE CITIZENSHIP

149-223

This section focuses on active citizenship in three units which include 16 lessons.

The material has been designed to be used flexibly so that schools can select specific units and lessons according to their priorities, and use them alongside other materials and activities.

The units and lessons are generally suitable for use with pupils across the key stage 4 age range and can be adapted for use with particular groups. Extra flexibility can be achieved as the units can be taught in any order.

You and the legal system

Objectives

- To discuss the purpose of having laws in society.
- To inform students about the legal position of young people.
- To role-play situations which demand the exercise of legal responsibilities.
- To inform students about their rights if arrested.

Resources

Worksheets: *You and the legal system – Opinions and facts* (p 151), *You and the legal system – situations* (p 152)

1 Give a brief introduction, explaining the objectives. Discuss and establish the difference between a rule and a law. Give the students copies of *You and the legal system – opinions and facts* and discuss the opinions.

2 Divide the class into groups of six and ask them to allocate parts and read the worksheet *You and the legal system – situations*. Then they should answer the questions to prompt analysis of the behaviour of the police and the young people.

3 A spokesperson from each group reports back to the class. Note suggestions on the board. Read 'The Facts' on the first worksheet and expand upon opportunities to highlight concepts of power, justice and change.

- Is it necessary to give police the right to stop people and ask them questions?
- Are there some laws which protect/benefit everyone?
- Is the law enforced fairly? Discuss whether young people and young black males are more likely to be stopped and searched than other people.

You and the legal system
• Opinions and facts •

OPINIONS

'I think laws are there to protect everyone'

'I think a law won't work if people think it's a bad law'

'I think you should always obey the law'

'I think it's all right to break the law if it's unfair'

'I think passing a law against something doesn't stop people doing it'

'I think you have to have laws or there'd be chaos'

THE FACTS

Rules are made by any organisation. Laws are made by Parliament and if you break them you can be prosecuted.

The police don't make the law. They are there to protect life and property and enforce the law.

Governments change and make new laws. Individuals can try to change the law by political action. Sometimes individuals break the law to make a point.

When the government wants to make a law it publishes a bill. There is a lot of debate. Individuals or groups can try to change the bill. It passes through a lot of stages in the House of Commons and the House of Lords before it finally becomes an act and is the law of the land.

The police have laws to guide them in their job. They can stop and search you if they have reasonable suspicion that you have committed an offence:

- they can use reasonable force;
- they can ask you questions including your name and address;
- they can ask you to remove your coat, jacket and gloves;
- they can search you if they suspect you of having drugs, birds' eggs, stolen goods, offensive weapons or tools for burglary.

If the police stop and search you they must provide a written notice of why you were stopped, who searched you and what the result was.

You and the legal system
• Situations •

▷ In your groups, assign parts and read through the play.

Cast

Carl, *a black 15-year-old* **Elaine**, *Carl's girlfriend* **Paul**, *Carl's friend* **Sharon**, *another friend*
PC Andrews **WPC Williams**

Scene: The four young people are walking through a car park at night. Carl is carrying a portable CD. They are fooling about. Two police officers approach them.

PC Andrews	Can I ask where you're going?
Carl	We're just on our way home. This is our short cut.
PC Andrews	What have you got there?
Paul	It's mine. What's it to you? We haven't done anything.
PC Andrews	OK. I'd like to have a look at it. *(Carl passes it over)* Right. Thank you.
WPC Williams	Can you give me your names and addresses?
Sharon and Elaine	We don't have to tell you. He's told you what we're doing.
WPC Williams	There have been a number of thefts from this car park recently. We have the right to stop and search you. Now tell me your names and addresses.
Sharon	Madonna, Windsor Castle. *(All giggle.)*
WPC Williams	I'm going to ask you again and I advise you to tell me the truth. You can appreciate we have to do our job.

They all give their names and addresses and cooperate when the officers ask them to remove their coats and jackets and empty their pockets.

PC Andrews	OK. There doesn't seem to be any problem. You do have the right to call at the police station tomorrow for a written notice of why you were stopped, who we are and what the result was. Off you go. Don't hang around the car park.

▷ In your group answer and record the following questions:

1 What, if anything, did the police do

  a wrong?

  b right?

2 Why were the young people stopped?

3 How was the young people's reaction

  a bad?

  b good?

4 How might the young people have made it worse for themselves? What effect would this have had?

My rights and responsibilities

Objectives

- To inform students about the legal position of young people.
- To role-play situations which demand the exercise of legal responsibilities.
- To inform students about their rights if arrested.

Resources

Worksheets: *You and the legal system – situations continued* (p 154), *Your rights at a police station* (p 155), *What you do know about the law?* (p 156)
Information sheet: *What do you know about the law?* (p 157)
Self-assessment sheets

1 Recap on the previous lesson. Divide the students into groups and ask them to look at the worksheet *You and the legal system – situations continued*. They can either discuss it in groups or choose one of the situations and role-play it.

2 Check that the students have understood the information on their responsibilities under the law and have applied it to the situations.

3 Ask the students to test each other about the information on the worksheet *Your rights at a police station*. Then ask them to complete the questionnaire *What do you know about the law?* Check the answers.

4 In groups, ask the students to choose a law they would like changed. Discuss how they could go about doing this.

5 Ask the students to complete self-assessment sheets.

You and the legal system
• Situations (continued) •

Sometimes we find ourselves in situations in which it seems that we are under suspicion. Let's assume that the best thing to do is to act in a way which will not make the situation worse.

Either write out five dos and don'ts for each of these situations on a separate sheet of paper, or role-play a situation, first showing how it should be handled, then showing how it should not be handled.

You have seen a bike being taken from the school bike shed by someone you know. You suspect it is not theirs.	You are stopped by police at 6.00 pm. They say you fit the description of someone who has committed a theft in the neighbourhood. They want you to help with their enquiries.	You have been given a CD by a friend. Someone says, 'Hey, that's just like the one our Sheila had stolen from her bag on Wednesday. I recognise that mark on it. Where did you get it?'

Your responsibilities under the law

You have to report: crimes, road accidents in which someone is injured, any suspicious behaviour which you see taking place. You must hand in property you find which is not yours. If you keep it you are guilty of theft. You must not waste police time or give false information. Maximum fine £500 or six months in prison.

You have to prevent crimes. Don't make crime easy, don't encourage others to break the law.

You have to act as a witness. Tell the truth in court. If you lie you are guilty of perjury and can be sent to prison. As a witness your words are evidence. You must tell the court what you know or have heard or seen, not what someone has told you has happened.

You have to serve on a jury when called. Once you are 18 you may be called to do jury service. You and 11 others will be called on to 'deliver a verdict according to the evidence' – decide whether an accused person is guilty or not. A fair legal system depends on ordinary people being involved like this.

Your rights at a police station

Complete this worksheet in pairs or groups of four.

Test each other by reading out the quote and asking whether it is true or false.
Then check against the facts in the boxes.

	My rights at a police station	'You can tell someone of your arrest.'				True or false
A1	The custody officer should tell you your rights. He/she should make sure you are treated properly. He/she writes a custody record. This tells you why you are being detained. You can ask for a copy of this when you are released.	You can consult a solicitor.	You can tell someone of your arrest.	You can read the Codes of Practice which explain what the police can and can't do.	If you are a juvenile (under 17) your parents must be told where you are.	

	My rights at a police station	'After 12 hours you can go home.'			True or false
A2	For a minor offence you can be held for up to 24 hours For a serious offence the police can ask a magistrate for permission to hold you for up to 92 hours.	At the end of this time you must either be charged or released.	You may be asked to return to the police station later when police have finished their checks.	If you are juvenile the Juvenile Bureau will decide whether to caution you or send you to court.	

	My rights at a police station	'You have the right to be represented by a solicitor.'		True or false
A3	If you are charged you will either be detained until the next morning to appear in court or released on police bail.	Bail means you must go back to the court/police station when you are told to.	You are entitled to be legally represented in court.	

What do you know about the law?

▸ **Complete this worksheet on your own or in pairs.**
Check it against the answer sheet.

At what age can you legally...

	Your answer	Correct answer
1 consent to medical treatment?		
2 get a part-time job?		
3 vote?		
4 be convicted of a criminal offence?		
5 get married with your parents' consent?		
6 drive a bus?		

Are the following statements true or false?

	Your answer	Correct answer
1 You can leave school as soon as you are 16.		
2 Children can drink alcohol at home under their parents' supervision.		
3 You have to pay for dental treatment as soon as you are 16.		
4 The age of consent is different for homosexuals and heterosexuals.		
5 Children of 12 can buy cigarettes for adults.		

What do you know about the law?
• answers •

Use this information to check your knowledge of the law.

5 years old

You must go to school.
You must pay child fares on public transport.

7 years old

You can open a bank account and withdraw money.

10 years old

You can be convicted of a criminal offence provided you knew what you were doing was wrong.

The police can search you, fingerprint and photograph you. They should only interview you if your parent or another adult is with you.

13 years old

You can get a part-time job but can't work for more than two hours on a school day.

14 years old

You can go to a pub, but can't buy or drink alcohol there.

A boy can be convicted of rape or unlawful sexual intercourse with a girl under 16.

A boy can be sent to a detention centre.

17 years old

You can drive a car.
You can buy a gun.
You can be put on probation.
You can be sent to prison for a serious offence.

19 years old

Until this age you are entitled to full-time, free education at a school or college.

21 years old

You can become an MP or a councillor.
You can drive a bus or a heavy goods vehicle.

18 years old

You are an adult in the eyes of the law.
You can buy and drink alcohol.
You can vote. You can buy a house.
You can bet and play bingo.
You can apply for a passport.
You can change your name.
You can be sued for money.
You can serve on a jury.
You can donate your body to science.
You can apply for legal aid.
You have to pay for dental treatment unless still in full-time education.
You can see your birth certificate if you are adopted.
If you are male you can consent to have sex with another male over 18.

16 years old

A girl can consent to sexual intercourse with a man or a woman.
You can marry with your parents' consent
You can leave school.
You can claim benefits.
You can consent to medical treatment including contraceptive treatment.
You can buy cigarettes and fireworks.
You have to pay for prescriptions and full fare on trains and buses.
You can ride a moped.

A boy or a girl of any age can be treated at an STI clinic in complete confidentiality.
Young people do not need their parents' consent to buy condoms.

Punishment and crime

Objectives

- To know and understand the role and operation of the criminal and civil justice systems.
- To apply students' understanding actively to school-based/local/ national or global issues.
- To negotiate, decide and take part responsibly in school- and community-based activities.

Resources

Worksheets: *What is crime?* (p 160), *Punishment and crime* (p 161), *Sentences* (p 163)
Information sheet: *Sentences – the facts* (p 162)

1 Explain the first two objectives and remind the class of the previous session with regard to how it felt to consider our legal responsibilities, eg as a witness and our rights, eg at a police station.

2 Ask the students to look at the worksheet *What is crime?* Read it through and ensure the students understand the language.

3 Divide the class into groups. Each group is to discuss their own attitudes to breaking the law. Which laws are widely respected and kept? Which are not? Why? Collect conclusions. Discuss the importance of enforcement as a deterrent. Apart from the police force what other kinds of deterrent or crime prevention are there? (Building design, street lighting, CCTV, neighbourhood watch schemes, traffic calming, youth clubs and other activities, jobs, education, etc.)

4 Ask the students to read the two case studies on the worksheet *Punishment and crime*. As individuals they should mark the functions of punishment out of 5. Lead a class discussion:

- How did responses differ?

- Did anyone find their attitudes were different towards case study 2?

- Are we more likely to favour 'retribution' if an issue directly affects us?

5 Introduce the idea of taking the law into your own hands, kangaroo courts, and vigilantes. Explain that in this country criminal investigations and trials are carried out by the publicly-funded police and the judicial system to avoid these.

6 Ask the students to read the information sheet *Sentences – the facts* on the court system and punishments. They should go on to complete the activities on the worksheet *Sentences* on aggravating and mitigating factors.

continued on page 159

Punishment and crime • continued •

7 Lead class feedback and sum up conclusions. If time allows encourage the students to undertake one of the following extension activities as a citizenship activity or as the basis of coursework for one of the GCSE short courses in citizenship.

Extension activities

School/community

Investigate the practice in your school of dealing with anti-social behaviour such as bullying or stealing. Some schools involve pupils in bully courts. How does this work? Is it effective? How can problems such as unfair trials or witness intimidation be avoided? Could it work in your school? Why/why not?

Local

Visit a local magistrates' court or crown court as a member of the public. Courts are in session during most school holidays. You have to go through security measures. You can ask the advice of the clerks in reception as to which would be the most interesting cases to attend.

Local/national/global

Make a collection of cuttings from local newspapers about local court cases. Follow a big case of national importance and, if possible, an international dispute involving the law. Evaluate what you have found. Do you consider that justice has been done?

What is crime?

Crime is breaking the law.

There are at least three different kinds of law in the UK.

Criminal law concerns anti-social acts such as crimes of theft, fraud, violence or murder. The police have a duty to investigate the case if this law is broken, to identify the offender, and collect evidence against him or her. The case is prosecuted by the Crown as representative of the public interest in dealing with crimes against the public. Cases are heard first in magistrates' courts and then, if serious, in higher courts such as crown courts or high courts. Taxpayers pay for the costs of the case. If pleading not guilty, a defendant is entitled to a fair trial, in which first the prosecution and then the defence state the case for or against the defendant and call witnesses. So that even the poor can have a fair trial, there is legal aid to pay for defence solicitors and barristers. In a jury trial 12 jurors decide on guilt or innocence, and then the judge acquits the defendant or passes sentence.

Civil law concerns private disputes between individual citizens, groups or companies. Usually these are not offences for which people are arrested, but often concern property or involve suing for compensation. Individuals can employ solicitors, but usually legal aid is not available and the costs of the case have to be covered by the plaintiffs (the people who bring the case to court). Small claims courts help keep the costs down.

Public law includes international law and constitutional law. It concerns disputes between countries or between a citizen and the state.

Democratic states are based on the 'rule of law' – a sort of contract between its citizens and the state. Each citizen agrees to obey the laws. In return laws should be passed democratically and carried out fairly. Laws are enforced by the police, the courts and prisons, who must be honest and even-handed, not favouring the rich and powerful or their friends. However, legal systems vary widely. There can be miscarriages of justice, and some systems seem to operate more fairly than others, eg towards women or minorities.

If laws are not enforced they can be widely ignored. People tend to keep to some laws only if they think they will be caught if they break them. An example is the 70mph speed limit on motorways. Other laws are almost universally accepted, eg compulsory wearing of seat belts.

Brainstorm examples of laws you know about that you know are often broken.

What are the factors which influence whether people break the law or keep it?

Punishment and crime

Punishments are set when individuals are found guilty and convicted by the courts.

Case 1

A man of 25 has been convicted of robbing a pensioner in her own home (using force or threat of force.)

What might be an effective punishment (a punishment that works)?
Your attitude to this will depend on which you think are the most important out of the possible functions given below.

Below are four possible functions of punishment. Give each function a mark out of five.
1   means extremely important;
2   means important;
3   means quite important;
4   means not very important;
5   means not important.

A   To punish the criminal and make him/her suffer in keeping with the suffering that has been caused to the victim/s of the crime (this is called retribution).

B   To persuade the criminal to give up crime and become a more useful/less anti-social member of society (this is called reform or rehabilitation).

C   To make it clear that this is such a bad crime that anyone who commits it can expect a very severe punishment, thus deterring others who might be tempted to carry out such a crime themselves (this is called deterrence).

D   To protect society from repeated offences by the individual.

Punishments can also be set by any organisation that has agreed rules, such as a school.

Case 2

A girl of 15 has taken an expensive mobile phone from her friend's bag and tried to sell it. Repeat the mark out of 5 according to what you want the effects of punishment to be. Have your attitudes changed? If so why do you think this is?

A   To punish the criminal and make him/her suffer in keeping with the suffering that has been caused to the victim/s of the crime (retribution).

B   To persuade the criminal to give up crime and become a more useful/less anti-social member of society (reform).

C   To make it clear that this is such a bad crime that anyone who does it can expect a very severe punishment, thus deterring others who might be tempted to carry out such a crime themselves (deterrence).

D   To protect society from repeated offences by the individual.

Sentences – the facts

In England and Wales all cases initially come to a magistrates' court. Magistrates are not trained lawyers, but are chosen from the community as being people of wide experience who can be trusted to serve the ideal of justice. Usually there are three magistrates on the bench who hear the evidence and pass sentence.

Sentences are set by the courts. Magistrates can set punishments for many offences. However, if a magistrate decides that he or she does not have adequate sentencing powers to punish the defendant if found guilty, the case is passed to a higher court where a judge presides. If the offence is eligible for a trial by jury and if the defendant pleads not guilty then the trial takes place in a higher court.

Thus offenders are only sentenced at a crown court or a high court if the offence is a serious one.

Factors that determine sentences

In the UK judges are independent and can make up their minds without consulting politicians or the government. However, they have to follow sentencing guidelines which have been laid down by Parliament, eg on maximum and minimum sentences for different kinds of crime.

Punishments used by the courts include:

- imprisonment (either immediate or suspended for a certain time – if the individual offends again he/she goes to prison for the original sentence as well as for the second offence);
- weekend prison;
- fines/confiscation of assets;
- community service orders;
- probation;
- being 'bound over';
- orders to attend courses such as parenting classes or anger management classes or to attend drug rehabilitation clinics;
- conditional discharge;
- driving ban;
- electronic tagging.

In the UK judges are no longer allowed to use capital punishment (the death sentence) or corporal punishment (flogging or maiming the offender, eg by cutting off a hand). The 1948 Declaration of Human Rights states in article 5 that: 'No one shall be subjected to torture or cruel, inhuman or degrading treatment or punishment.'

Which punishments are chosen and how severe they are depend on aggravating or mitigating factors.

Aggravating factors are described by the prosecution and make the crime more serious and the punishment harsher.

Mitigating factors make the crime less serious and the punishment lighter. Defence lawyers make a statement describing the mitigating factors to the best of their ability.

Sentences

Consider again case 1 on the *Punishment and crime* worksheet. A man of 25 has been convicted of robbing a pensioner in her own home (using force or threat of force). Mark whether these would be aggravating factors (A) or mitigating factors (M).

- He has been robbing the homes of other elderly people in the area for the last two years.

- He has a string of convictions since being caught shoplifting when 14. He has been in prison twice before.

- On this occasion he threatened, but did not use, violence.

- The woman he robbed is 85 and deaf.

- Recently he has tried to wean himself off hard drugs.

- He is now living back at home with his long-term girlfriend who is standing by him.

- The victim used to be independent but is now terrified to answer the door or go out.

- The defendant's mother is alcoholic and he used to care for his two younger brothers.

- He pleaded guilty at an early stage and thus saved the main witness any more stress and the system time and money.

- As well as her pension book, he took and spent the £200 cash that the victim had saved up to buy Christmas presents for her grandchildren.

Choose a selection of the factors to role-play in groups of three:

- the speech of mitigation for the defence;
- the statement of aggravating factors.

One of you should play the judge and pass a sentence that you think matches the crime and is just. Explain your reasons.

Curfew

Objectives

- To practise skills of group organisation to effect change.

Resources

Curfew poster (p 165) enlarged to A3 size
Worksheets: *Against curfew* (p 166), *For curfew* (p 167)
Self-assessment sheets

1   Start by explaining that this is a practical lesson which depends on everyone's participation. Explain what a curfew is and that local councils can introduce bye-laws which impose curfews on young people. Ask whether any students have experience of curfews imposed by their parents. If so, what was the aim of the curfew? Did it have the desired effect? Why/why not?

2   Go on to explain that some places have legal curfews designed to keep young people off the streets in the evening unless they are accompanied by an adult who is responsible for them, for example some American cities and some places in Britain where councils have a law and order problem. Display the *Curfew* poster at one end of the room and ask: if this happened here, what would your reactions be? Those who think it would be a bad idea go to the other end of the room. All students have to choose one end or the other – don't let anyone opt out. Don't worry if the groups are uneven in size. This makes it harder for the larger group to agree on tactics and doesn't automatically make it more likely to succeed.

3   Brief each group separately, giving them copies of the worksheet *Against curfew* or *For curfew*. Give them a time limit. You could also give them an optional resource pack with an A-Z street map, ward and constituency boundaries, details of local councillors and a phone book. The groups must make a list of people to consult and possible arguments, as well as guessing the methods that will be used by the other side.

4   The two groups hold a meeting to decide on their tactics. One member of the group acts as chair and the action agreed upon by all the group should be written down. However, surprise is important! The decisions should include whether to attend the public meeting, an action plan to prepare for the meeting, and, if appropriate, ideas for longer-term action.

5   Hold the public meeting, if both sides agree to attend, and chair it yourself. Follow with a vote on the issue. Then vote on which group had the more effective action plan and discuss how well each group worked.

6   Ask the students to complete self-assessment sheets.

Optional extension

Invite a local councillor to visit the class and be interviewed on the role of local government.

Concerned about the welfare of the young people of your town?

Then come to hear the views of
Councillor Sheila Smith
and her proposals for a
young person's curfew
7.30 pm-7.30 am

Place: Town Hall
Date: Wednesday 10 September
Time: 8.00 pm

Against curfew

▷ Use the following ideas to organise yourselves as a pressure group which is against the proposed curfew.

So you don't like the idea of a curfew here in your town? How can you best work to make sure it doesn't happen? You could attend the public meeting but if you do you will need to get well organised first. Here are some jobs to do. Sort out who is going to do what and when you will meet to agree tactics.

Why is the curfew a bad idea?
– a list of our arguments

A list of possible **allies**, ie people who might agree with us that a curfew is a bad idea.

Ways we could work against our opponents.

What arguments will our opponents, those who are in favour of a curfew, use? What methods will they use?

Hold a meeting of your group. Choose someone to chair it.
Agree on the tactics which your group will use. This must be a shared decision which is agreed by all.
Prepare for the public meeting. Who is going to say and do what?
What will you do after the meeting to achieve your aims?

For curfew

Use the following ideas to organise yourselves as a pressure group which is in favour of the proposed curfew.

So you like the idea of a curfew here in your town? How can you best work to make sure it happens? You could attend the public meeting but if you do you will need to be well organised. Here are some jobs to do. Sort out who is going to do what and when you will meet to agree tactics.

Why is the curfew a good idea?
– a list of arguments

A list of possible allies, ie people who might agree with us that a curfew is a good idea.

Ways we could work against our opponents.

What arguments will our opponents, those who are against a curfew, use? What methods will they use?

Hold a meeting of your group. Choose someone to chair it.
Agree on the tactics which your group will use. This must be a shared decision which is agreed by all.
Prepare for the public meeting. Who is going to say and do what?
What will you do after the meeting to achieve your aims?

Media factfile

Objective

- To explain to students the importance of a free press, and the media's role in society, including the Internet, in providing information and affecting opinions.

Resources

Copies of various broadsheet and tabloid newspapers, local and national.
Worksheets: *What is news?* (p 169), *Media factfile – questions* (p 171)
Information sheet: *Media factfile* (p 170)

1 Explain the objective. Divide the class into groups of four or five. Distribute four or five newspapers to each group. Each group should have at least one broadsheet, one tabloid and one local paper. Others could be regional, evening press, Sunday press, financial, etc. Explain instructions:

- each student within the group should take responsibility for looking at one newspaper and answering the questions on the worksheet *What is news?*;
- the working definition of 'news' should be information that concerns the making of political decisions that affect the public in some way;
- each student should refer to the *Media factfile* information sheet;
- students should be prepared to feed back their findings to the group and then to the class;
- following each activity students should record their personal judgements on the importance of the various newspapers in providing trustworthy news from local, national and global perspectives.

Circulate and help individual groups when required.

2 Lead class feedback:

- how much counted as 'news' in the various formats: tabloid, broadsheet, local, national, international?
- what evidence was found of a free press? (eg criticism of politicians or government, letters from members of the public, personal points of view, opinions, reporting of minority points of view?
- were there any abuses of the freedom of the press, eg attacks on personal privacy, unwarranted intrusion into private lives, unjustified criticisms of individuals or groups, sensationalist reporting which could have harmful consequences such as spreading alarm or prejudice?

3 Discuss how useful newspapers are when we seek information about what is going on in our world. How can they be used to research an issue? Make the point that back copies can be accessed, cuttings files can be gathered over time, the back copies of some broadsheets can be accessed online and searches made for keywords.

4 Anticipate the next lesson when students will use the Internet to access topical information.

What is news?

Name of newspaper ....

Type of newspaper (circle all those which apply)

aimed at a local / regional / national / international audience

printed every night / every morning / weekly / weekdays / Sundays

free / priced

broadsheet size / tabloid size

Number of pages ....

Number of pages with news items .... (the working definition of 'news' should be information that concerns the making of political decisions that affect the public in some way)

Front page headlines: underline the ones you think are news stories as above.

....

....

....

Other content: circle the headings which apply to your newspaper and count pages if appropriate

sport	puzzles, crosswords, cartoons, etc
celebrity lives	travel, holidays
TV listings or features	finance/business
advertisements	other

Can you find evidence that this is 'free press', ie not controlled by the government or army?
(eg criticism of politicians or the government, letters from members of the public, personal points of view or opinions, reporting of minority points of view?
yes/no   page ....

Can you find any abuses of the freedom of the press, eg attacks on personal privacy, unwarranted intrusion into private lives, unjustified criticism of individuals, sensationalist reporting which could have harmful consequences such as spreading alarm or prejudice?
yes/no   page ....

Overall how useful is this newspaper if you are seeking information about what is going on in the world? How could it be used to research an issue?

Useful for ....

Media factfile

Mass media (singular: medium)
The various ways of communicating with large numbers of people.

Newspapers
Since the eighteenth century newspapers have been widely read in Britain and are still an important medium of communication. During the twentieth century other media emerged.

Radio
National, regional, local and world services, some provided by the state, some by public service broadcasters and some by private companies or individuals.

Television
National, regional, local and world services, some provided by the state, some by public service broadcasters, some by private companies or individuals, and some by global companies, such as News International. This company owns several television companies such as Sky TV, newspapers in the USA and Britain, and book and magazine publishers in Europe, the USA and the Far East.

Internet
Electronic media allow individuals and groups to publish their own news and views on their websites. Of all the media this is the one that governments find it least easy to control, so it can be argued that it is the most free. On the other hand, there is no obligation for a website to tell the truth or put both sides of a story. If you are using the web to research an issue you need to use your judgement at all times and keep asking yourself: 'How can I check this information?'

Freedom of information

In some countries newspapers are strictly controlled by the government. The only news published is that which is favourable to the government. Other news is censored. A famous historical example of this is *Pravda* – meaning 'the truth' – which was the national newspaper of the former Soviet Union published by the Communist Party.

A democratic society operates on the principle of choice. It has to be possible for voters to change their government. They need to be able to make up their minds whether they think leaders are doing a good job and making the right decisions about how to run the country or the local area. They need trustworthy news about this. This means that newspapers (and other media) should be independent of the government and feel free to investigate and report the truth. These are the key features of a free press:

- no controlling links between the government or political parties and the newspapers (or other media);
- news is reported which is not favourable to the government (as well as news that is);
- many different opinions about controversial issues are expressed;
- readers can participate by contributing their own opinions;
- enough information is given in an unbiased way for readers to be able to make up their minds independently.

How free is the press in Britain? This is in itself a controversial issue.

Ask yourself this when you have analysed the newspapers on the *What is news?* worksheet.

Media factfile • questions •

Consider these points:

1 Were there enough news stories/different points of view to allow you to say that you know enough to be able to make up your mind fairly? Some newspapers have very little news coverage and report only a few opinions or facts. News from abroad, especially poor countries, is rarely given much space.

2 Was the reporting biased or one-sided? Did the newspaper report fairly on minority opinions?

3 Were there some stories which criticised decisions or policies? Was it clear what the newspaper's angle was?

4 Overall would you say you could tell which political party the newspaper supported?

5 In Britain no national daily newspaper is owned by a political party. However, most of them are owned by wealthy individuals or companies. Some of these obviously have their own political opinions. Do they use their control of the newspapers to slant the news so that the readers' opinions are influenced?

6 In Britain (unlike the USA) there are no legal or constitutional safeguards to protect the freedom of the press. Should there be?

7 Perhaps you found abuses of the freedom of the press, eg attacks on personal privacy, unwarranted intrusion into private lives, unjustified criticisms of individuals or groups. Are there effective ways of dealing with these abuses?

   • In Britain there are strict libel laws which can deter newspapers from criticising rich individuals in case they sue. Is this fair?

   • In Britain there is a code of conduct for the press. An individual can complain if they think their privacy has been invaded or the press has said something about them which is untrue. Is this enough?

8 Perhaps you found sensationalist reporting which could have harmful consequences such as spreading alarm or prejudice? These stories are designed to attract attention and so sell more newspapers. Are newspapers responsible about the consequences of whipping up public opinion? Do you think there should be limits on a free press?

Accessing information on the Internet

Objectives

- To explain to students the importance of a free press, and the media's role in society, including the internet, in providing information and affecting opinion.
- To enable students to understand the origins and implications of the diverse national, regional, religious and ethnic identities in the UK and the need for mutual respect and understanding.
- To research a topical, political, spiritual, moral, social or cultural issue or event by analysing information from different sources including the Internet.

Resources

Information/worksheets: *Media factfile* (pp 170-171)
Worksheet: *Research brief* (p 174)
PCs with Internet access
Bookmarked provision of www.learn.co.uk and other relevant web links.

1 Explain the objectives and remind the class of the findings of the previous lesson with regard to the reliability and usefulness of newspapers as sources of information on controversial or political issues which concern us as citizens. Refer to the *Media factfile* sheets and stress the importance of preparing the ground thoroughly before attempting an Internet search.

2 Divide the class into groups of four or five. Each group is to research an issue of current interest. Students should be prepared to plan their role within the group and agree which particular angle on the issue they are responsible for.

They will need to feed back their findings both to the group and then to the class, whether in oral or written form.

Note: The worksheet assumes that the research issue and case study will be immigration and asylum-seeking. If an issue has arisen which is more relevant or current then the worksheet can still be used with some minor amendments. Students will still need to plan their research and be briefed on the necessity for a highly critical approach to the reliability of websites.

3 Ask the students to complete the worksheet *Research brief*. Ensure that the groups have covered the angles and have a reasonable plan.

continued on page 173

Accessing information on the Internet continued

4 Lead class feedback and assess preparedness of groups/individuals. It is important to establish ground rules on printing – see below.

Students must understand that doing research does not mean being able to press a print button! It means scanning, sifting and discarding what is useless. A notepad is essential. A suggested compromise is to allow students to print only after they have asked permission.

5 Following each hit on a website, students should record their personal judgements on the importance and relevance of the site in providing trustworthy news from a personal, local, national or global perspective.

6 Prepare the practical arrangements for the following two lessons, including booking machines, logging on, bookmarking useful sites, booking technical support in case of problems and so on.

Research brief

Name ....

▷ **Complete this worksheet individually.**

The group is researching the topic of .... on the Internet (fill in title).
A report will be produced by the group. It will include websites visited and a description of their coverage and usefulness for this topic.

▷ **Each student should complete their own research brief.**

My contribution to this Internet research will be to (agree this with your group):

....

....

....

....

The key websites I shall visit will be (choose from key websites):

....

....

....

I also plan to use a general search engine to:

....

....

....

....

....

....

....

The net – whose word can you trust?

Objectives

- To explain to students the importance of a free press, and the media's role in society, including the Internet, in providing information and affecting opinion.
- To enable students to understand the origins and implications of the diverse national, regional, religious and ethnic identities in the UK and the need for mutual respect and understanding.
- To research a topical, political, spiritual, moral, social or cultural issue or event by analysing information from different sources including the Internet.

Resources

Worksheet: *Research brief* (p 174), *Internet notepad 1* (p 176)

PCs with Internet access

Bookmarked provision of www.learn.co.uk and other relevant web links.

1 Explain the objectives and remind the class of the responsibilities and roles agreed in previous lessons. Brief the students about the reliability and usefulness of websites as sources of information on controversial or political issues which concern us as citizens.

2 Ask the students to log on as pairs or individually, referring to their research brief. They should evaluate each website hit as they go on the worksheet *Internet notepad 1* and bookmark useful sites if they want to return to them. Circulate and suggest useful web links to follow up. Remind the students of the agreed ground rules on printing.

3 Ask the students to complete their *Research brief* worksheet. After each website hit, students record their personal judgements on the importance or relevance of the site in providing trustworthy news from a personal, local, national or global perspective.

4 Plenary: agree targets for the following lesson which will fulfil and complete their research brief. Students should bookmark useful sites and/or prepare to widen their search to include alternative views.

Internet notepad • 1 •

Name ....

Log here each new site you visit.

www.	Name of group/person	How useful? 5 ticks = brilliant 1 tick = little relevance

Making contact via the net

Objectives

- To explain to students the importance of a free press, and the media's role in society, including the internet, in providing information and affecting opinion.
- To enable students to understand the origins and implications of the diverse national, regional, religious and ethnic identities in the UK and the need for mutual respect and understanding.
- To research a topical, political, spiritual, moral, social or cultural issue or event by analysing information from different sources including the Internet.
- To express, justify and defend orally and in writing a personal opinion about such issues, problems or events.
- To encourage students to use their imagination when considering other people's experiences, and to be able to think about and explain views that are not their own.

Resources

Worksheets: *Research brief* (p 174), *Internet notepad 1* and *2* (pp 176 and 178), *Feedback to group* (p 179)
PCs with Internet access
Bookmarked provision of www.learn.co.uk and other relevant web links

1 Start by reminding the class of the objectives, responsibilities and targets agreed in the previous lesson, and set a time limit within which the students need to complete their research brief. The students then log on as pairs or individuals, refer to their *Research brief, Internet notepad* and *Feedback to group* worksheets and revisit useful sites to make notes or refine their search. If the students visit sites of groups or individuals with an obvious axe to grind they need to take this into account when assessing the usefulness of the site. Studies of primary and secondary sources during history lessons provide good experience for this. Circulate and provide assistance when required.

2 Students log off and report back to their groups with their findings. The group then completes *Feedback to group* worksheet. Has the group managed to reach a consensus on the issue they have researched or do individuals within the group still have different opinions? The group needs to present these opinions in an agreed format, eg orally, as a wall display, as a written argument.

3 Hold a whole-class plenary. Ask for group feedback, modelling tolerance of different individual viewpoints, and praising those who have, during research, engaged with views they may not agree with. Discuss the usefulness of the net when seeking information about what is going on in our world. What are the advantages and disadvantages of using it for research? How can the drawbacks be overcome? Compare findings to what the class said about newspapers. Make the point that good research has to be critical. This is especially true when using the Internet since there is no comeback if a website is not telling the truth, whereas newspapers have the libel laws and the Press Complaints Commission to worry about if they are not truthful.

Internet notepad • 2 •

Name ....

Evaluate each website you visit which is relevant to your research (three ticks or more).
Use extra sheets if necessary.

Website address..

Nature of website (eg a person or pressure group which represents refugees, or a political party against further immigration, personal view, government view)

....

....

1   What was the relevance of this website? (eg gave lots of information about what's going on, gave a personal viewpoint, is aimed at people like me, is aimed at people who need support or advice, is aimed at the general public).

....

....

2   Was the website useful from a personal, local, national, global perspective? (underline which applies)

3   How reliable do you consider the information on the website to be? Explain your answer.

....

....

....

....

4   To check out this information or find alternative views, I need to:

....

....

....

Feedback to group

Name ....

The websites I visited which were good were:

....

....

....

This was because:

....

....

....

Groups discuss the feedback from each group member.

Prepare to summarise findings for the class on whether you were successful in using the Internet to research this topic. Write your summary here.

....

....

....

....

....

List the advantages and disadvantages of using the Internet for researching controversial issues.

Advantages	Disadvantages

Immigration and asylum-seeking case study

Objectives

- To enable students to understand the origins and implications of the diverse national, regional, religious and ethnic identities in the UK and the need for mutual respect and understanding.
- To research a topical, political, spiritual, moral, social or cultural issue or event by analysing information from different sources including the Internet.
- To express, justify and defend orally and in writing a personal opinion about such issues, problems or events.
- To encourage students to use their imagination when considering other people's experiences and to be able to think about and explain views that are not their own.

Resources

Information sheets: *Ground rules for democratic debate* enlarged and displayed as a wallchart (p 181), *Immigration and asylum-seeking – facts and issues* (p 182), *Advantages and disadvantages of immigration* (p 183), *Admitting asylum-seekers* (p 184)
Worksheet: *Case study debate plan* (p 185)

1 Go through the wallchart *Ground rules for democratic debate* and remind the class of the ground rules when discussing controversial issues. Ask the students if they agree with the ground rules and emphasize that everybody is responsible for ensuring that they are kept. Tell the students you will not be forcing your own views on them. Of course you have your own personal opinions. It is up to you whether you disclose them to your students.

2 Divide the class into groups to prepare for the debate. Decide whether it is to be an oral debate and/or whether you want the students to write an essay on the subject. Individuals don't necessarily have to agree with the debate statement. Make it clear that they will develop their own view and might change their minds. At least one group should explore further each of these debate statements:

- legal immigration to this country needs to be increased and made easier;
- legal immigration to this country needs to be restricted and made more difficult.

3 Ask the students to complete the worksheet *Case study debate plan*. First they should read the information sheet *Immigration and asylum-seeking* and use highlighters to mark three points which support their case.

4 Hold the class debate, then ask for oral feedback. Ask the students to consider their original point of view. How have their opinions changed?

5 The next lesson will focus on the possibilities for individual, school, or community action on some of the issues raised.

Ground rules for democratic debate

These ground rules will allow a democratic debate.

Honesty
It is a basic human right to be able to hold opinions and express views.

Tolerance
Discussion means dialogue.
Other views must be listened to and taken seriously.

Respect for difference
Everyone is of equal worth within the group.
There must be no put-downs.

Sensitivity
Think before you speak!
Make sure your views are not expressed in a hurtful way. Back up your opinions with reasons.

Immigration and asylum-seeking
• facts and issues •

We, or our ancestors, all came to be citizens of this country through immigration.

Immigrants are people who come into a country to settle down permanently.

The history of the British Isles has seen many waves of immigrants coming here to settle. Here are just some of them, not in any particular order:

Celts	Africans	Bangladeshis	Flemish people
Romans	Russians	East-African Asians	Anglo-Saxons
Afro-Caribbeans	Chinese	Vikings	Pakistanis
Turkish Cypriots	Normans	Indians	Greek Cypriots

First-generation immigrants are the people who immigrated. They were not born here but came to live here.

Second-generation immigrants are the children of first-generation immigrants. They were born and brought up here.

Third-generation immigrants are the children of second-generation immigrants, and so on. People who know the country in which their family origins lie sometimes describe themselves as being of that heritage. For example: Irish-American heritage or African-British heritage.

So immigration is nothing new. A small amount of legal immigration and emigration is still going on. Nowadays there are laws which control immigration, nationality and rights of residency.

A British citizen is someone who was:

- born in Britain of British parents or of a parent legally settled in Britain;
- born overseas who has at least one British parent or grandparent.

Some people have dual citizenship.

The issue

Some people want to change the laws to make immigration easier and increase it. Others want to change these laws to make immigration harder and restrict it. This is a citizenship issue because it concerns the whole idea of community and identity.

It is a political issue because it concerns our rights as citizens and a possible change in public policy and the law. The government is concerned; political parties disagree and there are various pressure groups who have their own viewpoints and policies. Probably everyone in your class will have a slightly different opinion once they have completed the case study.

Asylum-seeking is a related but different issue. Some people want to settle in this country because they are frightened of what their own government will do to them if they stay in their own country. If they can prove that they have a 'well-founded fear of persecution' then they can be given the right to remain here indefinitely. This is one way of being a legal immigrant. However this is also a controversial issue with many different views being held by different groups such as political parties and refugee groups.

Advantages and disadvantages of immigration

Advantages of immigration	Disadvantages of immigration
Some arguments to support increased legal immigration.	Some arguments against increased legal immigration.
A country which accepts legal immigrants benefits in many ways:	A country which accepts legal immigrants may have some of the following problems:
• Immigrants tend to be young and hard-working. They pay taxes and don't claim many benefits or old age pensions. • They are often enterprising, ambitious, and make the most of their opportunities. • They create jobs and contribute to overall economic growth. • They help do necessary work where there is a shortage of workers in one area, for example teachers. • There is a skills shortage in Europe, including Britain. • Immigrants bring new ideas and cultures which help society improve and adapt to change. • A good mix of cultures, religions and ethnic groups enriches society, making it more outward-looking and interesting for everyone. • If you allow legal immigration you have fewer problems with people trying to get round the rules by attempting illegal immigration or applying for political asylum instead. • Immigrants send money back to their original countries – far more than the overseas aid budget. • There are moral arguments about why people from poor countries should be allowed to move to richer ones. We all try to better ourselves and our families. Why shouldn't we all have the right to move around freely? Isn't this a basic human right?	• Resentment from some existing citizens: some people may be anxious about what they see as increased pressure on housing, jobs or education. They may blame or scapegoat the immigrants for society's problems such as crime or poverty. • Pressure on community relations – in local areas there can be increased suspicion if the relative number of a particular ethnic/religious group rises and others feel that the balance has changed somehow. Some argue that hostility and racism increase. • Different cultures and lifestyles can be threatening to the 'old order'. • Educated workers from poor countries are needed in their own countries. Rich countries shouldn't be poaching their best people. • The young and enterprising need to use their skills in their own countries to develop their economies, bring new ideas and help society improve and adapt to change. It isn't practical to allow people to move around freely between countries.

Admitting asylum-seekers

Advantages of having generous systems for admitting asylum-seekers

- There are many wars and cases of political persecution around the world.
  It should be possible for people who are genuine refugees to apply to a country for a safe haven where they are free from torture and danger to their lives.
  Civilised countries should offer this right out of respect for human rights.
  Human rights are rights that all human beings should have.

- Asylum-seekers need time to produce the evidence to back their cases.
  They may have had to leave in a hurry, without passports, money or documentation.

- There may be people who try to wrongly claim asylum when actually they are 'economic migrants' – people who want to improve their prospects by coming to a rich country. However, this is not a reason to make life hard for genuine refugees or to take away the human rights and dignity of any of the applicants.

Disadvantages of having generous systems for admitting asylum-seekers

- A large and increasing number of people are applying for asylum. Most of them do not succeed in their applications because, according to the rules, they are not genuine refugees, but are economic migrants. Generous systems encourage people to apply, but most are disappointed.

- Civilised countries should offer respect for human rights, but need to deter those who do not have a well-founded fear of persecution.

- It should be possible to process applications quickly and send back those whose applications are not successful.

- Other countries should take their fair share of refugees.

- Tougher systems would deter the economic migrants, but those who are desperate will still apply.

- It is necessary to reduce the overall number of applicants because the system is overwhelmed.

- Some areas of the country where asylum-seekers are concentrated may have difficulties in providing enough support or in helping newcomers fit in.

- Asylum-seekers may experience hostility or racism on top of the problems they have trying to fit into a new culture.

Case study debate plan

1　Write here the debate statement you are supporting.

....

....

....

....

2　Use a highlighter to mark those points on the *Immigration and asylum-seeking* information sheets which support your case. If you personally don't agree with any of them mark these with a different colour.

3　Consider other information and opinions you can use – personal experiences, information from newspapers or TV, or information you discussed during your Internet research.

4　Plan at least five main points you wish to make. How can you back these up with evidence or make them more persuasive?

5　Write down your own personal viewpoint on the issue at the moment.

6　Write notes for your speech (if you are preparing an oral presentation) or write out your statement as an essay.

7　Take part in the class debate.

After the debate

Has your personal viewpoint on this issue changed? If so, how?

Discrimination – policies and safeguards

Note: two lessons will be needed for this work

Objectives

- To enable students to understand the origins and implications of the diverse national, regional, religious and ethnic identities in the UK and the need for mutual respect and understanding.
- To research a topical, political, spiritual, moral, social or cultural issue or event by analysing information from different sources including the Internet.
- To express, justify and defend orally and in writing a personal opinion about such issues, problems or events.
- To encourage students to use their imagination when considering other people's experiences and to be able to think about and explain views that are not their own.
- To negotiate, decide and take part responsibly in school and community-based activities.

Resources

Students' names written on slips of paper, A3 sheets of paper
Copies of your LEA equal opportunities policy
Information sheets: *Discrimination – the law* (pp 188-189), *Official bodies which promote racial equality* (p 190), *Equal opportunities policies* (p 191), *Political action* (p 192).
Worksheet: *Do the safeguards work?* (p 193)
Self-assessment sheets.

1 Review the previous lesson and the potential for community conflict and prejudice. Consider whether there are any human rights which should be common to everyone. Make the point that race and culture can be the subject of prejudice and conflict. Explain that this lesson will look at what safeguards there are to deal with this.

2 Put the names of the class into a box and draw out random groups of four students. Explain the need to work in random mixed groups in which the students may need to listen to the points of view of other people who they may not usually talk to. Remind the groups of the ground rules:

- no put-downs or abuse within the group;

- everyone has the right to be listened to.

Ask each group to elect a scribe and a person to report back to the class.

continued on page 187

Discrimination – policies and safeguards • continued •

Then each group brainstorms the questions:

- what is prejudice?
- what are the causes of prejudice?

They go on to list examples of prejudice on sheets of A3 paper.
The students feed back to the rest of the class and discuss their examples.

3 Raise the question of whether all societies need safeguards to protect
the rights of individuals and minorities. Ask the students to consider:

- examples of places or situations they know where the safeguards are
  insufficient;
- the results of not having mutual respect for others or safeguards to protect
  minorities and the rights of individuals.

4 Ask the students to read the information sheets *Discrimination – the law,
Discrimination – more law, Official bodies which promote racial equality, Equal
opportunities policies* and *Political action*, plus your LEA's equal opportunities
policy. Then ask them to consider the question:

- What safeguards are there in this country to protect us from prejudice
  and discrimination on the grounds of race and gender?

Within their groups, individual students read out one of the sheets to the
rest of the group in turn, after which they discuss how effective they think
the safeguards are. Circulate and join in.

5 Review the racial and cultural issues which were discussed in the previous
lesson, as well as the issues of equal opportunities and safeguards for
individual rights. Explain that in this follow-up lesson the students will
consider the effectiveness of present rules and laws, and will be asked to
make suggestions for improvements.

6 In pairs, ask the students to complete the worksheet *Do the safeguards work?*
Then ask for feedback on ideas for improving:

- local and national safeguards;
- a school rule.

7 Ask the students to complete self-assessment sheets.

Discrimination – the law

Q Are there any safeguards in Britain to protect people from prejudice?

A Laws have been made which might help to do this:

1 The criminal law

It is a criminal offence to:

- **use violence against others**

- **use threatening behaviour**

- **cause a breach of the peace**

- **damage or steal the property of others**

This applies equally to everyone.

If anyone is the victim of a criminal offence they may make a complaint to the police. The police have to collect evidence that a particular person has committed this offence. Where there is evidence that someone has broken these laws, he or she can be:

- arrested by the police (or by private citizens)

- charged with an offence

- tried in a court of law

- if found guilty, sentenced to a penalty chosen by the courts.

The victim may also claim compensation from the Criminal Injuries Compensation Board.

2 The Race Relations Act 1976

This law, passed by Parliament, makes it an offence to discriminate against someone because of their ethnic or national origin, their colour or their race. This applies to employment, housing, education and all other aspects of public life.

Racial discrimination can be direct:

- One person is treated less favourably than another because of his or her race.

- *Example*: a firm employs no black people and appoints people with fewer qualifications than black applicants.

Racial discrimination can be indirect:

- A rule which applies to everyone but in practice means that it is more difficult for people from one ethnic group to meet that rule.

- *Example*: an employer states that 'previous similar experience is required' when advertising a job, even when this isn't really necessary. If most people in that type of work already are white then it will be harder for black people to meet this requirement.

The act made it a criminal offence to 'incite to racial hatred' by 'saying or writing anything which is threatening, abusive or insulting, and which is likely to stir up hatred against any racial group'.

i Discrimination – the law • continued •

3 The Human Rights Act 2000

This says that everyone in this country is free:

- **to hold opinions and express views**

- **to hold a wide range of values, beliefs and thoughts**

- **to assemble with other people in a peaceful way**

- **to associate with other people and join a trade union**

- **to marry and start a family.**

Sexual discrimination can be direct:

- ie one person is treated less favourably than another because of his or her gender.

- *Example*: a person is repeatedly passed over when applying for a promotion, when he/she has exactly the same qualifications, skills, abilities and experience as other applicants, or the advert states 'person' but the employer intends to recruit from only one gender.

The Equal Opportunities Commission

This organisation is a public body set up by Parliament to prevent people being treated unfairly simply because of their sex.

- *Example*: you feel you have been unfairly treated because of your sex. The EOC gives you help and advice.

- *Example*: pension rights are different for men and women. The EOC investigates the facts, publishes a report and takes a test case to the European Court of Human Rights.

4 The Sex Discrimination Act 1975/86

This law, passed by Parliament, makes it an offence to discriminate against someone because of their gender or their marital status. This applies to employment, housing, education, facilities, services, advertising and victimisation.

Official bodies which promote racial equality

Q Are there any safeguards in Britain to protect people from racial prejudice?

A There are official bodies set up by Parliament which might help to do this.

1 The Commission for Racial Equality

This investigates ways in which the Race Relations Act is working (or not working)

Examples

- Do some employers stop some people even coming for an interview on the grounds of race? The commission investigates the facts.

- Is council housing allocated fairly? The commission investigates the facts. They publish their results in reports.

If a person or a group of people feel that they have suffered from racial discrimination they can make a complaint to the Commission for Racial Equality. The CRE sometimes supports an individual's claim to have been discriminated against and takes the case to court on his or her behalf.

2 Community Relations Councils

These local organisations employ officers who work with local councils, health authorities and employers to represent minority communities and draw up policies which safeguard rights.

Local Community Relations Councils also support people in local situations who feel they have suffered discrimination, and write reports.
Similar discrimination on grounds of disability is outlawed by the Disabled Persons Act 1944.

As yet there are no similar official bodies to protect people from religious prejudice or anti-gay prejudice. Should there be?

Equal opportunities policies

1 City council policy on equal opportunities

A policy is something which a council says ought to happen in any places the council controls, eg:

- schools (see Equal Opportunities policy statements);

- council housing;

- employment with the council.

2 School Equal Opportunities Policy Statements

Many schools have their own policy statements on equal opportunities. These cover what the school thinks ought to happen to bring about equal opportunities for its pupils. They give details of the sorts of action the school can take.

Q Are there safeguards in Britain to protect people from discrimination?

A Some organisations have policies which might help.

Many councils are committed to 'positive action' to help those groups in society, for instance women, who do not have, and never have had, a fair deal. They produce booklets such as Equal Opportunities in Employment which describe this in more detail. The booklets tell you who the policy covers and what safeguards there are for ethnic minorities. Booklets cover the following areas:

- recruitment to jobs; promotion
- harassment
- display of offensive material
- training
- monitoring.

The right to complain

Anyone who thinks they have been treated unfairly by the council – in schools, council housing, etc – can make a complaint. There must be an investigation of the complaint.

All school students need to be involved, along with staff, governors, parents and others who have an interest in the school, in the drawing up of such a policy and regular checks on whether it is being carried out.

If, after reading this, your group has something to say about what should be in the policy or how it is being carried out, note down your ideas for your form representative and form teacher.

Political action

Q Are there any safeguards in Britain to protect people from discrimination?

A Some kinds of political action might help to do this:

---

1 Join a political party

Anyone can join a political party or can form a political party and put up candidates.

- Political parties exist to represent people's views. They want to change the policies of government and the law: they do this by trying to get elected to Parliament or on to local councils.

- Even individuals can be elected as Independents on to local councils, though they stand more chance in a recognised party.

---

2 Vote

Everyone over 18 has a vote which they can use to change local councils, the government and our representatives to the European Parliament.

- Listen to the news.

- Find out what particular policies of individual parties are and what they believe in.

- Vote for someone who will represent your interests and those of the country.

---

3 Join a trade union

Anyone may join a trade union. These exist to support the rights of their members and to help their members:

- negotiate with their employers

- complain against unfair treatment at work

- complain against unfair dismissal.

---

4 Join a pressure group

Anyone may join a pressure group. These exist to bring about a change on behalf of their members or to voice their members' interests to those who make decisions.

Examples of pressure groups which sometimes campaign to improve safeguards against discrimination include:
Liberty
The Indian Workers Association
Mind, local women's groups, Shelter
The Terrence Higgins Trust

---

5 Be an 'active citizen'

There are things you can do to look after your rights and prevent prejudice and discrimination:

- Know your rights.

- Find out the ways of taking action.

- Be assertive in defence of what you believe in. But remember that assertiveness is not the same as aggression.

Do the safeguards work?

In pairs discuss the questions below, and write down your answers. Try to agree upon how well the rules and safeguards you identify actually work. Then write down whether you think the rules and safeguards work very well, quite well, or not at all well. Be prepared to report back with your answers.

A Write down those local and national rules or laws and bodies which provide safeguards for people and help them to be treated equally and with respect.	**How well do you think they work?**		
	Very well	Quite well	Not at all well

B Choose one of the above which you think needs improving. Discuss how you think it could be made better and write down your ideas. What could you do to get involved in actively improving the situation?

C Write down the rules in the school which provide safeguards for people and help them to be treated equally and with respect.	**How well do you think they work?**		
	Very well	Quite well	Not at all well

D Write a school rule and a sanction for those who break it, which you think would provide a safeguard for people and help them be treated equally and with respect.

E Sometimes new students join the school during the school year. They may come from another place or another country. How well are newcomers to the school treated? Are they made to feel welcome?

Write a report on:
• what staff and students do/don't do to help;
• what should be done to help newcomers.

Think about who is responsible for improving the situation.

Opportunities to change things

Note: If this unit is to be used as the starting point for a citizenship activity to be entered as coursework for any of the GCSE short courses in citizenship, please ensure that the following requirements are met:

- guidance to candidates as directed;
- acceptable practice;
- structure of coursework report;
- planning stage;
- account of the activity (knowledge and understanding of events and roles);
- account of the activity (explanation and interpretation of evidence);
- evaluation stage.

Objectives

- To know and understand the work of Parliament, the government and the courts in making and shaping the law.
- To know and understand the importance of playing an active part in democratic processes.
- To contribute to group and exploratory class discussions and take part in formal debates.

Resources

Worksheets: *Decisions affecting you* (p 195), *Why have voluntary groups?* (p 196), *Categories of voluntary groups* (p 197).

1　Explain the objectives. Introduce the idea that politics is about social change and the decision-making that affects our everyday lives. Decisions are made at all sorts of levels from individual through to global. A range of people may be involved, and this gives us all opportunities to change things through getting involved actively. Divide the students into groups and ask them to complete the worksheet *Decisions affecting you*. The correct answers are: A 2, B 3, C 1, D 8, E 7, F 5, G 8, H 4, I 6. The Queen is head of state and head of the Commonwealth, but does not make any government decisions.

2　Read through and explain the worksheet *Why have voluntary groups?* Ask the students to brainstorm voluntary groups they have heard of in different categories (charities, environmental pressure groups, animal welfare groups, single-issue campaign groups, local amateur sport or hobby clubs, trade unions, political parties) and to complete the worksheet *Categories of voluntary groups*.

3　Optional research homework: students can add to their lists and categories by consulting the community information section at the front of the *Yellow Pages*, eg Helplines, Caring for your environment, Get active sections. Local libraries have extensive lists of such information.

Decisions affecting you

Complete this worksheet in groups.

All the following decisions would affect you. But who makes these decisions? Are they made at local, national, European or global level? How accountable are these people, ie how easy would it be for them to take any notice of your ideas?

Discuss between you who might make the following decisions. Then put the right number from the list below against the decision.

A   The menu of today's school dinner.   _____

B   Who to appoint as a replacement if your teacher leaves.   _____

C   Whether GM food can be grown in Europe.   _____

D   The content of the National Curriculum courses you follow at school.   _____

E   The wages received by the person who made your trainers.   _____

F   Which day your dustbins are emptied.   _____

G   The amount of child benefit your parents receive for you.   _____

H   The level of council tax your parents pay.   _____

I   Which bills are passed by Parliament and become new laws.   _____

---

1   The European Union

2   People who work in your school

3   The governors of your school

4   Elected councillors

5   Local government officers (people who work for the council)

6   Elected MPs

7   Managers employed by a multinational company

8   Ministers, eg the Chancellor of the Exchequer, the Secretary of State for Education

9   The Queen

10   The Prime Minister

Why have voluntary groups?

▷ **Complete this worksheet individually.**

A voluntary group is set up and run by its members. You don't have to join it. It is not run by the government. Members pay for their membership themselves and raise funds to cover the cost of organising it. Big groups might have some full-time paid employees, but most members are not paid and work for the group in their own time. Groups can be extremely small, local or temporary. Other groups can be very large with millions of members. Many big groups have a network of small groups within them.

Think about a voluntary group that you take part in or know about – it could be small and local or big: a society, a club, a religious group, a hobby group, a charity.

What is its name?...

– Think about what the group is for and why people belong to it.
– Tick the statements below twice if they definitely apply to your group.
– Tick the statements once if they apply a bit to your group.
– Cross out any statement that definitely does not apply to your group.

  • To get things done.
  • To run something local in the way people want.
  • To provide a local amenity or facilities.
  • To help others.
  • To help people like yourself.
  • To complain about things people don't like.
  • To prevent unwanted change happening.
  • To meet with like-minded people.
  • To share a common interest.
  • To entertain.
  • To keep an area beautiful/improve an area.
  • To take part.
  • To enjoy yourself.
  • Because it's interesting.
  • Because you learn things.
  • Because a group can do far more than one person on his/her own.
  • Because it fits your religious or moral beliefs.
  • To keep yourself occupied.
  • To use your talents in a useful way.
  • To make friends/meet new people.
  • To change and improve the world we live in.

Compare your group with someone else's group. Are some people members of lots of groups?

Categories of voluntary groups

Brainstorm voluntary groups you have heard of and list them under different categories.

charities	environmental pressure groups
animal welfare/wildlife groups	**single-issue campaign groups**
local amateur sport or hobby clubs	**self-help/community groups**
trade unions	**political parties**

Research homework: add to your lists/categories by consulting the community information section at the front of the *Yellow Pages*, eg the Helpline, Caring for your environment, Get active sections. Write down the telephone numbers, e-mail and website addresses of those which interest you. Local libraries have extensive lists of such information, or you can use the Internet.

Organisations which change things

Objectives

- To know and understand the work of Parliament, the government and the courts in making and shaping the law.
- To know and understand the importance of playing an active part in democratic processes.
- To know and understand the opportunities for individuals and voluntary groups to bring about social change locally, nationally, in Europe and internationally.
- To express, justify and defend orally and in writing a personal opinion about such citizenship issues.
- To contribute to group and exploratory class discussions and take part in formal debates.

Resources

Information sheets: *How do people try to change things?* (p 199), *Tactics of pressure groups* (p 200)
Worksheet: *Categories of pressure groups* (p 201)

1   Explain the objectives. Introduce the idea that being actively involved in issues which affect you and your community is the best way to get a grip on your life and to develop as an individual. We are social animals. We depend on each other and are affected by what happens to other people elsewhere. In turn we affect others. This is called interdependence.

2   Recall the previous lesson and remind students that it is possible to change things. What sort of things might be changed? What methods do groups and individuals use to achieve their aims? Look at the information sheet *How do people try to change things?* which describes the aims and characteristics of a range of voluntary groups. Some are pressure groups set up to campaign to achieve certain aims. Some are voluntary associations with particular roles (eg animal welfare or a sport or trade association) but also have a campaigning role (eg combatting global poverty – Oxfam) or conserving bird-friendly ecosystems (RSPB) or improving/maintaining local amenities such as sports grounds (cricket club). Some are set up directly to influence opinion and become the government (political parties). They all act as pressure groups at some stage.

3   Look at the information sheet *Tactics of pressure groups*. This describes the campaign methods used by the identified groups. Ask the students to read both sheets and match the tactics to the group. The correct answers are: Women's Suffrage A, Oxfam F, RSPB C, NFU B, Greenpeace G, Amnesty International E, local cricket and tennis club D, trade unions H.

4   Discuss the differences between groups and possible different ways of categorising them using the worksheet *Categories of pressure groups* in preparation for the following lesson.

How do people try to change things?

This sheet describes the aims and characteristics of a range of voluntary groups.
They all act as pressure groups at some stage.

Try to match each group to the tactics they use to achieve their aims
described in *Tactics of pressure groups*.

RSPB

A group for people who enjoy watching birds.
A large national group with local associations.
Quarterly magazine. Runs reserves where habitat
is conserved. Campaigns against harmful farming
techniques and for protection of endangered species.
Targets: European Union, national and local
government, farmers, the public.

NATIONAL FARMERS' UNION (NFU)

An association of farmers which promotes its
members' interests to the British government and
European Union.
The NFU has several paid regional officials who advise
members and lobby ministers and civil servants in
DEFRA and the EU on issues related to land
management. Has been highly influential.
Targets: DEFRA, European Union.

LOCAL TENNIS AND CRICKET CLUB

Set up 50 years ago to provide a cricket ground and
tennis courts for the area.
Teams compete in amateur league. Members' fees pay
for upkeep of grounds (vandalism a problem) but not
enough to keep going, so has to campaign for more
grants or will have to close and sell land to builders;
area will lose the amenity and the green space.
Targets: Sports Council, local council, sport
development bodies, Lottery, potential local members.

AMNESTY INTERNATIONAL

Campaigning group with worldwide network set up
to help prisoners of conscience – non-criminals
in jail for their political opinions.
Especially active in non-democratic countries
where there are no fair trials.
Targets: the public, British and other governments.

GREENPEACE

A group which campaigns on environmental issues.
Members are concerned individuals in local groups
plus a few full-time workers and volunteers. Has
successfully drawn public attention to issues such
as GM crops, saving the whale, nuclear dumping
and oil-drilling in Alaska.
Targets: the public and decision-makers at local,
national and global levels, including businesses.

OXFAM

National charity with local groups who run shops
through which volunteers raise money for famine
relief and projects in the Third World which support
sustainable development.
Campaigns on global poverty issues, eg debt relief,
women's health and education, unfair trade rules.
Targets: the public, British and other governments.

TRADE UNIONS

Organisations which negotiate with employers to
promote their members' interests.
Many unions have political funds which they use to
promote their members' political interests. Union
members can choose to pay into these. Some sponsor
MPs. Many unions are linked to the Labour Party and
they influence and help pay for it.
Targets: the public, employers, MPs.

WOMEN'S SUFFRAGE

A variety of organisations which worked to get the vote
for women in Britain. Set up between 1851 and 1903.
Law changed in 1918 to give some women the vote; in
1928 to give all women the vote. The different groups
used different tactics. They all relied on having large
numbers of committed members.
Target: British government.

Tactics of pressure groups

This sheet describes the campaign methods used by the identified groups. Match the tactics to one of the organisations on the information sheet *How do people try to change things?* Start a case study file with the results.

A Early groups tried to lobby MPs and influence them with petitions, letters and getting sympathetic MPs to introduce private members bills etc. Mass demonstrations and public meetings were held. Every attempt was made to persuade the public that their cause was just. Later some groups became militant and took action such as refusing to pay taxes and chaining themselves to railings. These actions broke the law but the groups accepted the punishments. In prison they went on hunger strike. A few damaged property.

B This group concentrates on keeping close links with civil servants, ministers and sympathetic MPs. It has close links with a political party since many of its members are also members of this party at local level. It spends a lot of time lobbying in Brussels to try to influence the Common Agricultural Policy of the EU. It is used by the government to give it information and advice on what its members think and how best to make changes in agriculture.

C This group lobbies MPs when legislation it wishes to affect is passing through Parliament. It organises its membership via a quarterly magazine and newsletters. It raises money to buy and conserve specific habitats as an example of its aims.

D This group has no full-time paid employees. Members elect a committee who meet in their spare time to organise fixtures, collect fees and run coaching, especially for young players. They research grant-giving bodies and make frequent applications to them. They try to involve local youth positively in sport. They are careful to make sure they have good relations with neighbours and the local press.

E This group asks members to adopt the cases of specific people and write, fax or e-mail the governments which are mistreating them. This publicity sometimes embarrasses governments into releasing them. The group researches the fairness of legal systems in different countries, and writes reports which are widely used by human rights organisations who monitor torture and other abuses.

F This group raises money in order to buy seeds and tools, dig wells, build homes, train local people, etc, in its overseas projects. People contribute by gift aid (through wage slips), disaster appeals and by buying from their shops. Volunteers give time to sort and sell books, clothes, etc. National officials campaign via the United Nations, the Department for Overseas Development and Earth Summits.

G This group uses non-violent direct action to try to prevent people from doing things it considers wrong. They sail into the path of whaling ships and stand in front of the harpoons. They also do independent scientific research. They take soil samples and analyse them for cross-contamination with GM crops. They organise consumer boycotts against targeted multinational oil companies. The group raises funds through its local members. It spends money on publicity and on its activities.

H These groups represent and organise their members at their place of work. They negotiate with employers to achieve the best deal for their members. Members elect shop stewards and paid officials to represent them. Groups may join political activities if this is asked for by their members. Some groups are affiliated to their local Labour parties and help to select their candidates. Their members sometimes take industrial action such as strikes and working to rule. They co-operate with workers in other countries to protect their members against the actions of multinational companies.

Categories of pressure groups

Discuss the differences between the groups you have studied so far. In preparation for the next lesson, decide which groups could fit under the following headings (some could fit in several):

Range

Which groups are local?

Which groups are national?

Which groups are global?

Power and influence

Which groups are 'insider groups'? These are groups whose role in society, advice, or members are important to governments and allow them relatively easy access to decision-makers.

Which groups are 'outsider groups'? These are groups whose role in society, advice, or members are not important to governments or their targets, so they have to find other ways of pressuring decision-makers by winning over public opinion.

Tactics

Which groups always work within the law?

Which groups would consider breaking the law? Would this be by non-violent direct action (eg demonstrations, sit-ins, boycotts, breaking what they consider an unjust law openly and taking the consequences) or by violence against people or damage to property?

Case study of a voluntary group

Objectives

- To know and understand the importance of playing an active part in democratic processes.
- To know and understand the opportunities for individuals and voluntary groups to bring about social change locally, nationally, in Europe and internationally.
- To express, justify and defend orally and in writing a personal opinion about such citizenship issues.
- To negotiate, decide and take part responsibly in school- and community-based activities.
- To use imagination in considering other people's experiences and to think about, express, explain and critically evaluate views that are not their own.
- To reflect on the process of participating.

Resources

Information sheets: *Pressure group methods – what works?* (p 204), *How do people try to change things?* (p 199)
Worksheets: *Case study of a voluntary group* (p 205), *School environment – survey* (p 206), *School environment – action* (p 207)

1 Introduce the idea of a values continuum. Ask the students to read through the information sheet *Pressure group methods – what works?*

2 Organise the values continuum as follows: number the corners of the room one to four. Tell the students that the corners represent the following views:

a Anything goes, ie any method can be used, including violence against people.
b Non-violent direct action, like Gandhi or Martin Luther King, ie breaking what campaigners consider an unjust law openly and taking the consequences.
c Do nothing.
d Work within the law to campaign, eg organise public support, contact decision-makers, get publicity, do research, etc.

Call out a range of situations and ask students to go to the corner which indicates their opinion of the best method for change.
- There are no youth clubs in the area.
- An unsuccessful asylum seeker and his family are being deported tomorrow, you believe unfairly.
- The headteacher increases the school day by one hour every day.
- You live in a dictatorship, have no vote and your best friend has been thrown in jail and may be tortured.
- Your country has been invaded by the army of another country.

continued on page 203

Case study of a voluntary group • continued •

- You don't like the present government, which has three years to go before the next election.
- The number 48 bus on which you depend has changed its route and no longer goes near your house.
- Another airport runway is planned which will damage the environment and cause air and noise pollution in your area.
- Yet another child has been knocked down on a busy road near you.
- The state of your school toilets is disgusting.

3   Divide the students into groups and set them a research and evaluation task: one group should cover a local organisation, one a national organisation, one an organisation with a global dimension and one should volunteer to act as a mini pressure group within school over an agreed issue. This might take forward action as part of a Healthy School programme.

4   Each group investigates their organisation using the worksheet *Case study of a voluntary group*. They could choose one of the groups described in the information sheet *How do people try to change things?* and the matching information in the information sheet *Tactics of pressure groups*. Alternatively, they could choose their own.

The group volunteering to act as a mini pressure group within school over an agreed issue needs to agree the issue with you or use the worksheet *School environment – survey and action*. Alternative ideas for this group:
- A group that wishes to change some aspect of school uniform.
- A group that wishes to change some aspect of school procedure, eg starting or finishing times.
- A group that wishes to change some aspect of school culture or behaviour such as improving safety and amenities in the lunch break.
- A group that wishes to engage with another school in a citizenship activity – a primary school, a special school or another secondary school.

5   Homework and/or dedicated time on the Internet will be necessary for groups to complete their tasks. Individuals need to make commitments to their group to carry out agreed research roles.

6   Whole-class evaluation: groups feed back their findings on their respective voluntary groups and make them available to others, eg in a class file of case studies. Each group needs to evaluate its own work – did they complete the plan? Were they able to contact the group directly? Did they succeed in analysing the group using the categories suggested? How effective is the group and its tactics? Do any individuals support the group and its aims and intend to become active in it? If so why? If not why not? As an extension students could produce an information leaflet on the pressure group or voluntary organisation they studied.

7   Individual evaluation: in what ways and how far did each individual contribute to the research and citizenship activity? Each individual should write a paragraph on each of the following:
- an outline of the planning that took place before the activity began;
- a description of their contribution to the activity and that of others;
- their evaluation of the activity and how they think it could have been improved.

Pressure group methods – what works?

Methods used by individuals, pressure groups and political organisations.

Method	Comments
Concentrating on influencing the public, eg going all-out to persuade the public of the justice of your case.	Useful in the long term but takes time, good organisation, a flair for publicity, etc. Not always successful, eg issue of capital punishment.
Concentrating on influencing decision-makers, eg through amendments to bills.	Only works if there is some reason they want to listen to you. Decision-makers change, eg governments. Second readings of bills are the best time to do this.
Damaging property and/or using violence or threat of violence against people.	Illegal and means arrest if caught. Instant publicity. May turn people against your ideas if they disagree with your methods. Police and army will try to arrest you.
Using terrorist methods, eg bombs, hijacking.	Innocent people are killed. Governments usually not affected in the way terrorists intend, ie methods are counterproductive and, many people consider, immoral.
Contacting a political party and trying to get it to adopt your idea as its policy.	Long-term. If it works it makes you dependent on the fortunes of that party.
Joining a political party whose ideas you agree with and working to elect it so that it makes the changes you want.	Long-term. Depends upon party's electoral success. Parties do not always carry out their policies once in power.
Finding a pressure group that is already committed to your ideas and joining it.	As effective as the pressure group.
Finding people who have the same ideas as you and forming your own pressure group. • Conducting your own research so you have something to tell the decision-makers. • Organising mass support and action, eg demonstrating, letter-writing, petitions, leafletting, e-mail campaigns. • Getting publicity through publishing your ideas in leaflets, magazines, websites, etc. • Holding public meetings to inform and involve people. • Doing something dramatic to draw attention to your cause.	Requires personal commitment, energy, skill and good organisation. Website and e-mail help. • A good tactic – gets you listened to. Requires time and relevant knowledge. • Can influence MPs and councillors. Difficult unless you are well organised and concentrated in a ward or constituency. • Requires finance. • Difficult to attract a good turnout unless there is public concern. Internet useful. • Gets short-term publicity.
Using non-violent direct action, eg: • making a nuisance of yourself (sit-down strike, occupation); • breaking the civil law, eg refusing to pay taxes.	Can attract public sympathy. Requires great personal commitment, eg willingness to go to prison. Can lose you the support of those who disagree with breaking the law.
Threatening to withdraw co-operation or labour.	Only effective if it would hurt the decision-makers. You/your members also suffer.
Making contact with potential allies who have more power than you.	Always useful. Can save time and effort. Time and effort needed to make the necessary contacts.
Running an efficient organisation.	Useful: impresses people and helps attract media coverage.
Using the law and legal casework.	Sometimes very effective. Takes a long time, skilled research and money to pay legal costs.
Helping the government, eg by giving it information or public support.	You need to have something they want if this is to work.

Case study of a voluntary group

You have chosen to research the group called ....

Your responsibility is to find out as many details in answer to the following questions as you can.

The deadline is ....

Use:
- primary evidence (information provided by the organisation, eg leaflets, information on website addresses, etc);
- secondary evidence (what other people have said or written about the organisation, eg in books or newspapers)
- first-hand evidence (through personal contact with the group or with a member).

1   What is the address, telephone number, e-mail, website address of the group?

2   What is the range – local, national, European, global, all of these?

3   What are the main aims of the group?
    Which of these could be described as campaign aims?
    Is the organisation mainly a pressure group or mainly something else (eg a charity, a sports club, a religious organisation, etc)

4   How many members does it have? Are there membership fees? How do you join?

5   Describe the organisation, eg does it have a formal constitution? Is it registered as a club or a charity? Does it have a bank account? Is there a local branch? If so who is the contact person?
    What is the structure? (eg any elected officers?) How is policy made in the group?

6   Are there any paid full-time workers for the group? If so what do they do?
    What do volunteers in the group do? Find out why they do this and what they say about the benefits of joining.

7   What are the main tactics of the group?

8   What successes can the group demonstrate?

Analyse for yourself what you have found.

9   How effective do you consider this group to be in bringing about change?
    Explain your answers.

10 Do you think this is a worthwhile group to join or support?
    Explain your answers.

School environment – survey

Complete this worksheet in pairs.

1 Using your knowledge of the state of the school, complete the chart below.

2 Add comments in the spaces provided.

AREA	CONDITION			COMMENT	PRIORITY
	good	fair	bad		(1, 2, etc)
school gates/signs					
school drives/pathways					
school grounds/yards					
playing fields					
entrance hall					
corridors					
notice boards					
assembly hall					
dining room					
science labs					
gymnasium					
toilets					
tutor room no.					
other					

What needs to be improved?

What can you be proud of?

Which decision-making body could you report to on this issue
eg school council, senior management, governors?

School environment - action

Use this survey to identify an area of concern around school. Work in small groups.

1   Agree on the area which concerns you most (and which could realistically be improved).
2   Write a description of the problem, including physical or personal evidence.
3   Think of some realistic suggestions to solve it.
4   Consider how your group could act as a pressure group on this issue.
5   Write a plan for group action. Here are some ideas to get you going.

Planning stage

- What is the aim of your group?
- Who are the decision-makers on this issue – do they include any of the following: pupils, school council, heads of year, headteacher, governors, LEA, others?
- What tactics could you best use to influence these people? How can you persuade them that there is a problem and that your group can help with a solution?
- What further evidence or information would help you?
- How will you approach the decision-makers? In what order? What do you need to do first?
- What are the different jobs to be done and roles to be taken within your group?
- Do you need a leader or main speaker? Who will do what?
- How long will this take? What resources are needed? How often will you meet to make sure the jobs are done?
- What are the likely obstacles? How can you reduce these?

Action stage

- Show your teacher your plan.
- Carry out your plan.
- Log the main things that happen at each stage.
- Note each individual's contribution.
- Present your findings to your class.

Evaluation stage

- Was your group successful and effective?
- Did you achieve any of your aims?
- If so, which ones and why?
- If not, why not?
- If you were to try this again what would you do differently?
- What have you learned by doing this citizenship activity?

Parties and elections

Objectives

- To know and understand the work of Parliament, the government and the courts in making and shaping the law.
- To know and understand the importance of playing an active part in democratic processes.
- To contribute to group and exploratory class discussions and take part in formal debates.

Resources

Worksheets: *Free and fair elections – the issues* (p 210); *What if elections aren't free and fair?* (p 211); *Conditions for free and fair elections* (pp 212-213)
Information sheets: *Political parties and elections* (pp 214-215), *Websites* (pp 216-217), *Ground rules for democratic debate* (p 181)

1 Explain the objectives of the lesson. Introduce the idea that empowering yourself as a citizen means knowing and understanding the way the UK democratic system largely works through parties and elections.

2 Discuss and complete as a class the worksheet *Free and fair elections – the issues*. Then ask individuals to complete the worksheet *What if elections aren't free and fair?* Be prepared to defend universal morals, eg the ends do not justify the means, innocent civilians should not be the targets of political resistance. However these issues are not black and white. Aim at least for group understanding that individuals can agree to differ.

3 In groups or as a whole class complete the worksheet *Conditions for free and fair elections*. Be prepared to provide topical or historical examples, eg Zimbabwe, bribery and non-secret ballots in British elections before the 1870s.

4 Look at the information sheet *Political parties and elections*. Agree on research activities and allocate homework time to complete them. Use the information sheet *Websites*. The whole class should choose an idea to pursue from the extension list on page 209 as a further research and citizenship activity.

5 Hold a formal debate, mock election or survey. First create a poster display and agree the ground rules for a democratic debate (see *Ground rules* sheet).

6 Lead class feedback and sum up conclusions. Students could follow up these ideas as the basis of coursework for one of the GCSE short courses in citizenship.

continued on page 209

Parties and elections • continued •

7 Extension ideas.

After further study of the issues hold a formal debate. Some ideas for motions:

- This house believes there should be compulsory voting with non-appearance punishable by a fine (as in Australia, Belgium and Greece).

- This house believes there should be a different system of voting in general elections from the current first-past-the-post system.

- This house believes there should be all-postal elections in order to increase voter turnout.

- This house believes people should have the vote from the age of 14.

- This house believes there should be state funding of political parties.

Hold a mock election. Good background resources on how to do this are available from the Institute for Citizenship www.citizen.org.uk and their free booklet *Learning Through Elections*. Survey voter intentions among parents or a year group. You could ask for party affiliations or you could ask (as polling organisations do) which party has the best policies on a named issue. Check opinion polls for question design and how to choose a valid and representative sample.

Free and fair elections - the issues

Many countries are governed without having elections.
You may have heard the following terms:

military dictatorship
totalitarian state
absolute monarchy
theocracy
anarchy

▷ Write down what you think they mean.

Then check in a dictionary and write down their definitions in your own words.
Can you give examples of states which have been ruled in these ways now or in the past?

What if elections aren't free and fair?

A democracy must hold elections and they must be free and fair.

This is to make sure that people vote for the people and policies they really want, which should ensure that the government elected as a result reflects the will of the people. Sometimes there are elections which are not like this. Then there are complaints that the government is not legitimate – that it does not have the right to govern or make laws. If people do not have the opportunity to express their views openly or to choose their government, then they are likely to reject that government, refuse to obey its laws and organise campaigns against it. These people may become freedom fighters or underground activists.

Do you think it is ever right for people to use violence or go to war to overthrow their government in these circumstances?

....

....

....

....

....

....

....

....

....

....

What is the difference between resistance and terrorism?

....

....

....

....

....

....

....

....

....

....

Conditions for free and fair elections • 1 •

Think about the conditions that are necessary for free and fair elections.
What has to happen first if there is to be a peaceful transfer of power?
Remember that all countries have struggled to make themselves democracies
and many are still doing so. Many argue that Britain only became a full democracy in
1928. Others argue that the British electoral system is still not fully democratic.

Discuss whether the following conditions are essential (E), desirable (D) or unnecessary (U).

First mark each sentence with a letter. Then when you have agreed, place them in the
relevant columns on the blank sheet. Be prepared to explain your choices.

- There is more than one party or candidate.
- There are more than four parties or candidates.
- There is a secret ballot (nobody can find out how you voted).
- Men and women can vote.
- Only residents can vote.
- Children can vote.
- All citizens must vote by law.
- Elections are held regularly, eg every four years.
- Candidates must be able to campaign openly and express their views freely.
- Candidates/parties publish their manifestos and tell everyone what they want to do if elected.
- Candidates can spend what they like on their election campaign, eg TV advertising.
- There are strict limits on the amount of money candidates/parties may spend on the campaign.
- The media are impartial – they do not support one particular party or candidate.
- There are significant differences between the parties/policies/candidates.
- The losing party/candidate agrees to accept the result.
- The winning party/candidate agrees not to persecute the losers.
- There are safeguards for the losers, especially ethnic or religious minorities.
- There is a fixed period of time for voting, eg a polling day or week.
- Everyone can get to a polling station or post their vote.
- It isn't possible to vote twice (one person one vote).
- Candidates can give money to, or buy drinks for, voters.
- There is no violence or intimidation at the polling station.
- The ballot boxes can't be tampered with or lost.
- All votes are counted.
- Votes are counted fairly by independent people.

Conditions for free and fair elections • 2 •

Essential	Desirable	Unnecessary

Political parties and elections

In the UK mass modern political parties developed in the twentieth century and are
a key part of representative democracy and the parliamentary and government systems.

What are they for?

Political parties aim to be elected and thus to have the power to govern (run things).
They do this because they have core beliefs which they consider right for the country,
and they want their ideas to be carried out in the interests of the public.

What do they do?

In order to compete in elections effectively and attract support and votes, parties develop policies on
a whole range of issues. There is organisation and fund-raising at local, regional and national level.
People can join their local party and join in discussions on what those policies should be. They can
then work to get their party candidates elected at local, devolved, national or EU level. Local groups
at ward and constituency level raise funds, discuss issues and policies, send delegates to national
conferences, select candidates and work to get them elected by canvassing, delivering leaflets,
ferrying supporters to the polls, etc.

Party members usually have direct elections for the party leader. National organisations run
publicity campaigns, make party political broadcasts, hold conferences and do research. To be
successful parties must make sure that they represent public opinion on important issues and that
they show themselves to be trustworthy, competent and capable of running things if they are elected
to form a government.

Elections and government

In the UK the government is formed from the party with the most seats in the House of
Commons. In a general election (which must be held at least every five years) we vote directly for
our constituency MPs. The leader of the party which gains a majority is asked by the Queen to
form a government and become Prime Minister. Since 1945 governments have been either
Conservative or Labour. Since the 1970s other parties have gained more voter support.
However the electoral system used for UK general elections – first past the post – means that:

a) the two largest parties win more seats per vote than others and thus tend to have clear
majorities;

b) smaller parties are not invited into coalitions and so can suffer from the 'wasted-vote effect'
and tactical voting – voters who might have put them as a first choice don't because they
want to support whichever of the larger parties is nearest their views and likely to beat the
party they don't support.

Political parties and elections
• continued •

Political parties

Here are some political parties which put up candidates in general elections (elections of MPs to the House of Commons at Westminster). Each candidate has to put up a £1000 deposit (lost if he/she gets less than 1% of the vote) and be nominated by local people.

Conservative Party, Labour Party, Liberal Democrats

These three parties put up candidates in every English, Welsh and Scottish constituency. They also compete in local elections (for the 468 county, borough, district and unitary councils), mayoral elections (eg for the London mayor), elections for the Greater London Authority, the National Assembly of Wales, the Scottish Parliament and the European Parliament.

The Green Party, The Natural Law Party

These minority parties and other single-issue parties put up candidates in some constituencies and may also compete in elections for local councils, elections for the Greater London Authority, the National Assembly of Wales, the Scottish Parliament and the European Parliament.

Scottish Nationalist Party

This party puts up candidates in every Scottish constituency and competes in elections for local councils, the Scottish Parliament and the European Parliament, as well as general elections.

Plaid Cymru – Welsh Nationalist Party

This party puts up candidates in every Welsh constituency and competes in elections for local councils, the Welsh Assembly and the European Parliament, as well as general elections.

Ulster Unionist Party, Democratic Unionist Party, Progressive Unionist Party, Social Democratic and Labour Party, Sinn Fein, Alliance Party

These parties put up candidates in every Northern Ireland constituency and compete in elections for local councils, the Northern Ireland Assembly and the European Parliament as well as general elections.

To understand more you need to find out some more about the major parties and ideally follow a general election campaign.

Contact the parties via their websites (see *Websites* information sheets). Find out more about their local and national and global policies. There has been a major problem for parties in recent years – declining mass membership and voter apathy. This means fewer people bother to follow the issues, register to vote or turn out to vote. As a consequence they are all very keen to get in touch with young people and will be delighted to give you information. They may offer to send a representative to answer your questions. You need to consider a range of opinions on different issues before you can decide where you stand. Be careful to study a broad spread of political views. But be aware that your school has the right to refuse material which is offensive or likely to damage good community relations. Before any debate starts make sure everybody agrees to follow the ground rules for democratic debate.

Websites

These are some of the key websites for researching this topic further.

General search engines (type in the name of the organisation/issue)

Yahoo	*http://www.yahoo.com*
AltaVista	*http://www.altavista.com*
Google	*http://www.google.com*
Ask Jeeves	*http://www.ask.co.uk*

International organisations of which Britain is a member

United Nations	*www.un.org/*
NATO	*www.nato.int/*
Commonwealth of Nations	*www.thecommonwealth.org/*
European Union	*www.europa.eu.int/*
The European Commission	*www.cec.org.uk*

Governments and parliaments

The House of Commons and the House of Lords	*http://www.parliament.uk*
Parliamentary Education Unit	*www.explore.parliament.uk*
Central Office of Information	*http://www.coi.gov.uk*
The European Parliament	*www.europarl.org.uk*
National Assembly of Wales	*www.wales.gov.uk*
Scottish Parliament	*www.scottish.parliament.uk*

Political Parties

Conservative Party	*http://www.conservatives.com*
Labour Party	*http://www.labour.org.uk*
Liberal Democrats	*http://www.libdems.org.uk*
Green Party	*www.greenparty.org.uk*
Scottish Nationalist Party	*www.snp.org.uk*
Plaid Cymru (Welsh Nationalist Party)	*www.plaidcymru.org.*

Polling organisations

MORI	*http://www.mori.com*
NOP	*http://www.nop.co.uk*
Gallup	*http://www.gallup.com*
ICM	*http://www.icmresearch.co.uk*

Websites • continued •

Newspaper/TV websites

These run their own sites and keep articles going back several years.
Type in a search word to find articles. They also do special reports.

http://www.guardian.co.uk

http://www.channel4.com/learning/ (Channel 4 current affairs programme with multimedia)

An excellent general provider of ready-made resources on the net is *http://www.learn.co.uk/topical*
This provides two topical lesson packs per week for students and teachers.

Groups which promote global citizenship

Groups which advise on environmental/global citizenship issues.

Commonwealth Institute	*www.commonwealth.org.uk*
Council for Education in World Citizenship	*www.cewc.org.uk*
Council for Environmental Education	*www.cee.org.uk*
Institute for Global Ethics UK Trust	*www.globalethics.org*
Eco-Schools	*www.encams.org*

Pressure groups

Groups which promote global action on poverty, human rights, the environment.

Oxfam	*www.oxfam.org.uk*
Amnesty International	*www.amnesty.org/*
Greenpeace International	*www.greenpeace.org*
Friends of the Earth	*www.foe.co.uk*
Red Cross	*www.icrc.org./*
Save the Children	*www.savethechildren.org.uk/*
Survival International	*www.survival-international.org*

General citizenship websites

These could be useful for finding out about how students can take part in debates or get involved in
practical activities. Many current issues are available.

Citizenship Foundation	*http://wwwcitfou.org.uk*
Online debating chamber	*http://www.explore.parliament.uk*
CSV (Community Service Volunteers)	*http://www.csv.org.uk*
Institute for Citizenship/CC	*http://www.citizen.org.uk*

Global issues

Objectives

- To know and understand the work of Parliament, the government and the courts in making and shaping the law.
- To know and understand the United Kingdom's relations with Europe, including the European Union, and relations with the Commonwealth and the United Nations.
- To know and understand the wider issues and challenges of global interdependence and responsibility, including sustainable development and local Agenda 21.
- To express, justify and defend orally and in writing a personal opinion about such citizenship issues.

Resources

Information sheets: *Agenda 21* (p 220), *What does the future hold?* (pp 55-57)
Worksheets: *How can you make a difference?* (pp 221),
How can governments implement Agenda 21? (p 222)

1   Agenda 21 is a programme for action developed by the United Nations. Read the preamble 1.1 of Agenda 21 reproduced on the information sheet *Agenda 21*. Do students agree with this statement? If any dispute the facts, refer them to the worksheets *What does the future hold?*

2   Make the link between global inequality and poverty and other problems – war, terrorism, global warming, illegal immigration, pollution, depletion of natural resources such as fish and minerals. Rich countries can't ignore these. However there are many problems in persuading world leaders to commit themselves to the concrete action that the UN says is needed. Political and business pressures at home mean some want to delay or avoid what might be unpopular decisions such as cutting fossil fuel use (and private motoring) or giving more overseas aid.

3   Look at the worksheet *How can you make a difference?* Ask the students to complete the worksheet individually by ticking the boxes as directed. Feed back on the levels of commitment displayed within the class.

4   Look at the worksheet *How can governments implement Agenda 21?* Students taking a GCSE short course in citizenship will need to thoroughly know and understand this information on government structures. Divide the students into groups and ask each group to take an example of an area for action on sustainable development. If examples are needed refer them to the information sheets *What does the future hold?* The students should suggest laws or policies which would help achieve the target. Which governmental structures would have to be involved and at what level? Highlight these on the sheet.

Global issues • continued •

5 Lead class feedback and sum up conclusions.
Optional: hold a class debate, compose a speech or write an essay
on a contentious issue, eg:

- This country should spend a greater proportion of taxpayers' money on
overseas aid;

- The government should do everything within its power to discourage use
of private cars and encourage use of public transport.

- Private enterprise is more likely to save the planet than elected
governments.

Students could follow up these ideas as the basis of coursework for one
of the GCSE short courses in citizenship.

Agenda 21

Section 1.1 of the preamble to Agenda 21 reads as follows:

Humanity stands at a defining moment in history. We are confronted with a perpetuation of disparities between and within nations, a worsening of poverty, hunger, ill health and illiteracy, and the continuing deterioration of the ecosystems on which we depend for our well-being. However, integration of environment and development concerns and greater attention to them will lead to the fulfilment of basic needs, improved living standards for all, better protected and managed ecosystems and a safer, more prosperous future. No nation can achieve this on its own; but together we can – in a global partnership for sustainable development.

How can you make a difference?

Do you agree with Agenda 21? Will it help all citizens of the world? Governments have to implement it at national and local level. As a result individuals will have to make personal decisions and changes to their lives. Consider the following ways that you could take action as a citizen to support the Agenda 21 programme. Which do you agree with? Which will you actually do? Tick the box.

1   Through your lifestyle and choices as a consumer you:

	Agree with	Will do
• buy products/services which do not pollute the environment or exploit the poor but do invest in clean technology;	☐	☐
• boycott companies and products which act unethically and pollute the environment, exploit their workers or poorer countries, or waste energy;	☐	☐
• reduce your consumption of fossil fuels, eg by travelling less by car, flying less, using public transport, walking or cycling;	☐	☐
• reduce your use of electricity, gas and coal;	☐	☐
• switch to cleaner technology and renewable sources of energy;	☐	☐
• reduce your personal pollution, eg by not dropping litter, refusing unnecessary packaging and plastic bags, recycling.	☐	☐

2   Through your actions as a citizen you:

• support with your money and time voluntary organisations which promote the environment, sustainable development, campaign for the disadvantaged and against inequality, or support peaceful development and conflict resolution;	☐	☐
• follow developing issues in the news and discuss them with others, and use persuasion to change public opinion to agree with the need for these changes and priorities;	☐	☐
• use opportunities to make decisions and exercise choice, eg voting for candidates who share your views – from school council representatives to MPs;	☐	☐
• join a political party locally, participate in policy-making, work to get your party elected to local councils, at Westminster or the European Parliament so that the big decisions that you want are made at government level.	☐	☐

3   Through your actions at work you:

• use your influence in your workplace to promote science, clean technology and sustainable economic development;	☐	☐
• use your influence in your workplace to prevent exploitation of the poor at home or abroad, further inequality, pollution of air or water, wasteful use of energy.	☐	☐

How can governments implement Agenda 21?

Agenda 21 is a programme for action developed by the United Nations. World summits like the one held in Johannesburg in 2002 are an opportunity to tackle long-term problems. But will the governments of the richer countries commit themselves to take the action promised? Can they persuade their voters that this is necessary – even if the voters don't like all the implications?

Governments need to co-operate in international agreements to solve global problems. But following a policy through at all the levels of government means having the co-operation of elected representatives, the executive and the bureaucrats right down to local level. Follow the chart to see how we are actually governed. Then explain and give examples of laws or policies that would help carry out sustainable developments. Which bodies would need to be involved?

	Parliaments/assemblies are **legislatures**. They debate, legislate and consult. They are elected representatives or delegates.	Governments are **executives**. They make policies and decisions. They are made up of senior politicians.	Officials are **bureaucrats**. They implement policies They are paid, non-elected, public servants.
Global	**UN General Assembly** Delegates from each country debate and pass resolutions. Can impose sanctions.	**UN Security Council & Secretariat** Decide on action. Can veto action. Can send in UN troops.	**UN Agencies, eg UN Food Programme** Carry out agreed programmes.
European	**European Parliament** Directly elected by voters in each member country.	**Council of Ministers** Senior ministers from each member country.	**European Commission** Paid, non-elected officials who suggest new laws or directives.
National	**House of Commons** MPs are directly elected by voters in each constituency. They debate and pass laws. House of Lords are not currently elected. They can amend laws.	**Prime Minister & Cabinet** Senior MPs from the majority party.	**Civil servants** They are paid non-elected officials who advise ministers, run prisons, etc. Government agencies run many services
Devolved	**Northern Ireland Assembly Welsh Assembly Scottish Parliament** Directly elected by voters in each constituency.	**Ministers** agree a programme of legislation/policy.	**Scottish Executive Scottish Office,** etc, run devolved services.
Local	**Local councils: county, district, borough, unitary** Directly elected by voters in each ward.	**Leaders of the council, committee chairmen**	**Local government officers** Administer services, eg education according to policies agreed by councillors
Quangos	Local representation on public authorities Health authorities, etc	Water authorities, Police authorities,	Employees

Useful addresses

ABC (Anti-Bullying Campaign)
185 Tower Bridge Road
London SE1 2UF
020 7378 1446
http://www.bullying.co.uk or help@bullying.co.uk
Support for victims of bullying and victims' parents

KIDSCAPE
2 Grosvenor Gardens
London SW1W ODH
020 7730 3300
http://www.kidscape.org.uk
Information on bullying and child protection

TERRENCE HIGGINS TRUST
52-54 Gray's Inn Road
London WC1X 8JU
020 7831 0330
http://www.tht.org.uk
Leaflets/posters/videos/speakers on HIV/AIDS

NATIONAL AIDS HELPLINE
0800 567 123

ACE (Advisory Centre for Education)
1C Aberdeen Studios
22 Highbury Grove
London N5 2DQ
020 7354 8318
http://www.ace-ed.org.uk
Useful information sheets on different topics,
eg bullying, sex education

NATIONAL CHILDBIRTH TRUST
Alexandra House
Oldham Terrace
London W3 6NH
0870 444 8707
http://www.nct-online.org
Provides information and speakers on aspects of
parenthood, birth, feeding and child development

FPA (Family Planning Association)
2-12 Pentonville Road
London N1 9FP
0845 310 1334
http://www.fpa.org.uk
Leaflets, videos, teaching packs, speakers on
relationships, sexuality, abuse, learning difficulties
and physical disability

LESBIAN AND GAY YOUTH MOVEMENT
BM/Gym
London WC1N 3XX
http://www.queery.org.uk
Teaching packs, resources

BROOK ADVISORY CENTRE
Studio 421, Highgate Studios
51-79 Highgate Road
London NW5 1TL
0800 0185 023
http://www.brook.org.uk or
information@brookcentres.com
Large range of resources on sex and personal
relationships, unplanned pregnancy and
contraception

CHILDLINE
0800 1111
http://www.childline.org.uk

SAMARITANS
08457 90 90 90 (links callers to the nearest
Samaritans office)
http://www.samaritans.org.uk

HEALTH DEVELOPMENT AGENCY
Holborn Gate
330 High Holborn
London WC1V 7BA
020 7430 0850
http://www.hda-online.org.uk
Teaching packs, resources

HEALTH PROMOTION
See under local health authority in phone directory.
A good contact for advice and resources

COMMUNITY HEALTH COUNCIL
As above

CITIZENS' ADVICE BUREAUX
As above

HEALTH EDUCATION AUTHORITY
Marston Book Services Ltd
PO Box 269
Abingdon
Oxfordshire OX14 4YN
01235 465500
Teaching packs, resources

Useful addresses

DEPARTMENT OF HEALTH
DEPIS (Drug Education and Prevention Information Service)
www.doh.gov.uk/drugs/depis
Drugs and health information website

WIRED FOR HEALTH
www.wiredforhealth.gov.uk
Gives information on health issues, as well as information about the National Healthy School standard.

DRUGSCOPE
32-36 Loman Street
London SE1 0EE
020 7928 1211
http://www.drugscope.org.uk or
enquiries@drugscope.org.uk

TACADE (The Advisory Council on Alcohol and Drug Education)
1 Hume Place
The Crescent
Salford
M5 4QA
0161 745 8925
http://www.tacade.com or ho@tacade.demon.co.uk
Information on drugs and smoking

DEVELOPMENT EDUCATION CENTRE
EOCC Princes Street
Oxford OX4 1DD
01865 790 490
http://www.rmplc.co.uk or odec@gn.apc.org

DEVELOPMENT EDUCATION PROJECT
801 Wilmslow Road
Didsbury
Manchester M20 2QR
0161 445 2495
http://www.dep.org.uk or depman@gn.apc.org
Particularly good on gender, bullying and race issues

EQUAL OPPORTUNITIES COMMISSION
Arndale House
Arndale Centre
Manchester M4 3EQ
08456 015 901
http://www.eoc.org.uk
Key literature about gender discrimination laws and regulations

COMMISSION FOR RACIAL EQUALITY
Elliott House
10-12 Allington Street
London SW1E 5EH
020 7828 7022
http://www.cre.gov.uk or info@cre.gov.uk

Look at the Help and Support section in Useful Numbers at the front of your phone book for local contacts.